3. SESSION PLAN

This heading introduces the step-by-step lesson plan. With careful planning, you can easily tailor each session to the amount of class time you have.

4. BEFORE CLASS BEGINS

This is a convenient list of any special preparation or materials required.

5. ATTENTION GRABBER

Who knows what lurks in the minds of your students as they file into your room? The **Attention Grabber** will stimulate their interest and focus their thinking on the theme of the lesson.

The **Attention Grabber,** as well as other parts of the **Session Plan,** often—but not always—contain an additional alternate activity. These alternates are identified by the titles **CREATIVE OPTION, OPTIONAL** or similar designations. Choose the activity that best suits the needs of your class and fits your time schedule.

6. BIBLE EXPLORATION

The **Bible Exploration** is the heart of your class session because it involves each learner directly in the study of God's Word. It is during this period that you will invite the students to explore and discover **what the Bible says and means** and to discuss **how it applies to each student.**

SESSION PLAN

BEFORE CLASS BEGINS: Photocopy the Scratch Sheet and Fun Page. Provide felt pens, poster board or newsprint, tape or tacks and scissors. You will need envelopes if you play the second version of the game described in step 4 of the EXPLORATION.

Attention Grabber

ATTENTION GRABBER (3-5 minutes)

Materials needed: Felt pens, poster board, tape, scissors, scratch paper, inexpensive rewards.

Before class, write several messages on poster board. These might be the announcements for the day or a message about today's study such as, "The wall can tell an interesting story" or a silly saying or joke. Cut each message apart so that each word of each message is on a separate piece of poster board. Scramble the order of the messages and attach them to the walls of your room—one or two messages on each wall.

As students arrive, ask them to take a piec scratch paper and a felt pen or pencil and try together as many of the messages as they ca time limit and give inexpensive rewards to th who correctly figure out the most messages.

Say, **Today we are going to look at a in which the people involved spent a lo time looking at the walls trying to und a message that they couldn't read and they couldn't understand.**

Bible Exploration

EXPLORATION (35-50 minutes)

Materials needed: Newsprint or poster board, felt pens for use in the first step.

Step 1 (10-12 minutes): Have your students form six groups. Have them look at the "Party Time" section of the Scratch Sheet. Assign to each group one of the Scriptures in "Party Time" and explain, **Create a cartoon strip with one or more panels depicting the events you about in your assigned Scripture pas Draw big, because we will form a co story by putting all our cartoons tog the wall.**

(If drawing cartoon strips is not appro your situation, students may outline and

7. CONCLUSION AND DECISION

Each **Session Plan** provides this opportunity for students to deal with the questions, **What does the Bible mean to me? How can I put what I just learned into practice in my own life?** Be sure to leave enough time at the end of each session for the **Conclusion and Decision** activity.

8. NOTES

Every page of the **Session Plan** allows space for you to jot notes as you prepare for class. Also, you will find **important reminders** and **suggestions** listed in **bold type** to catch your attention.

NECESSARY CLASSROOM SUPPLIES

The Session Plan Bible study activities require that you make the following items readily available to students:

• A Bible for each student (Essential!) • Paper and pencils or pens • Felt markers • Butcher paper for posters • Transparent tape • Scissors

You will need a chalkboard and chalk, or overhead projector, transparencies and transparency markers.

Special requirements will be listed in the proper **Session Plans.**

THE SCRATCH SHEET STUDENT WORKSHEETS

The Scratch Sheet helps students focus on Bible truths.

The page immediately following most Session Plans is the Scratch Sheet worksheet for your students. Here's how to use the Scratch Sheet:

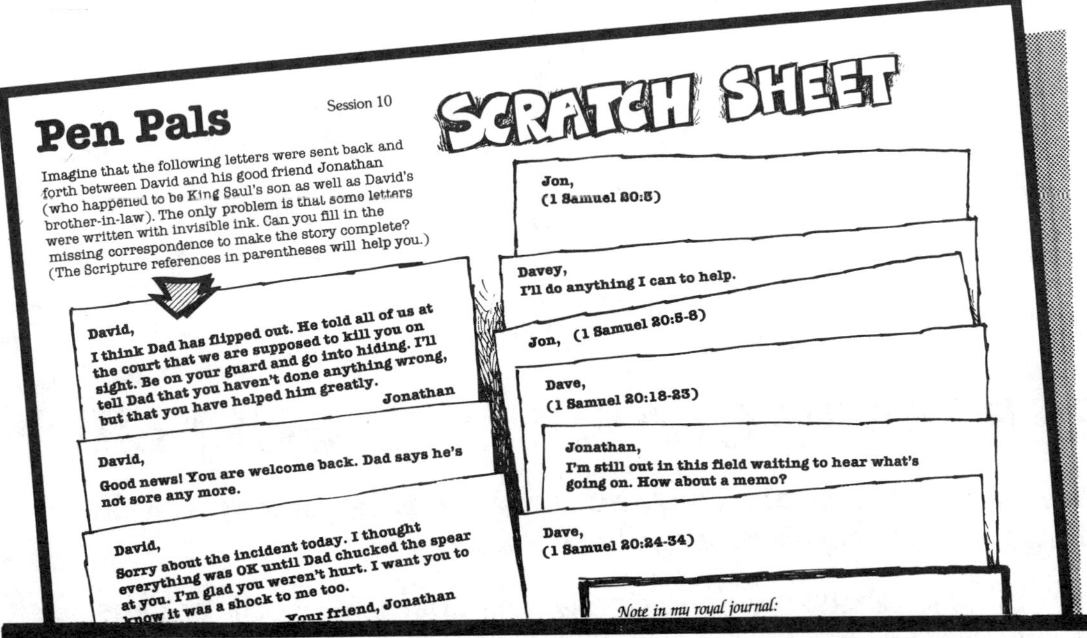

SCRATCH SHEET

Pen Pals

Session 10

Imagine that the following letters were sent back and forth between David and his good friend Jonathan (who happened to be King Saul's son as well as David's brother-in-law). The only problem is that some letters were written with invisible ink. Can you fill in the missing correspondence to make the story complete? (The Scripture references in parentheses will help you.)

David,
I think Dad has flipped out. He told all of us at the court that we are supposed to kill you on sight. Be on your guard and go into hiding. I'll tell Dad that you haven't done anything wrong, but that you have helped him greatly.
Jonathan

David,
Good news! You are welcome back. Dad says he's not sore any more.

David,
Sorry about the incident today. I thought everything was OK until Dad chucked the spear at you. I'm glad you weren't hurt. I want you to know it was a shock to me too.
Your friend, Jonathan

Jon,
(1 Samuel 20:5)

Davey,
I'll do anything I can to help.

Jon, (1 Samuel 20:5-8)

Dave,
(1 Samuel 20:18-23)

Jonathan,
I'm still out in this field waiting to hear what's going on. How about a memo?

Dave,
(1 Samuel 20:24-34)

Note in my royal journal:

Each session's Scratch Sheet features that session's memory verse (which is also printed on the Fun Page take-home paper). If you have a little extra time at the end of the lesson, review the memory verse with your students.

1. Before class, photocopy enough worksheets for your learners and a few extra for visitors. There is never more than one **Scratch Sheet** worksheet per session—some sessions have none at all.
2. The **Scratch Sheets** are generally used throughout each **Session Plan.** The best time to distribute them to students is when the **Session Plan** first calls for their use. Always keep a copy for yourself.
3. Be sure to have plenty of blank paper for students' written assignments—the **Scratch Sheets** don't have much extra space.
4. It may help to have your students fold their **Scratch Sheets** into their Bibles if there is a gap between uses of the worksheet. This will aid you in avoiding the dreaded Paper Airplane Syndrome!
5. Collect and save the worksheets once every few weeks. (Do not collect worksheets that contain private confessions to God or the like.) You can follow the progress of your students by examining their work. Parents, too, will want to see what their kids are learning.

Editor

Tom Finley

Consulting Editors

Marian Wiggins
Annette Parrish
Carol Eide

Contributing Writers

Brian Blandford
Jennifer Sudderth
Miriam Mohler

Designed and Illustrated by Tom Finley

Also used is: *KJV—King James Version*

GREAT OLD TESTAMENT LEADERS

NUMBER 10 IN A SERIES OF 12

INTRODUCTION

This book contains everything you need to teach any size group of junior high students about the leadership abilities and sensitivity to God displayed by Abraham, Moses, David and Daniel. Thirteen sessions, with complete session plans for the leader, reproducible classroom worksheets and reproducible take-home papers. Also, thirteen lecture-oriented Bible study outlines based on the same themes, to provide your students with needed reinforcement from a fresh perspective. And— dozens of action games and ideas to round out your youth program, plus a special section of clip art featuring illustrations to promote your Bible studies and dress up your announcement handbills.

Contents

Bible Studies:

OVERVIEW
OF THE PARTS AND PIECES

There is a ton of great teaching tools in this book, including object lessons, Bible games, memory verses, discussion questions, stories, worksheets, comic cartoons and more! Here's an overview of it all:

The **SESSION PLAN** contains two essential ingredients for a meaningful Bible study all students will enjoy: a commentary section to provide the leader with important biblical information and to set the stage for the lesson; and a lesson plan filled with Bible Learning Activities to help students retain spiritual truths. **FOR A DETAILED DESCRIPTION, TURN TO PAGE 6.**

The **STUDENT WORKSHEET,** called the **Scratch Sheet,** allows the student to learn by doing rather than just sitting and listening. Photocopy as many sheets as you need. **SEE PAGE 8 FOR COMPLETE DETAILS.**

Daniel's Stand SESSION 3

WHAT THE SESSION IS ABOUT
Christians must be willing to speak and live the truth even when it is unpopular.

SCRIPTURE STUDIED
Daniel 5:1-30; Romans 1:16

KEY PASSAGE
"I am not ashamed of the gospel, because it is the power of God for the salvation of everyone who ... r the Jew, then for ... mans 1:16

INSIGHTS FOR THE LEADER

To be a godly teenager is a tough assignment in any period of history. To continue to be a godly teenager when exposed to pressure from a world system committed to pagan philosophy is an assignment infinitely tougher. To begin as a teenager in such an environment and yet rise to a position of high honor without compromising truth, despite several changes of government and at the frequent risk of life, is to fulfill the toughest assignment of all. Yet that is the story of the book of Daniel.

Background
Daniel's story occurs near the end of the Old Testament history of the Jewish people. After Abraham's lifetime, his descendants grew into a nation of people as God had promised. Famine drove them to Egypt where they eventually became slaves. God used Moses to get them out of Egypt; we'll study his life in future ... ears of wandering in the ... land

Daniel and his three friends, Shadrach, Meshach and Abednego, were royal princes of the tribe of Judah, and are described in the first chapter of Daniel as "young men without any physical defect, handsome, showing aptitude for every kind of learning, well informed, quick to understand, and qualified to serve in the king's palace" (Dan. 1:4). These splendid young men serve as a good example for the young people of any era. They stood true to their principles in the midst of great pressure, drawing upon God's help to remain faithful against all odds.

The central figure of the four is Daniel, whose personal history is traced through four changes of dynasty in the first six chapters of the book of Daniel, and whose remarkable visions are given to us in chapters 7-12.

Daniel won respect and honor from the kings he served. He was eventually made the highest administrator of the entire province of Babylon (see Dan. 2:48 regardi... King Nebu... and 6:3 regardin...

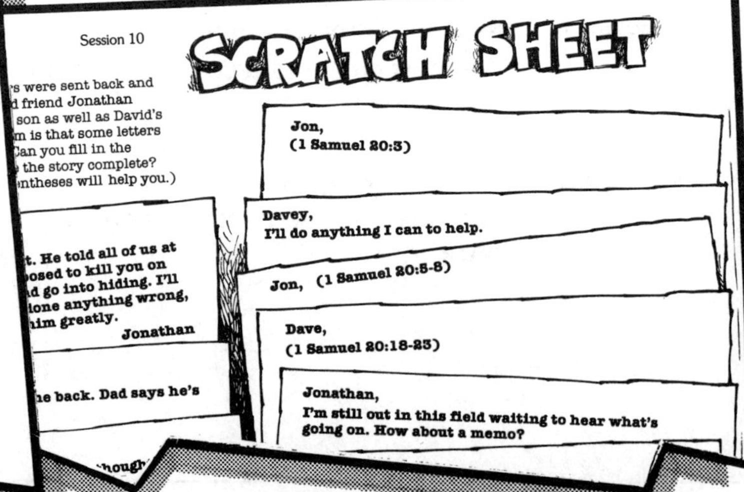
Session 10

SCRATCH SHEET

...s were sent back and
...d friend Jonathan
... son as well as David's
...m is that some letters
...Can you fill in the
... the story complete?
...ntheses will help you.)

Jon,
(1 Samuel 20:3)

...t. He told all of us at
...osed to kill you on
...d go into hiding. I'll
...done anything wrong,
...him greatly.
Jonathan

Davey,
I'll do anything I can to help.

Jon, (1 Samuel 20:5-8)

...he back. Dad says he's

Dave,
(1 Samuel 20:18-23)

Jonathan,
I'm still out in this field waiting to hear what's going on. How about a memo?

...hough...

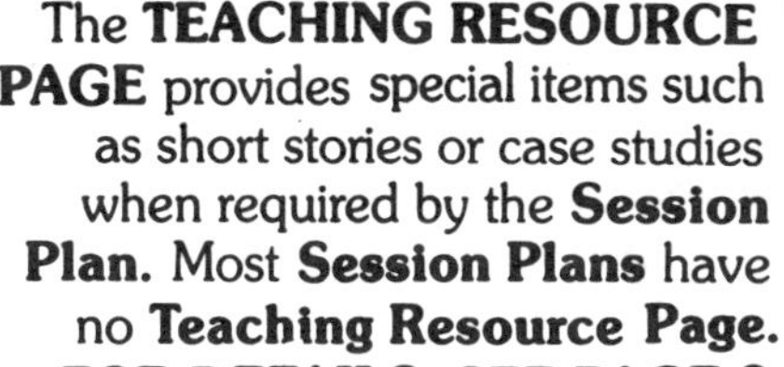

The **TEACHING RESOURCE PAGE** provides special items such as short stories or case studies when required by the **Session Plan.** Most **Session Plans** have no **Teaching Resource Page.** **FOR DETAILS, SEE PAGE 9.**

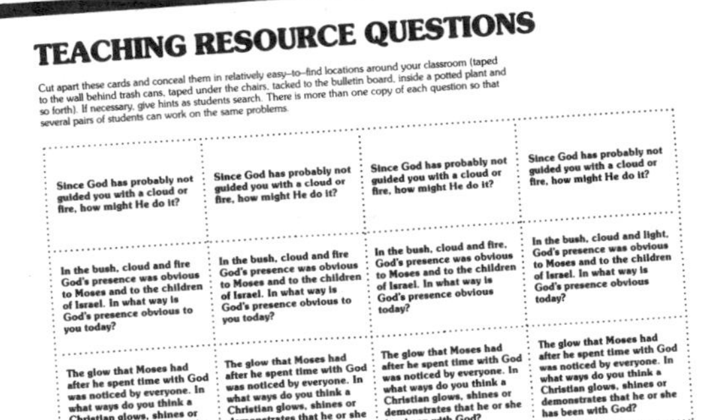

TEACHING RESOURCE QUESTIONS

Cut apart these cards and conceal them in relatively easy-to-find locations around your classroom (taped to the wall behind trash cans, taped under the chairs, tacked to the bulletin board, inside a potted plant and so forth). If necessary, give hints as students search. There is more than one copy of each question so that several pairs of students can work on the same problems.

Since God has probably not guided you with a cloud or fire, how might He do it?	**Since God has probably not guided you with a cloud or fire, how might He do it?**	**Since God has probably not guided you with a cloud or fire, how might He do it?**	**Since God has probably not guided you with a cloud or fire, how might He do it?**
In the bush, cloud and fire God's presence was obvious to Moses and to the children of Israel. In what way is God's presence obvious to you today?	**In the bush, cloud and fire God's presence was obvious to Moses and to the children of Israel. In what way is God's presence obvious to you today?**	**In the bush, cloud and fire, God's presence was obvious to Moses and to the children of Israel. In what way is God's presence obvious today?**	**In the bush, cloud and light, God's presence was obvious to Moses and to the children of Israel. In what way is God's presence obvious today?**
The glow that Moses had after he spent time with God was noticed by everyone. In what ways do you think a Christian glows, shines or demonstrates that he or she has been with God?	**The glow that Moses had after he spent time with God was noticed by everyone. In what ways do you think a Christian glows, shines or demonstrates that he or she has been with God?**	**The glow that Moses had after he spent time with God was noticed by everyone. In what ways do you think a Christian glows, shines or demonstrates that he or she has been with God?**	**The glow that Moses had after he spent time with God was noticed by everyone. In what ways do you think a Christian glows, shines or demonstrates that he or she has been with God?**
...ent time with God.	**Moses spent time with God. How do we spend time with God and what do we do when we are with Him?**	**Moses spent time with God. How do we spend time with God and what do we do when we are with Him?**	

The **TAKE-HOME PAPER,** called the **Fun Page,** features a newspaper theme, comic strip, Bible game (such as a maze or crossword), daily devotional questions and a memory verse for motivated students. **FOR MORE ABOUT THE FUN PAGE, TURN TO PAGE 10.**

Session 3

The TOWN CRIER

KING SAUL: AFRAID TO TELL OTHERS!

Based on 1 Samuel 10

Israel—His name was Saul. The Bible describes him this way: ". . . an impressive young man without equal among the Israelites—a head taller than any of the others" (1 Samuel 9:2).

Now God told His prophet Samuel that He was about to make Saul king of Israel. When Saul learned this he grew very nervous indeed.

Thousands of people had gathered at Mizpah to see Saul crowned king. Everyone was excited and filled with awe at seeing Israel's very first king.

But they almost didn't see him. The great Saul had hidden himself in the huge piles of baggage the crowds had brought with them to the airport . . . er, camelport.

The people looked everywhere for the reluctant king-to-be, but no one could find him. Finally, the people prayed to God and He, through His prophet, told them where Saul was.

So Saul was crowned king and lived happily ever after . . . uh, until he started going bananas and was eventually eliminated! But that's another story.

"Therefore everyone who hears these words of mine and puts them into practice is like a wise man who built his house on the rock." Matthew 7:24

Are you a wise person? Is your life built on Christ, the solid Rock? Are you prepared for anything that may go wrong in life? Just for fun, here's a game about some natural disasters that befall humanity from time to time.

Instructions: Each person below is shouting the name of some natural disaster. Unfortunately, they are all so scared, they've messed up the words! Your job is to split each word into **three parts,** and then stick each part back with two correct parts, to find the actual disasters. For example, *Earthquake, volcano* and *flood* can be split up and rewritten as earcand, flthqo and volooauke! Answers are below, but don't peek until you're finished!

Don't wait until you face a disaster before you get your life straightened out with God. If you haven't done yet, get right with Him right now!

Answers: Quicksand, earthquake, landslide, hurricane, tornado, avalanche, flood, volcano.

DAILY THINKERS

Day 1 Read Psalm 51:1,2. Does David's request seem sincere? How would you ask God the same thing?
Day 2 Psalm 51:10-12. List what David asks of God.
Day 3 Psalm 103:1. David indicates the depth of his love for God by saying what?
Day 4 Psalm 103:8-13. What are some characteristics of God? What does He do about our sin?
Day 5 Psalm 103:13-18. In light of these verses, what are the things in a person's life that have eternal value?
Day 6 Psalm 108:1-5. Write a song or poem of praise using this psalm as a model.

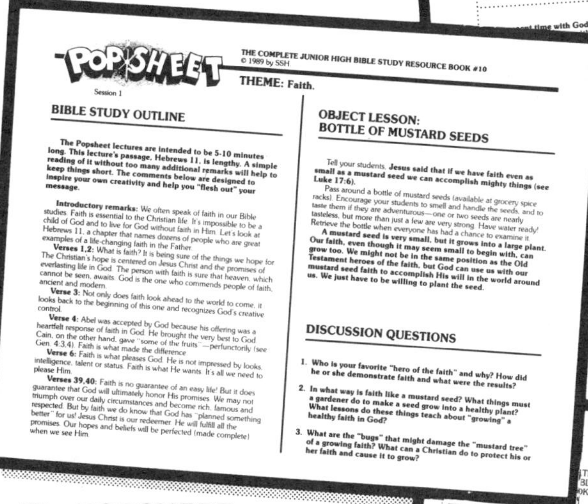

POPSHEET

Session 1

THE COMPLETE JUNIOR HIGH BIBLE STUDY RESOURCE BOOK #10
© 1989 by SSH.

THEME: Faith.

BIBLE STUDY OUTLINE

The Popsheet lectures are intended to be 5-10 minutes long. This lecture's passage, Hebrews 11, is lengthy. A simple reading of it without too many additional remarks will help to keep things short. The comments below are designed to inspire your own creativity and help you "flesh out" your message.

Introductory remarks: We often speak of faith in our Bible studies. Faith is essential to the Christian life. It's impossible to be a child of God and to live for God without faith in Him. Let's look at Hebrews 11, a chapter that names dozens of people who are great examples of a life-changing faith in the Father.

Verses 1,2: What is faith? It is being sure of the things we hope for. The Christian's hope is centered on Jesus Christ and the promises of everlasting life in God. The person with faith is sure that heaven, which cannot be seen, awaits. God is the one who commends people of faith, ancient and modern.

Verse 3: Not only does faith look ahead to the world to come, it looks back to the beginning of this one and recognizes God's creative control.

Verse 4: Abel was accepted by God because his offering was a heartfelt response of faith in God. He brought the very best to God. Cain, on the other hand, gave "some of the fruits"—perfunctorily (see Gen. 4:3,4). Faith is what made the difference.

Verse 6: Faith is what pleases God. He is not impressed by looks, intelligence, talent or status. Faith is what He wants. It's all we need to please Him.

Verses 39,40: Faith is no guarantee of an easy life! But it does guarantee that God will ultimately honor His promises. We may not triumph over our daily circumstances and become rich, famous and respected. But by faith we do know that God has "planned something better" for us! Jesus Christ is our redeemer. He will fulfill all the promises. Our hopes and beliefs will be perfected (made complete) when we see Him.

OBJECT LESSON: BOTTLE OF MUSTARD SEEDS

Tell your students, **Jesus said that if we have faith even as small as a mustard seed we can accomplish mighty things (see Luke 17:6).**

Pass around a bottle of mustard seeds (available at grocery spice racks). Encourage your students to smell and handle the seeds, and to taste them if they are adventurous—one or two seeds are nearly tasteless, but more than just a few are very strong. Have water ready! Retrieve the bottle when everyone has had a chance to examine it.

A mustard seed is very small, but it grows into a large plant. Our faith, even though it may seem small to begin with, can grow too. We might not be in the same position as the Old Testament heroes of the faith, but God can use us with our mustard seed faith to accomplish His will in the world around us. We just have to be willing to plant the seed.

DISCUSSION QUESTIONS

1. **Who is your favorite "hero of the faith" and why? How did he or she demonstrate faith and what were the results?**
2. **In what way is faith like a mustard seed? What things must a gardener do to make a seed grow into a healthy plant? What lessons do these things teach about "growing" a healthy faith in God?**
3. **What are the "bugs" that might damage the "mustard tree" of a growing faith? What can a Christian do to protect his or her faith and cause it to grow?**

The **POPSHEET** is a lecture-oriented version of the **Session Plan,** based on a different portion of the Scriptures. Use it as an alternative to the **Session Plan,** at another meeting later in the week, or combine it with the **Session Plan** as you see fit. **SEE PAGE 12.**

The **Popsheet** features **GAMES AND THINGS,** dozens of action games, special suggestions and ideas for your students to enjoy. **PAGE 14 CONTAINS DETAILS.**

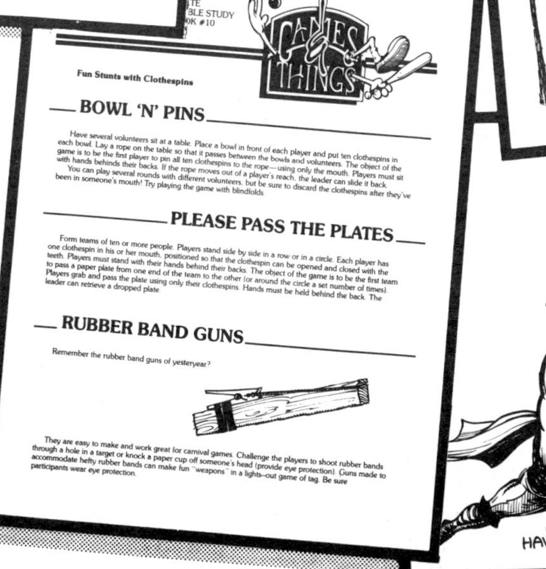

...TE
...BLE STUDY
...OK #10

Fun Stunts with Clothespins

BOWL 'N' PINS

Have several volunteers sit at a table. Place a bowl in front of each player and put ten clothespins in each bowl. Lay a rope on the table so that it passes between the bowls and volunteers. The object of the game is to be the first player to pin all ten clothespins to the rope—using only the mouth. Players must sit with hands behinds their backs. If the rope moves out of a player's reach, the leader can slide it back.

You can play several rounds with different volunteers, but be sure to discard the clothespins after they've been in someone's mouth! Try playing the game with blindfolds.

PLEASE PASS THE PLATES

Form teams of ten or more people. Players stand side by side in a row or in a circle. Each player has one clothespin in his or her mouth, positioned so that the clothespin can be opened and closed with the teeth. Players must stand with their hands behind their backs. The object of the game is to be the first team to pass a paper plate from one end of the team to the other (or around the circle a set number of times). Players grab and pass the plate using only their clothespins. Hands must be held behind the back. The leader can retrieve a dropped plate.

RUBBER BAND GUNS

Remember the rubber band guns of yesteryear?

They are easy to make and work great for carnival games. Challenge the players to shoot rubber bands through a hole in a target or knock a paper cup off someone's head (provide eye protection). Guns made to accommodate hefty rubber bands can make fun "weapons" in a lights-out game of tag. Be sure participants wear eye protection.

RETIREMENT CENTER

MINISTRY

BIBLE

UH... WHEN WE SAID OUR BIBLE STUDIES ARE SUPER, WE DIDN'T HAVE EXACTLY THIS IN MIND!

DON'T FORGET TO SIGN UP

The **CLIP ART AND OTHER GOODIES** section at the back of the book contains special art you can use to dress up your newsletters. **SEE PAGE 16 FOR COMPLETE INFORMATION.**

THE SESSION PLANS

How to squeeze the most out of each Bible study.

Every Session Plan contains the following features:

1. INTRODUCTORY INFORMATION

WHAT THE SESSION IS ABOUT states the main thrust of the lesson.

Your students will examine all verses listed in **SCRIPTURE STUDIED.**

The **KEY PASSAGE** is also the memory verse given on the **Scratch Sheet** student worksheet (when space allows) and the **Fun Page** take-home paper.

AIMS OF THE SESSION are what you hope to achieve during class time. You may wish to privately review these after class as a measure of your success.

Daniel's Stand

SESSION 3

WHAT THE SESSION IS ABOUT

Christians must be willing to speak and live the truth even when it is unpopular.

SCRIPTURE STUDIED

Daniel 5:1-30; Romans 1:16

KEY PASSAGE

"I am not ashamed of the gospel, because it is the power of God for the salvation of everyone who believes: first for the Jew, then for the Gentile." Romans 1:16

AIMS OF THE SESSION

During this session your learners will:

1. Retell the incident of Daniel and Belshazzar;
2. Identify areas where taking a stand for the faith is difficult;
3. Pray for God's help and strength in those difficult situations.

INSIGHTS FOR THE LEADER

To be a godly teenager is a tough assignment in any period of history. To continue to be a godly teenager when exposed to pressure from a world system committed to pagan philosophy is an assignment infinitely tougher. To begin as a teenager in such an environment and yet rise to a position of high honor without compromising truth, despite several changes of government and at the frequent risk of life, is to fulfill the toughest assignment of all. Yet that is the story of the book of Daniel.

Background

Daniel's story occurs near the er... Old Testament history of the Jewis... After Abraham's lifetime, his descen... into a nation of people as God ha... Famine drove them to Egypt wher... tually became slaves. God used ... them out of Egypt; we'll study his life i... sessions. After 40 years of wanderin... desert, the people fi...

Daniel and his three friends, Shadrach, Meshach and Abednego, were royal princes of the tribe of Judah, and are described in the first chapter of Daniel as "young men without any physical defect, handsome, showing aptitude for every kind of learning, well informed, quick to understand, and qualified to serve in the king's palace" (Dan. 1:4). These splendid young men serve as a good example for the young people of any era. They stood true to their principles in the midst of great pressure, drawing upon God's help to remain faithful against all odds.

The central figure of the four is Daniel, whose personal history is traced through four changes of dynasty in the first six chapters of the book of Daniel, and whose remarkable ... are given to us in chapters 7-12. ... Daniel won respe...

2. INSIGHTS FOR THE LEADER

This part of each lesson is background for you, the leader. Study this section with your Bible open and watch for useful information and insights which will further equip you to lead the class session.

Things to note about the Session Plan:

The **Session Plan** makes heavy use of **Bible Learning Activities**. A Bible Learning Activity (BLA) is precisely what it sounds like—an activity students perform to learn about the Bible. Because action is employed, the student has a much greater chance of **comprehending** and **retaining** spiritual insights. And because you, the leader, can see what the student is doing—whether it's a written assignment, skit or art activity—you can readily **measure** the student's comprehension. The BLA allows you to **walk about the classroom** as students work, answering questions or dealing with problem students. Furthermore, it's **easier to teach well** using BLAs. If you've never used BLAs before, you will quickly find them much simpler to prepare and deliver than a whole session of lecture.

The **Session Plan** provides guided conversation—suggestions on what to say throughout the class time. Notice that the guided conversation is always printed in **bold type** in the **Session Plan.** Regular light type indicates instructions to you, the teacher.

THE TEACHING RESOURCE PAGES

Special goodies to help you teach.

A few sessions require extra teaching tools such as board games or scrambled Bible verses. These are provided by the **Teaching Resource Pages** which follow the **Scratch Sheet** student worksheet in the appropriate sessions.

The **Session Plans** and the **Teaching Resource Pages** contain complete instructions.

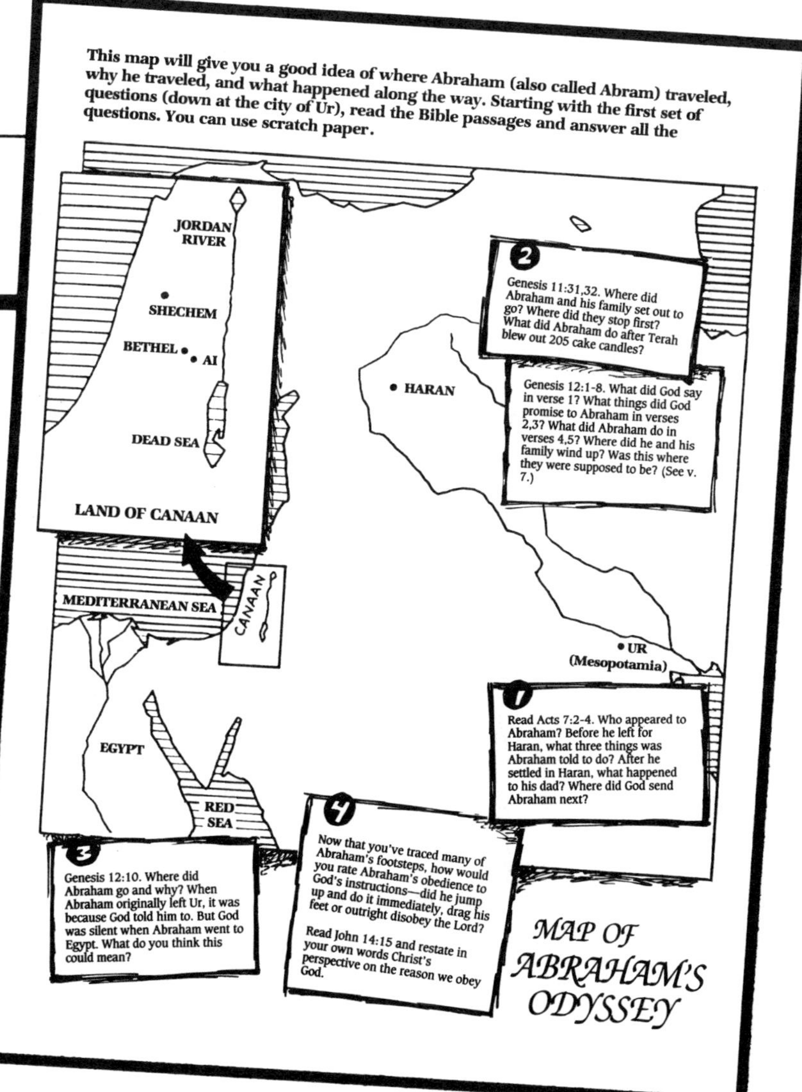

THE FUN PAGE
TAKE-HOME PAPERS

Give your students a treat! The Fun Page combines games, cartoons, short stories, memory verses and daily devotional studies into an enjoyable, fun-filled take-home paper.

KING SAUL: AFRAID TO TELL OTHERS!

Based on 1 Samuel 10

Israel—His name was Saul. The Bible describes him this way: " . . . an impressive young man without equal among the Israelites—a head taller than any of the others" (1 Samuel 9:2).

Now God told His prophet Samuel that He was about to make Saul king of Israel. When Saul learned this he grew very nervous indeed.

Thousands of people had gathered at Mizpah to see Saul crowned king. Everyone was excited and filled with awe at seeing Israel's very first king.

But they almost didn't see him. The great Saul had hidden himself in the huge piles of baggage the crowds had brought with them to the airport . . . er, camelport.

The people looked everywhere for the reluctant king-to-be, but no one could find him. Finally, the people prayed to God and He, through His prophet, told them where Saul was.

So Saul was crowned king and lived happily ever after . . . uh, until he started going bananas and was eventually eliminated! But that's another story.

Features:

Each **Fun Page** is designed to amplify the insights gained in the classroom. The **Fun Page** has a newspaper motif, with a set of cartoon reporters who attempt to dig out the truth about each session's subject.

"Therefore everyone who hears these words of mine and puts them into practice is like a wise man who built his house on the rock." Matthew 7:24

Are you a wise person? Is your life built on Christ, the solid Rock? Are you prepared for anything that may go wrong in life? Just for fun, here's a game about some natural disasters that befall humanity from time to time.

Instructions: Each person below is shouting the name of some natural disaster. Unfortunately, they are all so scared, they've messed up the words! Your job is to split each word into **three parts,** and then stick each part back with two correct parts, to find the actual disasters. For example, *Earthquake, volcano* and *flood* can be split up and rewritten as earcand, flthqo and voloouake! Answers are below, but don't peek until you're finished!

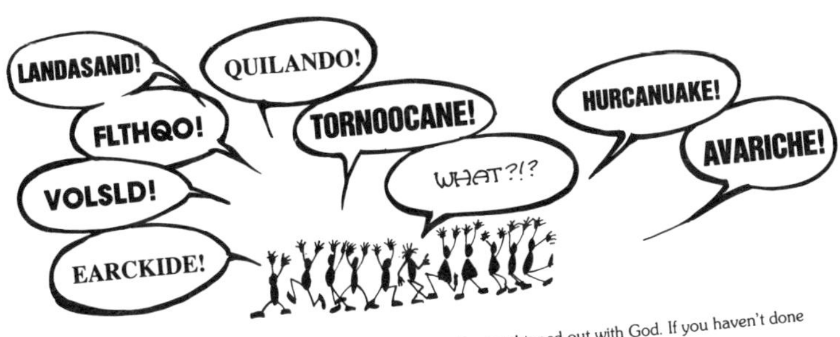

Don't wait until you face a disaster before you get your life straightened out with God. If you haven't done it yet, get right with Him right now!

Answers: Quicksand, earthquake, landslide, hurricane, tornado, avalanche, flood, volcano.

DAILY THINKERS

Day 1 Read Psalm 51:1,2. Does David's request seem sincere? How would you ask God the same thing?

Day 2 Psalm 51:10-12. List what David asks of God.

Day 3 Psalm 103:1. David indicates the depth of his love for God by saying what?

Day 4 Psalm 103:8-13. What are some characteristics of God? What does He do about our sin?

Day 5 Psalm 103:13-18. In light of these verses, what are the things in a person's life that have eternal value?

Day 6 Psalm 108:1-5. Write a song or poem of praise using this psalm as a model.

You'll also find Bible games that your students will love: mazes, crosswords, word searches—games ranging from the simple to the extremely challenging. Again, they are all designed to reinforce what the students have learned during the session time.

The **Daily Thinkers** section is a simple six-day devotional based on passages related to the Scriptures studied in class.

Today's Good News memory verse helps students lock the wisdom of God's Word into their minds and hearts.

How to use the Fun Page:

Photocopy both sides of the **Fun Page** back-to-back, just as it appears in this manual. (If your copy machine cannot do this, we suggest you copy each side on a separate sheet.) Make enough copies for your students plus a few extras for visitors. Note: You may like to occasionally save the **Fun Page** game for use during another Bible study time.

You can use the Fun Page several ways:

As a **take-home paper** to extend the classroom into the week. Hand out copies as students leave class.

As a special **Bible Learning Activity** during class. (Some of the games would make interesting **Attention Grabbers,** for example.)

Make it the **focal point of another Bible study.** For instance, if you used the **Session Plan** Sunday morning, you could reinforce the lesson during an informal midweek meeting by involving students in answering the questions in the **Daily Thinkers.**

Even absentees can be involved. Put the **Fun Page** into an envelope along with a personal note to that learner who needs a little encouragement.

THE POPSHEET LECTURE BIBLE STUDIES

"Pop" these **Popsheets** out of this book and give them to the leader of your youth group's other meetings. Great for an at-home Bible study, a camp retreat, games night or special event.

Youth groups come in all sizes and shapes. So do youth programs. Meetings vary widely in style—ranging from Sunday morning Bible studies with singing and announcements, to deeper discipleship programs for motivated students, to the fun and action of game nights with very short Bible messages.

The **Popsheets** offer a good source of creative thinking for whatever type of program you have. **Popsheets** are packed with Bible stories, object lessons, case studies, discussion questions and fast-paced games and other ideas aimed at the junior high "squirrel" mentality! Each **Popsheet** covers the same basic theme as the accompanying **Session Plan,** but the stories, verses, object lessons and case studies are all new and fresh.

The advantages?

- For students who attended the **Session Plan** class, a fresh new perspective on the topic. A great way to insure retention.
- For learners who missed the **Session Plan** class, a good way to keep current with the other students. This is a sound method to guarantee that all your youth group members explore every topic in a Bible study series.
- Or use your creativity to replace some of the Bible Learning Activities in the **Session Plans** with object lessons and short stories from the **Popsheets.**

THEME

Roughly the same theme as the accompanying **Session Plan.**

BIBLE STUDY OUTLINE

A suggested Bible passage with a list of important points to make during your lecture, the **Bible Study Outline** offers a ***basic* lesson plan** to stimulate your thinking as you prayerfully prepare your message. **Use your own creativity and ability to "flesh it out."** There is plenty here to help you create outstanding Bible messages your students will enjoy and remember.

Notice that the **Bible Study Outline** contains no **Bible Learning Activities.** The **Popsheet** is designed to be a short Bible message (five to ten minutes) that you can give at an informal games night, camp cabin devotional, or similar setting.

OBJECT LESSON

Each **Popsheet** has an object lesson, short story or case study. (A case study is a description of an event or situation a junior high student is likely to face in life.) These add spice to your messages. A good object lesson, for instance, and the spiritual truth it conveys, can be remembered for a lifetime.

THE COMPLETE JUNIOR HIGH BIBLE STUDY RESOURCE BOOK #10

Session 1

THEME: Faith.

BIBLE STUDY OUTLINE

The Popsheet lectures are intended to be 5-10 minutes long. This lecture's passage, Hebrews 11, is lengthy. A simple reading of it without too many additional remarks will help to keep things short. The comments below are designed to inspire your own creativity and help you "flesh out" your message.

Introductory remarks: We often speak of faith in our Bible studies. Faith is essential to the Christian life. It's impossible to be a child of God and to live for God without faith in Him. Let's look at Hebrews 11, a chapter that names dozens of people who are great examples of a life-changing faith in the Father.

Verses 1,2: What is faith? It is being sure of the things we hope for. The Christian's hope is centered on Jesus Christ and the promises of everlasting life in God. The person with faith is sure that heaven, which cannot be seen, awaits. God is the one who commends people of faith, ancient and modern.

Verse 3: Not only does faith look ahead to the world to come, it looks back to the beginning of this one and recognizes God's creative control.

Verse 4: Abel was accepted by God because his offering was a heartfelt response of faith in God. He brought the very best to God. Cain, on the other hand, gave "some of the fruits"—perfunctorily (see Gen. 4:3,4). Faith is what made the difference.

Verse 6: Faith is what pleases God. He is not impressed by looks, intelligence, talent or status. Faith is what He wants. It's all we need to please Him.

Verses 39,40: Faith is no guarantee of an easy life! But it does guarantee that God will ultimately honor His promises. We may not triumph over our daily circumstances and become rich, famous and respected. But by faith we do know that God has "planned something better" for us! Jesus Christ is our redeemer. He will fulfill all the promises. Our hopes and beliefs will be perfected (made complete) when we see Him.

OBJECT LESSON: BOTTLE OF MUSTARD SEEDS

Tell your students, **Jesus said that if we have faith even as small as a mustard seed we can accomplish mighty things (see Luke 17:6).**

Pass around a bottle of mustard seeds (available at grocery spice racks). Encourage your students to smell and handle the seeds, and to taste them if they are adventurous—one or two seeds are nearly tasteless, but more than just a few are very strong. Have water ready! Retrieve the bottle when everyone has had a chance to examine it.

A mustard seed is very small, but it grows into a large plant. Our faith, even though it may seem small to begin with, can grow too. We might not be in the same position as the Old Testament heroes of the faith, but God can use us with our mustard seed faith to accomplish His will in the world around us. We just have to be willing to plant the seed.

DISCUSSION QUESTIONS

1. **Who is your favorite "hero of the faith" and why? How did he or she demonstrate faith and what were the results?**
2. **In what way is faith like a mustard seed? What things must a gardener do to make a seed grow into a healthy plant? What lessons do these things teach about "growing" a healthy faith in God?**
3. **What are the "bugs" that might damage the "mustard tree" of a growing faith? What can a Christian do to protect his or her faith and cause it to grow?**

DISCUSSION QUESTIONS

You may wish to involve your students in your lectures by asking them about the issues and implications of the Bible study. Feel free to modify or add to the questions to more nearly suit your students' needs.

The **Popsheet** is intended to be folded and placed in a Bible for easy reference as the leader teaches.

GAMES AND THINGS

THE COMPLETE
JUNIOR HIGH BIBLE STUDY
RESOURCE BOOK #10

Fun Stunts with Clothespins

BOWL 'N' PINS

Have several volunteers sit at a table. Place a bowl in front of each player and put ten clothespins in each bowl. Lay a rope on the table so that it passes between the bowls and volunteers. The object of the game is to be the first player to pin all ten clothespins to the rope—using only the mouth. Players must sit with hands behinds their backs. If the rope moves out of a player's reach, the leader can slide it back.

You can play several rounds with different volunteers, but be sure to discard the clothespins after they've been in someone's mouth! Try playing the game with blindfolds.

PLEASE PASS THE PLATES

Form teams of ten or more people. Players stand side by side in a row or in a circle. Each player has one clothespin in his or her mouth, positioned so that the clothespin can be opened and closed with the teeth. Players must stand with their hands behind their backs. The object of the game is to be the first team to pass a paper plate from one end of the team to the other (or around the circle a set number of times). Players grab and pass the plate using only their clothespins. Hands must be held behind the back. The leader can retrieve a dropped plate.

RUBBER BAND GUNS

Remember the rubber band guns of yesteryear?

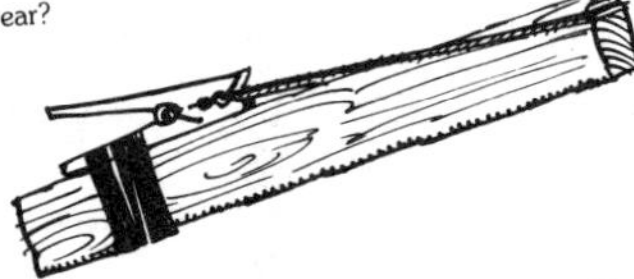

They are easy to make and work great for carnival games. Challenge the players to shoot rubber bands through a hole in a target or knock a paper cup off someone's head (provide eye protection). Guns made to accommodate hefty rubber bands can make fun "weapons" in a lights–out game of tag. Be sure participants wear eye protection.

On the reverse side of the **Popsheet** you will find **Games and Things,** a wonderful collection of:

1. Action activities for your games night, youth group activities, socials, youth Vacation Bible Schools, camps—wherever kids are gathered. Give a copy to the leader of the games night program; he or she will love you for it!
2. Creative suggestions for social events, community involvement and the like.
3. Paper games similar to the **Fun Page** games—Use them as the focal point of an at-home style Bible study for a nice change of pace.
4. Special ideas such as posters (which you can enlarge on a copy machine or opaque projector). These special ideas will appear occasionally in this and future **Junior High Bible Study Resource Books.**

EXCITING OPTIONS FOR THE SMALL YOUTH PROGRAM

Mix and match: Putting together a customized class time tailored to *your* students.

We hope that by reading these introductory pages you've come to realize how hard we are working to bring you a truly useful resource manual for your youth program. There is plenty here for your Sunday School classes, midweek Bible studies, games meetings and special events—even if you do all these things every week.

But what do you do with all these ideas if you're a small congregation with no youth staff (or one poor overworked "volunteer")? This is where **The Complete Junior High Bible Study Resource Book** really shines! By spending a few hours each week in preparation, you can mix and match the best features of each **Session Plan, Scratch Sheet, Fun Page, Popsheet** and **Games and Things** to build a wonderful classroom experience for your students. This illustration gives you some idea of the scope available to you:

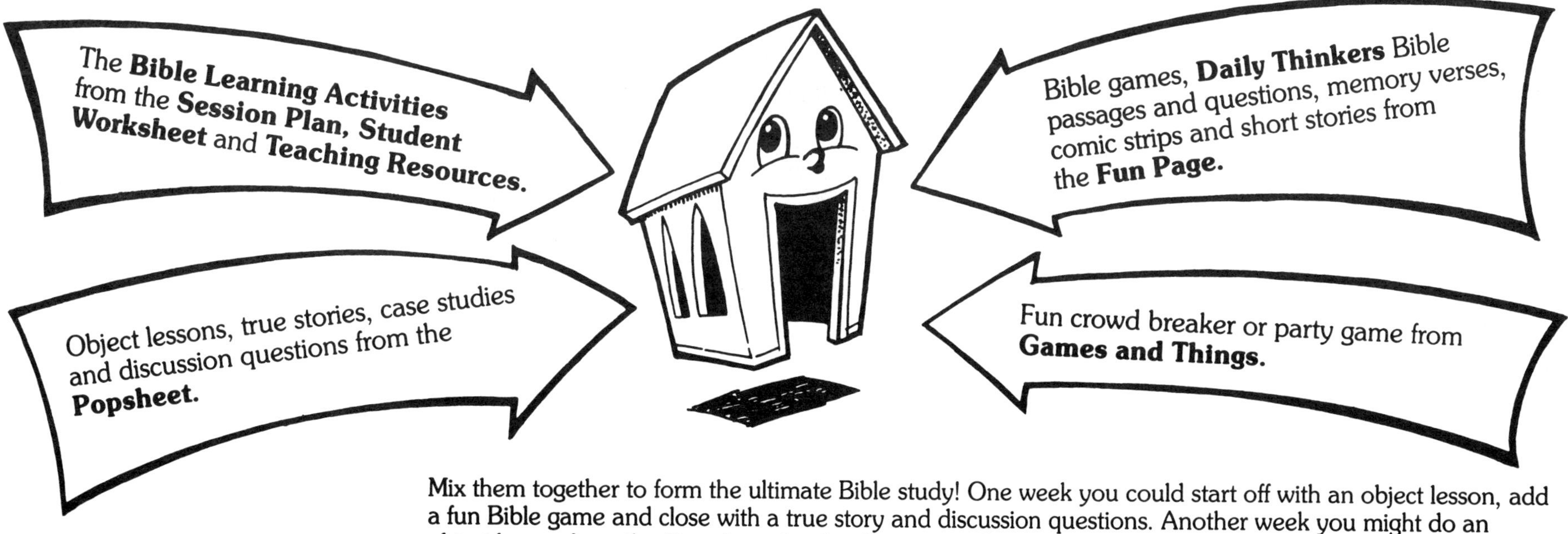

Mix them together to form the ultimate Bible study! One week you could start off with an object lesson, add a fun Bible game and close with a true story and discussion questions. Another week you might do an object lesson from the **Popsheet** for the **Attention Grabber,** Bible passages from the **Daily Thinkers** for the **Exploration** and finish with a party to celebrate God's provision. Each week can be a new and exciting experience that your students will look forward to.

INTRODUCTION TO CLIP ART

Good news for those who can't draw.

If you want your class or youth group to increase in size—and who doesn't— you'll welcome the Clip Art and Other Goodies section found at the rear of this book. Create your own terrific monthly youth group activity calendars, announcement sheets and posters. It's fun and easy! Simply follow the tips and techniques in the Clip Art and Other Goodies section; you'll produce great "promo pieces" that will attract kids to your Bible studies and other events.

Remember: Even if you can't draw cartoons, with the right promotional clip art you can draw kids!

Abraham's Faith SESSION 1

INSIGHTS FOR THE LEADER

WHAT THE SESSION IS ABOUT

Abraham's example shows that our faith can grow as we live in Christ day by day.

SCRIPTURE STUDIED

Genesis 12:1-4; 15:1-6; 16:1-6; 21:1-5; Jeremiah 17:7,8; Galatians 3:6-9; Hebrews 6:13-15; 11:11,12,17-19

KEY PASSAGE

"Abraham believed God, and it was credited to him as righteousness." Romans 4:3

AIMS OF THE SESSION

During this session your learners will:

1. Identify events that shaped Abraham's faith;
2. Describe ways believers' faith today can grow as Abraham's did;
3. Choose one practical way to help their faith mature.

Students often learn the facts about Bible characters without realizing how this information can or should affect their lives today. They need to see that there are answers to the question, "So what?"

This 12-week study of four Old Testament leaders will emphasize the "so what?" as strongly as it does basic facts about the lives of Abraham, Daniel, Moses and David. These "giants" are examined honestly for their strengths and their weaknesses, their triumphs and their failures. Applications to the Christian walk today are clearly shown.

While the studies are not arranged in strict chronological order, information is given to help you provide brief background sketches showing how the characters fit into biblical history.

The first two sessions center on Abraham. Session 1 shows Abraham's faith and how it grew through the experiences of his life. Session 2 deals with the ways in which he obeyed God.

Background

The Bible opens with four great events: the Creation, the Fall, the Flood, and the scattering of nations after the confusion of languages. Following these events, God focused on one man and his descendants. The man is Abraham, father of the Jewish people and recipient of three great promises from God (a land, descendants, and blessings) that are essential to His plan of bringing salvation to the world.

It is difficult to study the story of Abraham without feeling challenged right down to one's toenails. The faith of the man is so breathtaking in its daring and so mighty in its achievements that today's believers must feel humbled in its presence. And yet Abraham learned faith in a very human way, and not without stumbling.

(Note: Throughout these two sessions, it is important to remember that Abraham started out in life as Abram; when he was 99 his name was changed by God as part of the promise that he would have a son—see Gen. 17:5. It would be a good idea to give students this fact as you begin the BIBLE EXPLORATION.)

Abraham and the Book of Hebrews

The writer of Hebrews points to Abraham as a stimulus to New Testament Christian faith. In chapter 11, four specific demonstrations of the Patriarch's trust in the Lord are cited:

1. It was by faith that he was willing to be uprooted and go to an unfamiliar country (see v. 8).

2. He settled in what was to become the land of Israel (see v. 9). Though he lived the life of a nomad, his faith was undaunted because it looked forward to a marvelous future (see vv. 10,13). This is the very essence of faith: Like its inseparable ally, hope, it trusts

where it cannot see (see Rom. 8:24).

3. Abraham believed God could give him a son, in spite of his own advanced age and Sarah's barrenness. The strong steel core of this faith was Abraham's certainty of God's faithfulness to His promise (see Heb. 11:11). We learn something vital about true faith here: It depends not on its own strength, but upon an ever-increasing awareness of total reliability of God. Once certain of what God has said—and that He has said it to us—there is no need of fear that He will not carry it out.

4. Abraham was willing to give Isaac back again to God (see Heb. 11:17-19). By faith he received the gift of a son; by faith he must surrender him. The "even though" of verse 18 brings home the apparent nonsense of the challenge to Abraham. It seemed so illogical that God would take away what He had given, but here is where Abraham showed an important truth about biblical faith. It is not blindly irrational. It is always reasonable, even when it has to fly in the face of normal human reason. So Abraham "reasoned that God could raise the dead" (v. 19) and on that basis followed the awful inner compulsion that all but led to the death of his dear son. If God ever calls us to make some sacrifice in His name, be it giving up a relationship, a job, a career, our freedom or even life itself, He never expects us to do it without providing something better.

Faith That Grows

Faith like Abraham's does not suddenly appear at the wave of a magician's wand. It is a seed that has to be planted and nurtured, fed, pruned and trained. As we trace the Genesis accounts of Abraham's life, we find that is exactly what happened.

In Genesis 12:1—13:4 we have the account of Abraham's obedience to God's initial call. After Abraham arrived in the land of Canaan, there was a famine (see Gen. 12:10). How long this was after his arrival we are not told, but it was enough to send him scuttling out of his God–given territory to Egypt. Was this a falling away from his walk of faith, or was it legitimate prudence? We are not told, but there is no doubt that it opened him to a new temptation he would not have encountered if he had stayed in Canaan. He became afraid that his beautiful wife would be such an attraction that he would be seen as a very disposable husband by anyone with a lustful eye and a sharp knife. So he invented the shoddy little ruse of pretending that she was merely his sister. (She actually was his half-sister; see Gen. 20:12.) But the Lord would not tolerate such a thing. Sadly, innocent people suffered (see Gen. 12:17). The incident is especially sad because it arose out of Abraham's fear, and fear is the opposite of faith.

The story ends with Abraham back in the Promised Land, calling on the name of the Lord at the altar he had built at his first coming (see Gen. 13:3,4). What a comfort to know that there is restoration after backsliding—as long as there is repentance.

The Promise of a Son

The next test of Abraham's faith was over the promise God had made that Abraham would have a son. Time had gone on and on and on—and it hadn't happened. So Abraham and Sarah applied their human reason to the problem, without reference to God. Their solution was for Abraham to produce a son through Sarah's servant Hagar (see Gen. 16:1–4). But it meant trouble then (see vv. 4,5) and later (see Gen. 21:8–10). Once again, departure from faith was injuring innocent people. Abraham was learning to have faith the hard way.

When we turn to Genesis 17:17-22 we find a very human Abraham indeed. In spite of his tremendous trust in God the renewal of the promise of a son struck him as so ludicrous that he couldn't help laughing (see v. 17). It had been so long since the original promise—and besides, now he had Ishmael. Wasn't that enough? (See v. 18.) But God had something more to say: "Your wife Sarah will bear you a son" (v. 19), and the son's name, Isaac, which means "he laughs," will be a reminder of the time Abraham laughed. (Sarah laughed too: see Gen. 18:12; 21:6.) Abraham's faith was reassured. The proof of his faith was his obedience to the circumcision commandment (see Gen. 17:23).

However, circumcision was far from being the greatest evidence of the genuineness of Abraham's faith. The greatest was his willingness to sacrifice

Isaac, as James indicated in his discussion of the relationship between faith and deeds (see Jas. 2:20-22).

The story of Abraham's willingness to sacrifice Isaac is too long to comment on here in detail. But all that is needed is to read it carefully and prayerfully, and then worship God in awe at the faith He built into His servant Abraham. (See Gen. 22:1-18.) Having read the story, we should then ask ourselves, "How willing are we to sacrifice anything God may ask of us?" If we realize how far short we fall in our willingness, then let's remind ourselves that it all began for Abraham when he "believed the Lord, and he credited it to him as righteousness" (Gen. 15:6).

With that act of trust as a starting point, God helped Abraham's faith grow. He used not only Abraham's successes in practicing faith, but also his failures, to produce the "end product" of the strong belief that Abraham displayed in the later part of his life.

"Tall oaks from little acorns grow"! Encourage your students to plant their faith as Abraham planted his, and to let God make it grow.

SESSION PLAN

BEFORE CLASS BEGINS: Now is a good time to make sure that your classroom has all the supplies listed in the "Necessary Classroom Supplies" on page 7.

Make enough photocopies of the Scratch Sheet and the Fun Page take-home paper so that each student will have a copy of each. (Both immediately follow this Session Plan.) The Daily Thinkers on the Fun Page do not cover the same topics studied during the sessions. The purpose for this is to familiarize students with additional Old Testament personalities and their lives as people of God.

The ATTENTION GRABBER and ALTERNATE ATTENTION GRABBER call for special materials in addition to the writing paper, pencils, scissors and Bibles you should always have on hand. See step 1 of the EXPLORATION for a suggestion regarding an easy way to assign Scripture passages to students.

If this happens to be your first session with a new group of kids, we suggest you hand out photocopies of the "All About Me" questionnaire found in the "Clip Art and Other Goodies" section at the back of this book. The information will help you get to know your students. As you plan this session, be sure to allow for the time it will take students to fill out the questionnaire.

Attention Grabber

ATTENTION GRABBER (2-3 minutes)

Materials needed: A few baby toys such as a baby rattle, mobile and bathtub toy.

Show your students the toys. Ask students to raise their hands in response to these questions:

How many of you played with toys like these when you were young? How many of you play with them now?

Then say something like this: **As a person grows older, his or her interests change. There may have been a time when you longed for your birthday to come so that you could get a doll or truck. But now these things don't appeal to you like they did. You have grown and matured and your interests have matured, too. Today we are going to look at a very important part of Christian maturity: growing in our faith in God.**

Optional: This session is about faith. If you are not sure of each student's degree of commitment to God, spend a couple of minutes discussing the nature of belief in Jesus Christ.

ALTERNATE ATTENTION GRABBER (5-7 minutes)

Materials needed: Baby pictures of students and one of yourself; inexpensive prize.

Bring to class baby pictures of four or five students and one of yourself. Display pictures and have students try to guess which picture is whose. This will be a bigger challenge and even funnier if you can obtain the pictures from the parents without the students knowing about it. See if learners know what they looked like as babies.

Give an inexpensive prize to the student who correctly identifies the most pictures.

Talk about ways in which students have grown during the past dozen years or so. What if they had stayed the same? How is physical growth similar to Christian growth? What would be the results if people never grew as Christians?

Say something like, **Today we are going to take a look at the Old Testament personality of Abraham. We'll see how he changed over the years. We will see how his faith in God grew.**

Optional: This session is about faith. If you are not sure of each student's degree of commitment to God, spend a couple of minutes discussing the nature of belief in Jesus Christ.

Bible Exploration

EXPLORATION (30-40 minutes)

Step 1 (12-15 minutes): Have students form groups of two or three. Distribute Scratch Sheets to students. Direct attention to the Scratch Sheet section titled "The Faith of Abraham." Assign one or two of the Scriptures listed there to each group. (The fastest way to assign the passages is to circle the appropriate ones on the sheets before handing them out.) Say, **Most people had some way to measure how they had grown when they were young. Some put pencil marks on the wall, others used a printed growth chart. You are about to work on Abraham's growth chart of faith. In your groups, look up and read the Scriptures assigned to you. Then jot down how Abraham's faith may have been affected by the situations you read about. Then I want all of you to fill in the blanks in the statements at the bottom of the sheet.** (The answers to fill in the blanks are "righteousness," "children," "faith" and "blessed." As you discuss these answers, be sure your learners understand the meaning of the words "righteousness" and "blessed.")

Note: If your class is very small or for some other reason you feel uncomfortable with assembling students into small groups, simply read the various passages aloud and do the assignment as a class discussion. You can apply this alternative teaching method to many of the small group activities suggested throughout this manual.

After students have had time to work, reassemble the class and let pairs take turns sharing their responses, beginning with the acorn and working toward the top of the tree. Answer any questions and clarify any misunderstandings that may come up regarding the material, using information from the INSIGHTS FOR THE LEADER at the beginning of this session. Tell students, **The events in Abraham's life provided opportunities to trust God more and to grow in faith. These events tested his maturity. Sometimes he responded well; sometimes he failed. We can learn about faith from his successes and his failures.**

Step 2 (10-12 minutes): Place a few scissors within reach of the students. Explain, **Each person's life is made up of many different personal experiences—ordinary days, winning awards, flunking classes, births or deaths among family and friends, achievements, disappointments, relationships. Work individually to choose at least five of the cards on the Scratch Sheet—cards that reflect things that have happened in your life. Cut out the cards and jot down on a piece of paper how these events may have helped or hindered your spiritual growth. If your friend died, for example, how did your relationship with God help you deal with your pain? His help probably caused you to grow closer to Him.**

Optional: Have students glue or tape the cards onto a sheet of paper to form a time line of these events in their lives.

After students have had time to work, regain their attention and ask volunteers to describe how their experiences have affected their faith. Share an experience of your own.

Step 3 (8-10 minutes): Draw attention to the text of Jeremiah 17:7,8 on the Scratch Sheet. Read these verses aloud to the class. Say, **God wants our faith to grow. Our maturing faith will show up through our Bible study, prayer, fellowship, telling others about Jesus, worship, relationships and making sure our actions match what we claim we believe. We're going to list some ways we can grow in each of these areas.**

Lead a class discussion, guiding your students to suggest practical ways believers their age can help their faith grow in the areas just named. Offer further suggestions if needed. Encourage learners to make their ideas as practical as possible.

Here's an example: Worship. A student could try to listen to all the words of the hymns; concentrate during the prayer times in the service; at the beginning of the services, think about things God has done for him or her the past week.

Say, **Today we have seen that faith can grow, and we have looked at some things that will help nurture it. Let's write down some thoughts about our faith.**

Conclusion and Decision

CONCLUSION (1-2 minutes)

If you did the original ATTENTION GRABBER, show your students one of the toys again. Say something like this: **It's natural for a baby to play with toys, just as it's natural for that baby to eventually grow up. It's not hard to grow up physically; it just takes a little food, a little exercise, a little care. It's natural for baby Christians to grow up too. If you want to grow**

in your Christian faith, read the Word of God and obey what He tells you to do—that's your food and exercise.

Have students prayerfully and individually write one practical thing they could do to help stimulate the growth of their faith.

Close in prayer, asking God to help your students experience the sort of spiritual growth Abraham underwent in his life.

Distribute the Fun Page take-home paper as students leave the classroom.

ALTERNATE CONCLUSION (5-7 minutes)

On the chalkboard, write the word "faith" in descending fashion as shown below. Explain, **Write a poem to God about your faith, using each letter in the word "faith" as part of each line. Remember, poems don't always have to rhyme.** An example is given below which you can also write on the board.

F
A
I
T
H

Example:

Gives me everything
I give **O**bedience to Him
I talk to Him **D**aily

After students have had time to write, close in prayer.

You may want to collect the Scratch Sheets so that you can read the poems.

Distribute the Fun Page take-home paper as students leave the classroom.

SCRATCH SHEET

Session 1

"Abraham believed God, and it was credited to him as righteousness."
Romans 4:3

The Faith of Abraham

Abraham had to grow and mature in his relationship with God. (He didn't always act maturely, either!) Using this tree as a model of Abraham's life, write down what events occurred and what effect (good or bad) they may have had on the "growth" of Abraham's spiritual life.

Hebrews 11:17-19

Genesis 21:1-5; Hebrews 11:11,12

Hebrews 6:13-15

Genesis 16:1-6

Genesis 15:1-6

Genesis 12:1-4

Read Galatians 3:6-9 and fill in the blanks:

1. Abraham believed God and was credited with ____________________.
2. If we believe, then we are ____________________ of Abraham.
3. If we have ____________________, we are ____________________ along with Abraham.

In the Cards Department

Read these cards and then cut out five or more that describe something that has happened to you. Jot down how each event may have affected your relationship with the Lord.

- Had a prayer answered.
- Was in a fight at school.
- Graduated elementary school.
- Got a good grade in a hard class.
- First met best friend.
- Moved to a new place.
- Had an argument with folks.
- Was baptized.
- A stay in the hospital.
- Death of a friend.
- Death of a family member.
- Flunked a grade.
- Became a Christian.
- Went to a Christian camp.
- Won an award or prize.
- Abducted by aliens. (Just kidding!)

Jeremiah 17:7,8:

"But blessed is the man who trusts in the Lord, whose confidence is in him. He will be like a tree planted by the water that sends out its roots by the stream. It does not fear when heat comes; its leaves are always green. It has no worries in a year of drought and never fails to bear fruit."

FUN Page!

The TOWN CRIER

BUT NOOOOOO! I GET A REPORT THAT STARTS: "ABRAHAM WAS BORN IN A LOG CABIN IN 1809."

MANAGING EDITOR

Today's Good News:

"Abraham believed God, and it was credited to him as righteousness."
Romans 4:3

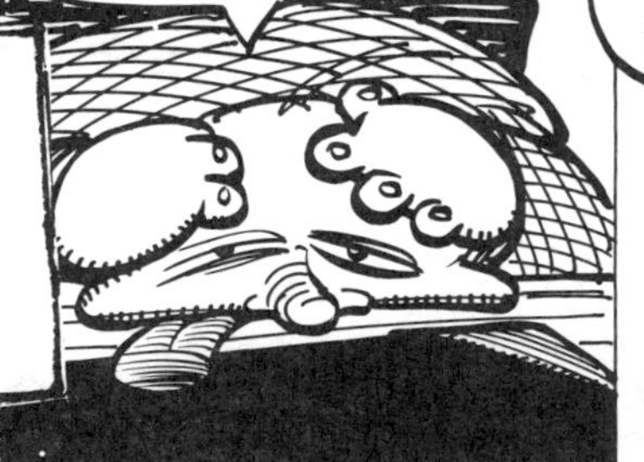

I DUNNO, CHIEF, BUT PIFONT GOT A GREAT PHOTOGRAPH OF ABRAHAM FOR THE FRONT PAGE!

A PHOTOGRAPH OF ABRAHAM? LET ME SEE THAT...

Continued . . .

HOW DOES ONE GET TO HEAVEN? BY BEING **RIGHTEOUS** IN GOD'S EYES. (AND THEN BY DYING!) HOW DOES ONE BECOME RIGHTEOUS IN GOD'S EYES? WELL, MANY PEOPLE BELIEVE IT'S BY BEING AS GOOD AS THEY CAN BE. BUT THE BIBLE SAYS, **"ALL OUR RIGHTEOUS ACTS ARE LIKE FILTHY RAGS."** ISAIAH 64:6

WE JUST AREN'T **GOOD ENOUGH** TO BE RIGHTEOUS IN GOD'S EYES! SO HOW DO WE DO IT? **BY OBEDIENT FAITH IN GOD!**

"If you have faith as small as a mustard seed, you can say to this mulberry tree, 'Be uprooted and planted in the sea,' and it will obey you." Luke 17:6

That's a pretty powerful faith! Is your faith growing, as a mustard seed grows into a large tree? If so, maybe your faith will become as strong as the faith of some of the famous Bible people in these

CLASSIFIED ADS

Instructions: Here are some ads taken out by familiar people from the Bible. You will find them all mentioned in Hebrews 11, so look up that chapter and see if you can match the name or incident with the proper ad. Answers are at the bottom of this page, but no peeking!

1. **MUST SELL IMMEDIATELY! One large ocean-going boat. Good condition, only used once. Buyer must transport boat from top of Mt. Ararat to ocean.**
2. **WANTED: Young person to baby-sit full time a newborn boy named Isaac. Mother is 99 years old and kinda pooped out.**
3. **FOR SALE: Huge number of quality building stones left over from the demolition of a city's outer walls.**
4. **FOR SALE: Brand new, never used coffin. I bought it for my old age, but as it turns out, I won't ever need it.**
5. **WILLING TO SACRIFICE: My son Isaac.**
6. **USED CHARIOTS! Slightly water logged, from trying to follow me across the Red Sea.**
7. **PERSONAL APPEARANCE: Hear the exciting story of this ex-harlot who became involved with a group of foreign spies!**

Answers: 1. Noah. 2. Sarah. 3. Joshua, the walls of Jericho. 4. Enoch. 5. Abraham. 6. Moses. 7. Rahab.

DAILY THINKERS

Day 1 Read Genesis 37:1-11. What would have been the wise thing for Joseph to do about his dreams? Why was Joseph hated by his brothers? Is this a good reason for hating someone? Why or why not?

Day 2 Genesis 37:12-22. What was the sarcastic name Joseph's brothers called him? What was Reuben's plan?

Day 3 Genesis 37:23-36. Write a short page from Joseph's journal showing how he might have felt.

Day 4 Genesis 39:1-6. Why did Joseph prosper? Why did Potiphar prosper?

Day 5 Genesis 39:7-10. Who did Joseph say he did not want to sin against? What would you do in a similar situation? What might be the results of your actions?

Day 6 Genesis 39:11-20. Describe how Joseph must have felt after this incident.

THEME: Faith.

Session 1

BIBLE STUDY OUTLINE

The Popsheet lectures are intended to be 5-10 minutes long. This lecture's passage, Hebrews 11, is lengthy. A simple reading of it without too many additional remarks will help to keep things short. The comments below are designed to inspire your own creativity and help you "flesh out" your message.

Introductory remarks: We often speak of faith in our Bible studies. Faith is essential to the Christian life. It's impossible to be a child of God and to live for God without faith in Him. Let's look at Hebrews 11, a chapter that names dozens of people who are great examples of a life-changing faith in the Father.

Verses 1,2: What is faith? It is being sure of the things we hope for. The Christian's hope is centered on Jesus Christ and the promises of everlasting life in God. The person with faith is sure that heaven, which cannot be seen, awaits. God is the one who commends people of faith, ancient and modern.

Verse 3: Not only does faith look ahead to the world to come, it looks back to the beginning of this one and recognizes God's creative control.

Verse 4: Abel was accepted by God because his offering was a heartfelt response of faith in God. He brought the very best to God. Cain, on the other hand, gave "some of the fruits"—perfunctorily (see Gen. 4:3,4). Faith is what made the difference.

Verse 6: Faith is what pleases God. He is not impressed by looks, intelligence, talent or status. Faith is what He wants. It's all we need to please Him.

Verses 39,40: Faith is no guarantee of an easy life! But it does guarantee that God will ultimately honor His promises. We may not triumph over our daily circumstances and become rich, famous and respected. But by faith we do know that God has "planned something better" for us! Jesus Christ is our redeemer. He will fulfill all the promises. Our hopes and beliefs will be perfected (made complete) when we see Him.

OBJECT LESSON: BOTTLE OF MUSTARD SEEDS

Tell your students, **Jesus said that if we have faith even as small as a mustard seed we can accomplish mighty things (see Luke 17:6).**

Pass around a bottle of mustard seeds (available at grocery spice racks). Encourage your students to smell and handle the seeds, and to taste them if they are adventurous—one or two seeds are nearly tasteless, but more than just a few are very strong. Have water ready! Retrieve the bottle when everyone has had a chance to examine it.

A mustard seed is very small, but it grows into a large plant. Our faith, even though it may seem small to begin with, can grow too. We might not be in the same position as the Old Testament heroes of the faith, but God can use us with our mustard seed faith to accomplish His will in the world around us. We just have to be willing to plant the seed.

DISCUSSION QUESTIONS

1. **Who is your favorite "hero of the faith" and why? How did he or she demonstrate faith and what were the results?**

2. **In what way is faith like a mustard seed? What things must a gardener do to make a seed grow into a healthy plant? What lessons do these things teach about "growing" a healthy faith in God?**

3. **What are the "bugs" that might damage the "mustard tree" of a growing faith? What can a Christian do to protect his or her faith and cause it to grow?**

Fun Bible Games

BIBLE RELAY

Assemble two or more teams, lined up behind a team captain at the end of the room. The teams must have equal numbers of players. On a chalkboard, write a list of Bible verses—as many verses as there are players on a team. Place Bibles on a chair at the other end of the room, one Bible per team. At a signal, the first person on each team runs to a Bible, looks up the first verse on the list and reads the verse and its reference at full volume, then runs back to the team and tags the next player. The next player repeats the process, reading the next verse on the list. The first team to read all the verses listed wins. If some players don't know the Bible well, you can simply photocopy a list of verses (and perhaps highlight the references) from which the players can read.

CUTTHROAT CROSSWORDS

Pit two or three players against each other on a Bible-based crossword puzzle. Here's how: Players take turns solving the clues and filling in the puzzle. Each player should use a colored pencil, a different color for each player. When the game is completed or no one can solve any more clues, players count how many clues each has correctly solved. The player with the most solved clues wins. If a clue is wrong and must be erased, the player who made the mistake loses a point. If in solving one clue a player also completes another word, he or she gets a point for the extra word.

Crossword puzzles based on the Bible can be purchased at any prominent bookstore chain or Christian supply store. The books generally have puzzles aimed at several age levels.

ASSEMBLE A VERSE

Here's a good one to play when you want to teach about a particular verse or passage. Write the verse on butcher paper in letters large enough to be seen by everyone in the classroom. Cut the verse into separate words, shuffle and place the words in a bucket or other container. You need to make as many copies of the verse, each in a bucket, as the number of teams you plan to have. Each team should have at least five players.

Line teams up single file behind a team captain. At the signal to begin, the captain of each team takes a word out of his or her team's bucket, runs to the far side of the room and tapes the word to the wall. The player then runs back and tags the next person on the team who repeats the process. Players may need to take more than one turn to arrange the words in the proper order.

The object of the game is to be the first team to tape the words in proper order. As more words are assembled, some players may be forced to use their turn to rearrange them to achieve the proper order. Only one word can be moved or added during each turn. Teams can shout advice as players tape words.

To speed things up a bit, have sponsors hand short lengths of tape to the players as they reach the wall. Also, you can drop a big hint by reading the passage just before the game begins.

Abraham's Obedience SESSION 2

WHAT THE SESSION IS ABOUT

God wants us to give Him our complete obedience.

SCRIPTURE STUDIED

Genesis 11:31—12:8,10; John 14:15; Acts 7:2-4

KEY PASSAGE

"If you love me, you will obey what I command." John 14:15

AIMS OF THE SESSION

During this session your learners will:

1. Examine specific Scriptures relating to Abraham's obedience to God's call;
2. Describe the possible results of complete obedience, partial obedience and disobedience;
3. Brainstorm ways they can be more obedient to God and pray, asking God's help to act more obediently.

INSIGHTS FOR THE LEADER

Our scene opens in the ancient city of Ur, with Abraham (then called Abram) living presumably happily with his father Terah, his wife Sarah (then Sarai) and his nephew Lot. It happens that Ur is one of the ancient biblical cities we know something about. Since the excavation of Ur by Sir Leonard Woolley in 1924, a picture has emerged of a prosperous place with a strong cult of the moon god. It surely is not too speculative to suggest that Abram and his family must have found it a very tense situation to be worshipers of the Lord among idolaters. One of the things they would have encountered, for example, was the practice of burying the dead not just with their material possessions, as was common in many ancient cultures, but with their servants too.

Abram Leaves Ur

But for all that, when God told Abram to leave (see Acts 7:2,3) it must have been hard. For all its faults Ur was a civilized place to live, with comforts that could never be enjoyed by a wandering nomad. But so strong was the call, Abram went.

With Terah, Abram's father, seemingly in charge (see Gen. 11:31), the group got as far as Haran and settled down for the time being.

Despite the time spent in Haran, the call and the promise (see Gen. 12:1-3) still reverberated in Abram's spirit with an insistence that would not go away. Finally Terah died (see Gen. 11:32; Acts 7:4), and off Abram went. He obeyed by faith (see Heb. 11:8), and went even though he still did not know where he was going. No maps, no travel books, nothing more than a few traders' tales could tell him what lay beyond the dip of the horizon. For him, it was a trek over the edge of the world. But he knew he had the call and the promise, and he obeyed.

Arrival at Shechem

Eventually they arrived at Shechem. Confirmation for the journey came with a vision, increasing the scope of the previous promise. God said, "To your offspring I will give this land" (Gen. 12:7). It is worth noting that even at that moment Abram had to take everything in faith. It was a promise for the future. He was not being given the land; it was being promised to his descendants. His only possession there would be his wife's grave (see Gen. 23:4; Acts 7:5,16; Heb. 11:9,10).

In Shechem Abram built an altar and worshiped, then continued his odyssey. He had arrived but it was not the end. Only the end of the beginning. His was to be a lifetime of traveling up and down the land of promise, pacing out the future domain of his descendants. He was claiming the land not only for his children but for the Lord, so at his next stop, between Bethel and Ai, he built another altar (see Gen. 12:8). Abram's walk with God would be a con-

tinuing experience of worship.

It is not difficult for the Christian to identify with Abram. There are many spiritual parallels with the saga of his journey. The person without Christ is, in a sense, in Ur with its idolatry; the gospel call to repentance and faith is like the call to Abram to "get up and go." As Bunyan showed so brilliantly in *Pilgrim's Progress,* the Christian life is a pilgrimage from darkness to light. But that call to start means leaving not only sin behind, but our comfortable life too. And that can be difficult.

Just as the fulfillment of God's promise involved Abram's willingness to continue in obedience, so our obedience to God allows us to progress in our walk with Him. If we settle in Haran and, unlike Abram, do not continue in obedience we will experience the frustrating, chafing tensions of being neither fully Christian in our actions nor fully pagan. We find a battle going on inside us. Paul summed this battle up in Galatians 5:17 when he said, "The sinful nature desires what is contrary to the Spirit, and the Spirit what is contrary to the sinful nature." Because of the conflict, "you do not do what you want." As long as we let our sinful nature have its way, we cannot fully obey and serve God.

Is there a time when we are completely free of the influence of sin in our lives? In one way there is not, at least on this earth, for we will never be fully free of our sinful nature until we are glorified in heaven (see Phil. 3:12). But in another way, there is. For Scripture shows us how to daily put the "old man" to death and open ourselves to the fullness of the Holy Spirit that Jesus might reign in our lives (see Rom. 7:24,25).

Believers' Freedom

In Romans 6:1-14 we read the critical fact that makes it possible: When we became Christians, our old selves were crucified and buried with Him. Hence we are liberated to lead a new life, not only at the future resurrection, but also here and now. The problem is how to make the theory fact, how to make actual what is stated in words. Paul's answer is to "count yourselves dead to sin but alive to God" and not to "let sin reign in your mortal body" (vv. 11,12). Plainly this is more than mind over matter advice. It does means a deliberate act of the will—keeping our hands, feet, eyes and everything else from evil sights, sounds and action and putting them to good works instead, using them for righteousness (see v. 13). But this, of course, will be impossible in our own strength. In chapter 8 of Romans, Paul shows that the answer is the Holy Spirit. "The law of the Spirit of life" sets us "free from the law of sin and death" (Rom. 8:2).

That is the way of complete obedience for us. We can now build our altar and worship Him, knowing we are heirs of God and co-heirs with Christ (see Rom. 8:17).

SESSION PLAN

BEFORE CLASS BEGINS: Photocopy the Scratch Sheet, the "Map of Abraham's Odyssey" Teaching Resource page and the Fun Page. If you wish, supply felt pens for students to color their copies of the Teaching Resource map.

Attention Grabber

ATTENTION GRABBER (3-5 minutes)

Tell students, **Turn to the "Oh, No, Doctor!" section of the Scratch Sheet and look over the doctor's orders on the page. Choose the order that would be hardest for you to obey. Not that we should disobey a doctor's instructions, but some people have a harder time with injections, while others may find it more difficult to be restricted to bed.**

Ask for students' responses. Then say something like this: **If we go to a doctor, we generally trust his or her advice and obey the doctor's orders even if they are unpleasant for us at the time. We do this because we are looking forward to the results of the treatment—getting better. Today we are going to look at an order from the Lord to Abraham that may have seemed much like a doctor's unpleasant order.**

ALTERNATE ATTENTION GRABBER (5-7 minutes)

Pass out slips of paper and tell students, **This morning we are going to try a little experiment called "True Confessions." I want you to write on this slip of paper approximately the amount of time that has passed since you were last disobedient to someone you know you should have obeyed. For example, if I disobeyed the speed law while driving this morning, my last disobedient act took place about half an hour ago. Maybe you were asked to mow the lawn yesterday, and you went on a bike ride instead. Write the amount of time since you were last disobedient, in hours or fractions of hours, on your paper. Do not sign the paper.**

After allowing time for students to write, collect the papers and read the times to the class.

Say, **It is obvious that most of us do not go very long without having some difficulty with obedience. Today we are going to look again at Abraham. Abraham was not perfect as we saw in our last session. But his obedience stands as a good example for Christians today.**

Bible Exploration

EXPLORATION (30-45 minutes)

Step 1 (15-20 minutes): Distribute copies of the "Map of Abraham's Odyssey" Teaching Resource page. The Teaching Resource assignment can be accomplished by students working individually or in groups of three or four—or you can lead a class discussion as students follow along on their individual copies of the map. Whichever method you choose, read the map's instructions to your students and be sure they all know what to do. Walk around the room to offer encouragement and advice as students work on the questions.

Optional Step 2 (5-7 minutes): Allow students to color their maps with felt pens for display.

Step 3 (3-5 minutes): When everyone has finished their maps, ask the students for their responses. Ask, **Do you think Abraham obeyed God? Why or why not?** You may get varying responses. Point out that Abraham obeyed by leaving Ur and heading to Haran. From there God led Abraham to the land of Canaan. Even though obedience had a cost (leaving home, not knowing destination, etc.) Abraham still chose to obey God.

Step 4 (10-15 minutes): Ask students to form groups of three or four. Direct attention to the "Obedience Opportunity" section of the Scratch Sheet and tell students, **Examine the chart and work together with your group to decide on the possible results of obedience, disobedience and so on.** (For example, one result of disobedience may be punishment.)

After groups have had time to work, reassemble the class and ask for their responses. Ask your students some questions like these:

Do you think that there is more to be gained by obedience or by disobedience?

Why do you think people disobey God?

What are some hard choices you may have to make in order to obey God?

How is partial obedience like disobedience?

Tell students, **We all tend to create problems when we disobey the one who loves or cares for us, whether that is God or a parent or some other person who has responsibility for us.**

Say something like, **You have demonstrated that incomplete obedience is still disobedience. If you are like me you probably find yourself obeying God when it is convenient for you, or putting off doing what you know you are supposed to do. Let's think about our own obedience to God for a moment.**

Conclusion and Decision

CONCLUSION (3-5 minutes)

Invite students to brainstorm with you ways in which they can be more obedient followers of God. Write their ideas on the chalkboard as they give them. Let each student privately choose one idea he or she wants to focus on. Close with a time of silent prayer in which students may ask God to help them be more obedient to Him this week.

Distribute the Fun Page take-home paper.

ALTERNATE CONCLUSION (5-10 minutes)

Now that students have traced the steps of Abraham as he obeyed God's guidance, ask them to work privately to create "maps" of their own life experiences with God. For example, perhaps they first heard about God at home, became Christians in a worship service, attend Bible studies in your classroom, invited a friend to a youth group activity or feel called to serve God in a foreign country. Students can plot these various "contacts" with God on a whimsical map of their own design. You might also suggest students plot times when they were disobedient to God.

Collect unsigned maps so that you can get a good idea of the spiritual experiences your class members have had.

Close in prayer and distribute the Fun Page take-home paper.

SCRATCH SHEET

Which of the doctor's orders below would you have the toughest time obeying? Why?

Tongue out, open wider, and DON'T GAG!

I think you are going to need stitches.

Looks like we'll have to start rabies shots!

You must pay this within 30 days.

You need to stay away from any physical activity for three months.

Obedience Opportunity

Choose two or three of the following situations and describe the possible results each kind of obedience would produce.

SITUATION	Obedience	Eventual Obedience	Partial Obedience	Disobedience
You are asked to take out the trash—NOW!				
Your homework assignment is due tomorrow.				
You know God doesn't want you to go to that party!				
You are asked to keep your phone conversations to three minutes.				
You know you should forgive that person who wronged you.				
You know you should keep away from that kind of centerfold magazine.				
Your folks ask you not to wear certain types of clothing, hairstyles or makeup.				
You know that you should try to make friends with a new kid in school.				

This map will give you a good idea of where Abraham (also called Abram) traveled, why he traveled, and what happened along the way. Starting with the first set of questions (down at the city of Ur), read the Bible passages and answer all the questions. You can use scratch paper.

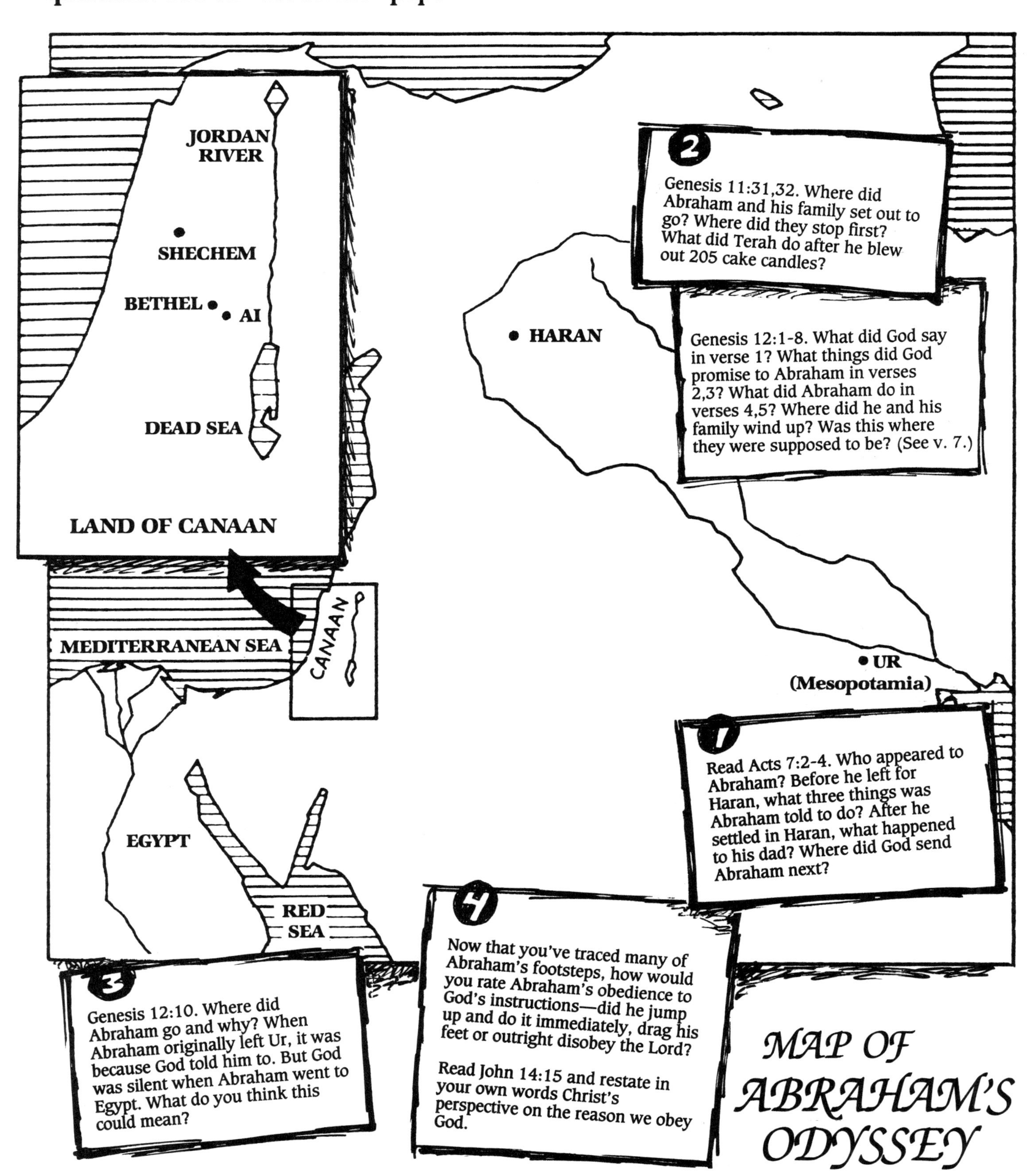

The TOWN CRIER

Today's Good News:

"If you love me, you will obey what I command." John 14:15

AMAZING DISCOVERY: THE DEVIL'S DIARY!!

By ace reporter Typo

Jerusalem—Stunned archaeologists have dug up what are apparently two very old parchment pages from a diary kept by Satan himself!

Professor Heinrich Nurmlinger, of the European University of Digging Up Very Old Stuff, who dug up the very old stuff, told this reporter:

"Jah, ve haff dug up some very old schtuff here. Ve haff translated it into English und it looks like it is from der Devil himself!"

The complete English translation for both pages is as follows:

From the desk of Satan:

Note to myself: Send a memo to Demon Unbelief reminding him how important to me it is that all humans DISOBEY GOD. A human who obeys God is a human who has defeated me. And I HATE to be defeated!

Make sure Unbelief understands that it is up to him to prevent them humans from praying, reading their Bibles, attending local church fellowships and other offensive things. It is also imperative that Unbelief causes them younger humans to disobey their parents, to deliberately do things they know are wrong and to generally be as obnoxious as possible!

The only good human is a disobedient one! Them are the kind I want to share eternity with.

We humans can learn two things about Satan from this diary excerpt. One, Satan loves to see people not obey the Lord. Two, Satan's grammar ain't so good.

INTERVIEW WITH THE APOSTLE PETER

By foreign correspondent Pifont
Based on John 18

Heaven—We informed the internationally–known apostle Peter of the discovery of the Devil's diary. Peter had this to say about the nature of obedience and disobedience:

"I learned about disobedience the easy way; I disobeyed. I had been a disciple of Jesus for many months. I honestly believed He was the Son of God. But suddenly Jesus was captured by the Roman soldiers. Afraid for my life, I denied to everyone that I had ever known Him. I lied to save my own skin.

"After that I was ashamed of myself and terribly depressed. Jesus was crucified for me, but I had denied Him.

"But praise God! I learned something of great importance that I want your readers to know: Jesus can forgive sin and disobedience!

"As my friend John wrote, 'If we confess our sins, he is faithful and just and will forgive us our sins and purify us from all unrighteousness' (1 John 1:9)."

Once a denying, disobedient disciple, Peter went on to become a fantastic example of an obedient believer!

SATAN AND JESUS IN COMBAT!

By the News Hound Based on Luke 4:1-13

The Wilderness—Eyewitnesses (namely two lizards I uncovered) report that Satan appeared to Jesus here in the wilderness. Satan tempted Him, hoping to make Him disobey Almighty God and thus ruin His mission here on earth.

But Jesus was too smart for the old rat! Every time Satan offered a new temptation, Jesus would respond with Bible truths!

The Bible says that Satan is a liar and the father of lies (John 8:44). When faced with the truth of the Bible and one who believes and obeys it, Satan runs in terror!

Speaking about obeying God, Jesus Himself said, "If you love me, you will obey what I command" (John 14:15). And He wants us to keep His commandments because He loves us!

TOWN CRIER EDITORIAL

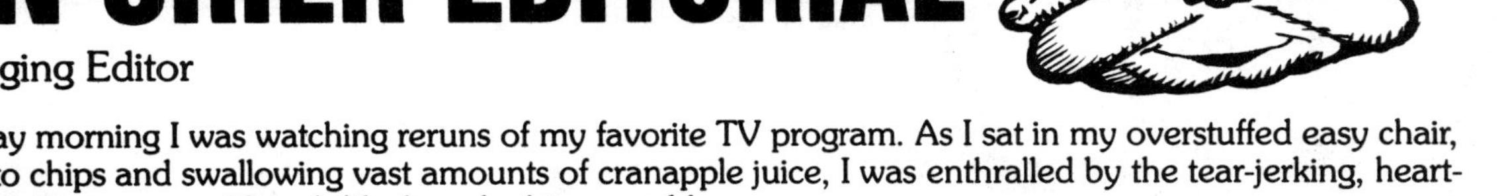

By the Managing Editor

Last Saturday morning I was watching reruns of my favorite TV program. As I sat in my overstuffed easy chair, munching potato chips and swallowing vast amounts of cranapple juice, I was enthralled by the tear-jerking, heart-rending saga unfolding on my 19-inch black-and-white portable.

One of the main characters, Wally Cleaver, turned to his younger brother and mouthed the immortal line: "Boy, Beaver, are you gonna get clobbered when Dad gets home!" Sheer poetry! I wiped a tear and blew my nose on my onion-dip-covered paper towel.

While the station took a short commercial break (some clown with a chimp selling used cars), my mind drifted into a fitful semiconsciousness.

In my daydream I recalled myself as a child. I recalled my sweet mother and my hard-working father. I recalled that it is a big mistake to fall asleep holding a plate of chips and dip and a cup of cranapple juice.

"Boy, am I gonna get clobbered when Dad gets home," I cried. But then I became fully awake and realized that my dad was long gone.

Is God like that? Does He "clobber" Christians who disobey?

The Bible says, "The Lord disciplines those he loves" (Hebrews 12:6), which means He may deal with you or me in a loving but serious way when we are off the track. Remember that God will only do things that lead to ultimate good for His children (see Romans 8:28).

★ ★ ★ ★ ★ ★

We here at the Fun Page are always striving for perfection. (Well, almost always.) And so we made "Obedience Charts" to help all our employees do good things and avoid bad things.

As you can see from this partially filled-out chart, one employee (who shall remain nameless to protect him, but his initials are "N.H.") has given us some trouble. He can't seem to sit still. His attention is always distracted. He has a hard time keeping his mind on his work.

To find out the reason WHY, connect the dots in the proper numerical order. The answer will appear.

Show up to work on time.
Keep the coffee breaks short.
Be happy with your miserable salary.
Eat no dog biscuits on the job.
No chasing cats.
No shedding.
No chewing the Chief's slippers.

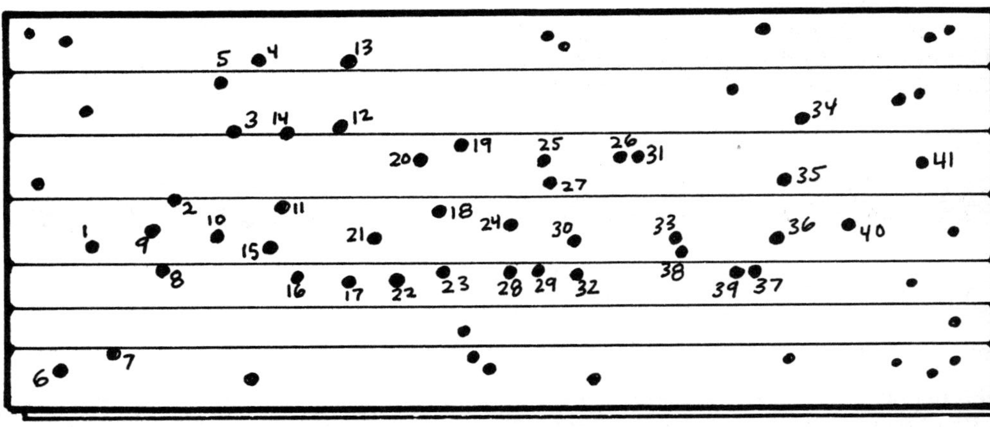

Now that you've completed our obviously absurd chart, we invite you to make some kind of serious chart of your own to test your spiritual "Obedience Quotient." List such things as the amount of time you spend talking to or thinking about God, the time you spend reading your Bible or Christian books, and any personal "goodness goals" you may have. If you keep your chart for a week or two, it'll give you a good idea of what you can do to improve your Christian life.

DAILY THINKERS

Day 1 Read Genesis 39:20-23. What did the Lord do for Joseph while he was in prison?

Day 2 Genesis 40:1-8. How did Joseph show kindness to the baker and the cupbearer?

Day 3 Genesis 40:9-15. What was the favor Joseph asked of the cupbearer?

Day 4 Genesis 40:16-23. What happened to the cupbearer, the baker and Joseph?

Day 5 Genesis 41:1-8. Why do you think ancient people put so much stock in dreams? Do you think God used them? How?

Day 6 Genesis 41:9-16. Who did Joseph say would interpret the Pharaoh's dream?

THEME: Obedient people never see death.

Session 2

BIBLE STUDY OUTLINE

Read John 8:51-59 to your students. Make the following remarks as time allows.

Introductory remarks: The Jewish leaders did not like Jesus. To them He was a heretic, a nut who claimed equality with God. Let's take a look at a typical clash between Jesus and the religious leaders.

Verse 51: Jesus brings up two major subjects in this sentence: obedience to His Word and death. To the obedient child, God will grant eternal life.

Verses 52,53: The Jews did not understand that Jesus was talking about spiritual death. He meant that people who love and obey Him will live forever in eternity. His obedient disciples—including those of us who have given our lives to Him and obey Him—are in no danger of missing out on eternal life. From other places in the Bible we know that we will spend an eternity of joy and love with Almighty God. But those who reject Jesus will be rejected by Jesus.

The Jews accused Jesus of being demon-possessed, an indication that they had no idea who they were talking to or what they were talking about. In an attempt to show how misguided Jesus was, they pulled out the "big gun"—Abraham, the venerated founder of the Jewish people and obedient servant of God. He obeyed God and so did the prophets, but they all died. "Who are you, Jesus, to build yourself up above these great people of the faith?" is what the Jews were saying.

Verses 54-59: Jesus pointed out that not only was He the object of Abraham's faith, obedience and desire, He was around long before Abraham was born! The phrase "I am" is a name that God the Father called Himself when He addressed Moses. To take the name upon Himself, Jesus was either a heretic—as the Jews thought—or truly God's Son. The Jews tried to kill Jesus, but He escaped. Later, they would play a part in Jesus' crucifixion. Jesus ultimately escaped that too by rising from the dead! (At this point, do the Object Lesson.)

OBJECT LESSON: COUNTERFEIT CASH

Show your listeners a five, ten or twenty dollar bill. Say, **This happens to be real, but there are people who make counterfeit versions. In order to be a good counterfeit, "funny money" must look real, feel real and seem real in as many ways as possible. It just can't BE real.**

All of us here believe that we are alive. But until we are made alive in Christ, we are spiritually dead; our lives are counterfeit. Counterfeit lives may look and feel real, but they are valueless compared to real life, eternal life. The Bible says that we were dead in our sins, and that God made us "alive with Christ" (Col. 2:13). Christians are truly alive, other people are still dead in their sins. Christians will never die this type of death again.

The Jews believed that they were alive, but they were counterfeits. Don't make the mistake they did. If you don't know if you are spiritually alive, talk to me after the meeting.

DISCUSSION QUESTIONS

1. **Why did the Jewish religious leaders dislike Jesus? Why do you suppose Jesus didn't try to make them like Him?**

2. **What does it mean to be obedient to God? What are some things that we must be doing to be obedient?**

3. **Why do you think God considers sinful unbelievers to be spiritually dead? How can a person be made alive?**

4. **We have said that a counterfeit life is a valueless one compared to real, eternal life. What is eternal life and why is it more valuable than our earthly lives?**

Unusual Props for Youth Work

STOCKS

Long ago, stocks were used to publicly punish offenders. The device looked something like this:

Nowadays, stocks can also come in handy in youth work. Not to punish, of course, but to play good-natured games.

The captain of a losing relay team, for example, could be placed in the stocks for two minutes. Anyone who goes in the stocks gets a cold soda or some other reward when coming out.

If you're having a slave contest, disobedient slaves can be brought back in line with the threat of time in the stocks.

Also, a youth leader locked in the stocks makes a good pie throwing target!

ANNOUNCEMENT TABLE

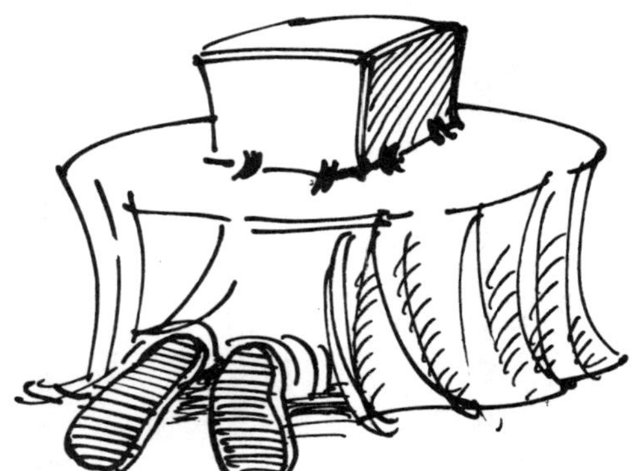

A table with a hole in the middle, covered with a box, makes a fun way to present important announcements and information. Tape your announcements to the inside of the box. Students crawl under the table one at a time to read the news. Hand them a flashlight or cut a small hole in top of the box to let light in. The announcement table can be placed in a central location for students to investigate when they arrive for your meeting. The box can also contain riddles, brainteasers, Bible passages and instructions for any game you want students to play.

GIANT NOSE

Years ago, one of the editors of THE COMPLETE JUNIOR HIGH BIBLE STUDY RESOURCE BOOK caused quite a stir at summer camp by bringing an eight-foot papier-mâché nose filled with prizes wrapped in green plastic! Kids could reach up a nostril to obtain a prize. His idea was published elsewhere but, although giant noses haven't exactly swept the youth world off its feet, we present it here again for your own possible edification.

You can make a smaller version that provides just as much fun. Use chicken wire mounted on a plywood backboard to form the shape, then cover the wire with paper soaked in starch. When the paper drys, spray the nose with flesh–tone paint, adding a wart here and there. Wrap prizes or announcements in pieces of green garbage bag covered with green slime—you can buy it at toy stores—or green gelatin.

The plywood board should have a hole in it—you can reach through and grab somebody's hand or pour some slime out a nostril. It's strictly junior high, but somebody's got to do it!

Daniel's Stand SESSION 3

WHAT THE SESSION IS ABOUT

Christians must be willing to speak and live the truth even when it is unpopular.

SCRIPTURE STUDIED

Daniel 5:1-30; Romans 1:16

KEY PASSAGE

"I am not ashamed of the gospel, because it is the power of God for the salvation of everyone who believes: first for the Jew, then for the Gentile." Romans 1:16

AIMS OF THE SESSION

During this session your learners will:

1. Retell the incident of Daniel and Belshazzar;
2. Identify areas where taking a stand for the faith is difficult;
3. Pray for God's help and strength in those difficult situations.

INSIGHTS FOR THE LEADER

To be a godly teenager is a tough assignment in any period of history. To continue to be a godly teenager when exposed to pressure from a world system committed to pagan philosophy is an assignment infinitely tougher. To begin as a teenager in such an environment and yet rise to a position of high honor without compromising truth, despite several changes of government and at the frequent risk of life, is to fulfill the toughest assignment of all. Yet that is the story of the book of Daniel.

Background

Daniel's story occurs near the end of the Old Testament history of the Jewish people. After Abraham's lifetime, his descendants grew into a nation of people as God had promised. Famine drove them to Egypt where they eventually became slaves. God used Moses to get them out of Egypt; we'll study his life in future sessions. After 40 years of wandering in the desert, the people finally moved into the land God had promised Abraham. They settled down, and were ruled first by judges and later by a series of kings. Eventually the people became so wicked that God had to teach them a lesson. To do this He used neighboring countries to conquer and capture the Hebrew people.

At this time a Hebrew young man named Daniel was taken as a captive to the land of Babylon which was ruled by Nebuchadnezzar.

Daniel and his three friends, Shadrach, Meshach and Abednego, were royal princes of the tribe of Judah, and are described in the first chapter of Daniel as "young men without any physical defect, handsome, showing aptitude for every kind of learning, well informed, quick to understand, and qualified to serve in the king's palace" (Dan. 1:4). These splendid young men serve as a good example for the young people of any era. They stood true to their principles in the midst of great pressure, drawing upon God's help to remain faithful against all odds.

The central figure of the four is Daniel, whose personal history is traced through four changes of dynasty in the first six chapters of the book of Daniel, and whose remarkable visions are given to us in chapters 7-12.

Daniel won respect and honor from the kings he served. He was eventually made the highest administrator of the entire province of Babylon (see Dan. 2:48 regarding King Nebuchadnezzar and 6:3 regarding King Darius).

Handwriting on the Wall

The fifth chapter of Daniel contains the story you and your students will look at in today's session. On the occasion of the annual feast of the gods, King Belshazzar invited a thousand of his lords and his wives and concubines to the palace. The licentious feast of Belshazzar reached its height when he called for

the golden vessels taken from the Temple in Jerusalem, and the king and his guests drank wine from the vessels, praising their pagan gods in deliberate blasphemy of the God of Israel. Immediately a supernatural hand appeared and wrote upon the plaster of the wall certain Aramaic words—*Mene, Mene, Tekel, Parsin*.

The party-goers were understandably frightened at this. The king was so terrified that he turned pale and his knees knocked. He called on all his wise men and offered rich rewards to the one who could read and interpret the writing. But no one could.

The queen heard the terrified voices of the king and his nobles and came into the banquet hall. She urged Belshazzar to send for Daniel since he had been able to interpret dreams that had baffled the kingdom's wise men in the past.

So Daniel duly arrived. He boldly rebuked the king for his evil ways and his persistent refusal to recognize the true God. Then he interpreted the inscription thus:

"*Mene:* God has numbered the days of your reign and brought it to an end.

"*Tekel:* You have been weighed on the scales and found wanting.

"*Peres* [The singular of Parsin]: Your kingdom is divided and given to the Medes and Persians" (Dan. 5:26-28).

And that very night, as history records, two Babylonian deserters led Persian invaders under the wall of the city where the Euphrates River had been diverted, and the defending garrison found itself attacked from within. That same night the king was slain as the Persian troops raged through the city.

Lessons from Daniel

The similarities of Babylon to the world we live in are obvious. God is often out of the question for many of the people around us in our jobs or schools; there is a party going on, the sails are full and the weather is clear. But let fear enter the picture, from whatever cause, and the people of the living God are brought out into the open and asked for counsel. The world's answers are seemingly fine—until the going gets tough.

Another point of comparison that has impact in our world is the fact that Daniel had to say the unpopular thing. No one likes to be told that he or she is a sinner. No one likes to be told that what he or she is doing is wrong. But sometimes it must be done. Of course those who do so must be sure that their lives, like Daniel's, are not incriminated by what they say.

Your students will have ample opportunity to take a stand for their faith by refusing to cheat or gossip and by explaining why they do not participate in some types of activities rather than shrugging their shoulders in embarrassment.

There is no question that Daniel's remarks were uncomfortable for the king and his court, and there should be no question that the speech and character of today's Christians should make those around them feel a little uncomfortable with their sinful condition. Christians should be channels of too much light for those trying to stay in darkness and too much power for those trying to puff themselves up to appear strong.

SESSION PLAN

BEFORE CLASS BEGINS: Photocopy the Scratch Sheet and Fun Page. Provide felt pens, poster board or newsprint, tape or tacks and scissors. You will need envelopes if you play the second version of the game described in step 4 of the EXPLORATION.

Attention Grabber

ATTENTION GRABBER (3-5 minutes)

Materials needed: Felt pens, poster board, tape, scissors, scratch paper, inexpensive rewards.

Before class, write several messages on poster board. These might be the announcements for the day or a message about today's study such as, "The wall can tell an interesting story" or a silly saying or joke. Cut each message apart so that each word of each message is on a separate piece of poster board. Scramble the order of the messages and attach them to the walls of your room—one or two messages on each wall.

As students arrive, ask them to take a piece of scratch paper and a felt pen or pencil and try to put together as many of the messages as they can. Set a time limit and give inexpensive rewards to those who correctly figure out the most messages.

Say, **Today we are going to look at an event in which the people involved spent a lot of time looking at the walls trying to understand a message that they couldn't read and that they couldn't understand.**

Bible Exploration

EXPLORATION (35-50 minutes)

Materials needed: Newsprint or poster board, felt pens for use in the first step.

Step 1 (10-12 minutes): Have your students form six groups. Have them look at the "Party Time" section of the Scratch Sheet. Assign to each group one of the Scriptures in "Party Time" and explain, **Create a cartoon strip with one or more panels depicting the events you read about in your assigned Scripture passage. Draw big, because we will form a continuing story by putting all our cartoons together on the wall.**

(If drawing cartoon strips is not appropriate for your situation, students may outline and summarize

the scriptural events.)

Step 2 (5-10 minutes): Ask students to share their finished cartoon strips. Call on the groups in order, starting with those who have the first verses in Daniel 5 and continuing through to the last verses. Post cartoons on the wall in order as soon as students have completed sharing them. When all groups have reported, use the posted cartoon strips as a visual aid for a quick review of what happened.

Step 3 (5-7 minutes): This step can be done as a class discussion or in this manner: Have students remain in their groups and work on "The Party in Question" section of the Scratch Sheet. Ask students to discuss the answers to these questions in their groups and be prepared to report to the rest of the class. After allowing a few minutes for work, regain students' attention and ask for their answers. Help them cover the following points:

Question 1: The people and their king had shown contempt toward God.

Question 2: She recognized that Daniel had a special relationship with God, although she did not have a clear picture of who Daniel's God really was.

Question 3: Daniel was not afraid to say the unpopular thing even though it could have cost him his life.

Step 4 (10-12 minutes): There are two ways you can play the Scratch Sheet's "In the Cards" game:

1. When ready to play, distribute scissors so each student can cut out the game cards on his or her worksheet. Each student shuffles all the number 1 cards and places them facedown in a stack. The number 2 and 3 cards are also shuffled and placed facedown in separate stacks. The student then takes a card from the top of each stack, turns the cards faceup and reads them in order: 1,2,3. Ask each student to read aloud the sentence formed by the cards. Sometimes the sentence will make sense, such as: "If someone offered me drugs I'd just say 'No.'" Sometimes it will be nonsense, for example: "If someone offered me the mall I'd ask him or her to watch a clean movie."

After the students have had a chance to read all or most of the sentences in their stacks of cards, move on to step 5.

2. Before class, cut out all the cards from each photocopy of the worksheet. Put each set of cards in an envelope. When ready to play, give each student one set of cards. Challenge the students to arrange the cards into five sentences that make sense (see the paragraph above for an example). Have volunteers read aloud some of their sentences.

Step 5 (5-10 minutes): Read Romans 1:16 to your students. Lead a class discussion on applying this verse based on the situations found in the game. Ask students to describe what they might say if faced with a given situation and what might happen if they said it. (Point out that the number 3 cards in the game do not necessarily contain the best possible response to the situation. For instance, a person who wants to shoplift may be helped more by hearing the gospel than by being offered a loan.)

Summarize students' contributions and say something like this: **We know that it is not always easy to stand up for our faith in tough situations. God's people in Bible times found that to be true, and God's people today—including you and me—will often find it to be true. But remember that God wants to help us be strong during difficult times! Let's take some time to turn to Him for that help.**

Conclusion and Decision

CONCLUSION (3-5 minutes)

Provide paper and pencils and tell students, **Without giving your name, write a description of a situation where you tend to chicken out rather than take a stand for your faith in Christ. If you cannot think of a situation, leave your paper blank. When you have finished writing, fold your paper.**

After allowing students time to write, collect the papers and redistribute them. Tell students, **I'd like you to pray for the person whose paper you received. Ask God to help and strengthen him or her the next time this situation comes up. If you received a blank paper, pray for that person anyway. Ask God to help him or her grow in faith.**

Close in prayer.

Distribute the Fun Page take-home paper.

Party Time

You have been assigned one of the Scriptures below. Draw a cartoon with one or more panels showing the events in your Bible passage.

Daniel 5:1-4
Daniel 5:5-9
Daniel 5:10-12
Daniel 5:13-17
Daniel 5:18-21
Daniel 5:22-30

The Party in Question

1. Why did Belshazzar get into this mess?
2. How did the queen of Babylon describe Daniel and his God?
3. In what way did Daniel display courage by reading and interpreting the inscription?

"I am not ashamed of the gospel, because it is the power of God for the salvation of everyone who believes: first for the Jew, then for the Gentile." Romans 1:16

In the Cards

Cut out all these cards and shuffle them as your teacher explains.

1. If someone offered me	**2.** drugs	**3.** I'd just say, "No."	**1.** If a friend asked me to watch	**2.** a dirty movie	**3.** I'd ask him or her to watch a clean movie.
1. If a friend asked me to help him or her cheat on	**2.** a test	**3.** I'd offer to help my friend study.	**1.** If I was asked to help a pal shoplift from	**2.** the mall	**3.** I'd offer to loan him or her some cash instead.
1. If a teacher told my class Jesus was a myth like	**2.** the Easter Bunny	**3.** I'd challenge him or her to let my youth minister talk about Jesus in class.	**1.** If my mom said I was a fool to believe in	**2.** Jesus	**3.** I'd try to explain the gospel to my mom.

The TOWN CRIER

KING SAUL: AFRAID TO TELL OTHERS!

Based on 1 Samuel 10

Israel—His name was Saul. The Bible describes him this way: "An impressive young man without equal among the Israelites—a head taller than any of the others" (1 Samuel 9:2). See photo.

Now God told His prophet Samuel that He was about to make Saul king of Israel. When Saul learned this he grew very nervous indeed.

Thousands of people had gathered at Mizpah to see Saul crowned king. Everyone was excited and filled with awe at seeing Israel's very first king.

But they almost didn't see him. The great Saul had hidden himself in the huge piles of baggage the crowds had brought with them to the airport . . . er, camelport.

The people looked everywhere for the reluctant king-to-be, but no one could find him. Finally, the people prayed to God and He, through His prophet, told them where Saul was.

So Saul was crowned king and lived happily ever after . . . uh, until he started going bananas and was eventually eliminated! But that's another story.

What if the typical North American kid did EVERYTHING he or she was told to do? I mean **EVERYTHING!**

Well, if he or she watched TV a lot and saw a lot of commercials, and he or she bought EVERYTHING sold on TV, then this is part of what he or she would buy in the course of a lifetime:

6,789,003 Toyota pickups;
1,937,910 pairs of 501 jeans;
91,788,932,495 cans of diet soda;
871,047 bottles of extra-strength pain relievers;
78,934,591 boxes of sugar-coated cereal;
Over 200 billion McDonald's hamburgers;
10,832,190 cans of decaffeinated coffee;
40,987,001 lipsticks and eyeliners;
78,933 Roach Motels.

You can add many more things to the TV list. And what about music? If our friend did everything he or she heard during a lifetime of music listening, he or she would . . .

suffer from 99,876,397 broken romances;
drive 6,574 low riders;
move to the beach and ride 10,746 waves (surf music);
commit 96,874 acts of mayhem and 1,874 suicides (heavy metal music or whatever it's called by the time you read this).

And what if he or she did everything that TV or movie actors do? Well, our friend would . . .

crash 9,786,946 cars;
destroy 10,112,019 police cars;
murder 47,875,927 people (worse than Hitler!);
tell 178,341,961,991 stupid jokes;
tell 37 funny jokes.

And what if our boy or girl did everything the school teachers said to do? He or she would . . .

read 178 boring old novels and write 8,473 meaningless book reports in English class;
run 99,932 laps in P.E.;
solve 17,398 equations in math class;
smash 871 fingers in shop class;
ruin 9,741 articles of clothing in chemistry class.

You may say to yourself, "Why so MANY of each thing?" Because the average person spends so MUCH time watching TV, listening to music and, yes, going to school.

But let's get serious for a moment. Most people spend very LITTLE time thinking or hearing about the most important truth of all: Jesus Christ. They won't hear much about Him on TV, they won't hear much about Him on the radio, and for sure they won't hear about Him from most school teachers. And yet, when a person receives Christ's promise of eternal life, he or she gets . . .

an infinite number of SMILES;
an infinite number of JOY-FILLED DAYS;
an infinite amount of LOVE, and so on.

But the painful truth is, many people miss out on eternal life—because no one takes the time to tell them about Jesus Christ.

Hey, a gift that you can give your friends simply by opening your mouth is to tell them the good news about Jesus. Tell them! Your kindness will count for eternity.

Today's Good News:

"I am not ashamed of the gospel, because it is the power of God for the salvation of everyone who believes: first for the Jew, then for the Gentile." Romans 1:16

DAILY THINKERS

Day 1 Read Genesis 41:17-24. Draw a picture of Pharaoh's dreams.

Day 2 Genesis 41:25-32. What were the messages of the dreams?

Day 3 Genesis 41:33-40. What happened to Joseph? What special things did the Pharaoh say about Joseph?

Day 4 Genesis 41:41-49. Write a brief biography of Joseph's first 30 years.

Day 5 Genesis 41:50-52. What clues do the names of Joseph's sons give you about his frame of mind?

Day 6 Genesis 41:53-57. How did Joseph's plan save lives?

Session 3

THEME: Speaking God's truth—the prophet who refused.

BIBLE STUDY OUTLINE

Read Jonah 1:1-17 to your students. Make the following comments as time permits. (For fun, you might want to hold up a fish from the grocery store and say, "Who does this remind you of?" Students will probably name everybody but Jonah!)

Introductory remarks: We've all heard about Jonah—his is the most famous fish story of all time. But do you remember how Jonah came to be swallowed by the fish? Let's answer that question by taking a look at the prophet of God who refused to speak the unpopular truth.

Verses 1-3: Why did Jonah run from God's command? Perhaps because he knew full well what the people of Nineveh were like—a cruel and bloodthirsty group who dominated the world by crushing their neighbors. They left inscriptions boasting of how they ruthlessly tortured and killed their enemies. Jonah must have envisioned a pretty horrible end to the mission God had given him—a horrible end to Jonah, that is (see Jon. 3:8).

Verses 4,5: God cannot be run away from, try as some people may. He's always there, knowing what goes on in our hearts and lives. He was there with Jonah even on the way to Tarshish, which was in what is now the country of Spain.

Jonah fell asleep, whether miraculously from the hand of God or for some other reason, we don't know. Who knows, he may have fainted from fright.

Verses 6-11: The sailors were religious pagans. They demanded that Jonah pray to his God, just as they were praying to theirs, in the hope that somebody's god might be powerful and kind enough to help out. They cast lots, a common way pagans tried to learn the will of their god or gods. The lot fell to Jonah. The sailors weren't any happier when they discovered that Jonah was trying to run from the very God who made the waters in which they were about to sink!

Verses 12-16: Jonah was valiant and brave (belatedly); he urged the men to throw him into the raging sea. Actually, he was probably convinced drowning would be a better way to go than to head back to Nineveh! The men were nice guys and tried to save his life, but in the end they tossed him over the side. Because it immediately grew calm, the sailors realized Jonah's God wasn't just some kind of myth. Even in the failure of Jonah, God pulled out a small victory in the lives of these men and glorified His name in their sight. Undoubtedly they returned to their homes bearing the astonishing tale of Jonah's miraculous death.

Verse 17: But Jonah didn't die! God had other plans for him. In fact, God had His original plan still in mind. Jonah, better late than never, was to tell the evil Ninevites about Almighty God.

(Read the third chapter of Jonah to conclude your study. Now do the Object Lesson.)

OBJECT LESSON: MAP

Display a road map, globe or atlas. Say, **Who can point out an area on this map where God cannot go? No matter where we look, God is there. Jonah made the mistake of thinking God should only be concerned about the area of the map called Israel. But God thought otherwise. Jonah thought a nice vacation in Spain might be a good way to get God off his back. Jonah learned otherwise. God is everywhere and cannot be avoided or fooled.**

There are people today who make the same mistake Jonah did. The non-Christians try to ignore Him, believing that an ignored problem is a solved one. Christians who want to avoid God's leading may ignore Him or become "too busy" for Him. Or they may say, "I'm too young (or old or sick or dumb) to be of any service to God." All these ways of avoiding God are doomed to failure. The best thing to do is to give God your life fully and allow Him to be your guide.

DISCUSSION QUESTIONS

1. **Why did Jonah try to run from God's command? Were his fears valid? Why not? Does God have power to protect us when we are afraid? Why are we sometimes fearful to allow God to guide our lives?**
2. **Even though Jonah's flight was wrong, something good came of it. What was it? (See Jonah 1:16 and 3:1-10.) God managed to glorify Himself despite Jonah's foolishness. What does this tell you about God's control over matters?**
3. **Could God have found someone else to do the job once Jonah sailed in the other direction? Why do you think He stuck with Jonah? What does this teach you about the sort of person God can use in His service?**

Here are a couple of postcards that you can mail to your students and their parents. Add your phone number and details as necessary. Photocopy the postcards onto card stock if your machine is capable, or make photocopies to paste to card stock. The *Games and Things* following the next session has two additional postcards.

We haVE YOUR kiD!

In our Sunday School, that is.

We invite you to worship with us this coming Sunday and every Sunday. Join us!

Major fun is happening NOW and we want you to join us!

Daniel's Character SESSION 4

WHAT THE SESSION IS ABOUT

Daniel had a personal relationship with God that he demonstrated publicly.

SCRIPTURE STUDIED

Daniel 6

KEY PASSAGE

"Now when Daniel learned that the decree had been published, he went home to his upstairs room where the windows opened toward Jerusalem. Three times a day he got down on his knees and prayed, giving thanks to his God, just as he had done before." Daniel 6:10

AIMS OF THE SESSION

During this session your learners will:

1. Discuss Daniel's characteristics as found in Daniel 6;
2. Describe the source of those characteristics and tell how they can be expressed in believers' lives today;
3. Compare their own characteristics with Daniel's and ask God's help to develop godly characteristics in their lives.

INSIGHTS FOR THE LEADER

Following the downfall of Belshazzar's reign, the political situation that Daniel became a part of was boiling and bubbling with intrigue and personal ambitions. Daniel, a foreigner and a former captive, was now being considered for a position of "second in command" in the land of his captivity. Yet the God of his people was still his master. Everything in Daniel's life had to flow around the immovable rock of that commitment to God.

Daniel's Character

When Darius took over the kingdom, he appointed three administrators, one of whom was Daniel, and 120 satraps ("protectors of the realm") under them. Daniel was a favorite of King Darius, probably because he was credited with helping to destroy King Belshazzar's reign through his fearless interpretation of the writing on the wall. (See Daniel 5.) Furthermore, "Daniel so distinguished himself among the administrators and the satraps by his exceptional qualities that the king planned to set him over the whole kingdom" (Dan. 6:3).

The presence of a foreign-born captive in a place of high authority must have caused anger and jealousy in the explosive political machinery that surrounded Darius. It became the passionate objective of Daniel's opponents to dislodge him from his position and bring him back to a place of servitude appropriate for a person of his "lowly" background. So the other administrators and the satraps began to scrutinize the speech and behavior of Daniel to see if they could discover some flaw upon which to impale his career.

Unlike his contemporaries, Daniel had a closet empty of skeletons. His record was flawless. Aside from pure fabrication on the part of Daniel's enemies, there was nothing that could lead to his dismissal as one of the king's most trusted men.

The central point of Daniel's life was his relationship with God. As his antagonists discovered, Daniel was never too busy to meet with his Lord. Three times a day he would kneel at his open window and pray, facing Jerusalem (the site of the Jewish Temple with its holy of holies). This was evidence of his private and personal faith. He came before the Lord not with an insincere piety, nor because of social pressure to appear spiritual, but because from the depths of his soul he longed for fellowship with his Creator. As a result of this longing and of his times in the Lord's presence, he was filled with the joy, sense of purpose and inner confidence that can come only from spending time with God because one wants to.

These traits were apparent to Daniel's fellow workers. They probably had difficulty figuring out what motivated Daniel. He seemed an odd fish, with none of the typical vices that weigh people down like anchors.

What they saw was faith in action. They looked for flaws, but they could find only his "exceptional qualities" and the fact that he was "neither corrupt nor negligent" (Dan. 6:4). Daniel's life-style was a public example of a private faith. He actually lived by the principles that he considered to be true.

The Plot Against Daniel

Finally Daniel's opponents decided that the only thing they could use to trap him was the thing he had built his life upon, his "religion." So they conceived a plot. They convinced the king to issue a decree stating that anyone who prayed to any god or man during the next thirty days, except to Darius, would be thrown into the lions' den. Darius willingly signed the decree, evidently not realizing that he was offering up his top man for sure destruction.

Many years after Darius, other followers of the true God would be cast to the lions for the crime of not worshiping a Roman Caesar as god. Surely these saints must have thought of their predecessor, Daniel, as they went to their fates.

Daniel worshiped the one true God, so in the face of sure death he went to his upstairs room. As usual, he opened his windows toward Jerusalem, got down on his knees, and "prayed, giving thanks to his God, just as he had done before" (Dan. 6:10).

Of course this is exactly what his enemies had hoped that he would do. They had found that his only vulnerable spot seemed to be his faith, but they did not realize they were about to touch the high voltage of the living God by tampering with His servant.

Daniel's opponents seized upon their opportunity and reported him to the king. The king was "greatly distressed" (v. 14), but there was nothing he could do. He had signed the decree, and according to the law of the land—the "law of the Medes and Persians"—even he could not annul it (v. 15).

So the king gave the order and the men brought Daniel and threw him into the lions' den. A stone was placed over the mouth of the den so that neither Daniel nor the lions could escape. The king returned to the palace and spent a sleepless night, without food and without entertainment.

The Lions Miss a Meal

King Darius probably had a worse night than Daniel did, for the lions lay tame that night, their mouths closed by an angel. What a mighty king was unable to accomplish, God did in rescuing Daniel.

At the first light of dawn the next day, the king hurried to the lions' den. "When he came near the den, he called to Daniel in an anguished voice, 'Daniel, servant of the living God, has your God, whom you serve continually, been able to rescue you from the lions?' " (Dan. 6:20). He was overjoyed to hear Daniel's affirmative reply, and to see his trusted administrator drawn from the den without a wound on him (see v. 23).

Implications for Today

A shake-up in the government soon followed, with Daniel's false accusers becoming breakfast for the hungry beasts who had been denied their feast on Daniel.

The example of Daniel, while familiar to many students since childhood, has many ramifications that may be more relevant to them now that they are in junior high.

Daniel, like Christians today, was a stranger in a pagan land. But he was consistent in turning toward God for his strength. Your students live in a world hostile to and often unfamiliar with what they really believe as Christians. "Religion" is not a proper topic of conversation in most junior high circles. Religious beliefs are thought to be better left within the walls of a church building.

The hostilities and misconceptions about our personal faith dissolve when we demonstrate our beliefs by our public "testimony" or life-style. This is not to suggest that we hide the fact that we pray and seek God's guidance; Daniel's habits in this regard were clearly known. But the thing that strikes those who come into contact with us should be similar to the things that were observed in Daniel: exceptional qualities, integrity, trustworthiness, responsibility. And if those around us wish to contend with us, let them contend with our God. His mighty power is still the same as it was for Daniel.

SESSION PLAN

BEFORE CLASS BEGINS: Photocopy the Fun Page. Make enough copies of the Teaching Resource crossword puzzle so that each pair of students can have one copy. There is no Scratch Sheet this time.

Attention Grabber

ATTENTION GRABBER (5-7 minutes)

Tell your students that you are going to play a game of "Twenty Questions." To play, students try to guess an object from the room that you have in mind. They do this by asking questions that can be answered yes or no. The class gets twenty chances to ask questions (though you can allow more if you like). Pick any object, preferably one within sight of the students, such as a pencil or door.

To help students warm up to the game, give them an example of an object and the questions that would help a person determine what it is. For example, to discover that the object is a pencil, it would help to ask questions such as, "Is it smaller than a bread box?" "Is it made out of wood?"

Feel free to drop a hint or two to help students discover the object you have in mind.

When time is up or the object is guessed, say something like this: **You had a good shot at discovering what the object was because of the characteristics that you asked about. The characteristics gave it away. Today we are going to look at Daniel, someone whose characteristics gave him away—in fact, his characteristics got him into deep trouble with the authorities!**

Bible Exploration

EXPLORATION (30-40 minutes)

Step 1 (15-20 minutes): Remind students, **In our last session we looked at the episode of the handwriting on the wall and saw how Daniel had the courage to give God's message to the king. Today we're going to look at another example of Daniel's courage and willingness to stand for the Lord.** Read Daniel chapter 6 to your class (or have volunteers read portions). Have students form pairs. Tell them, **Work together to complete the crossword**

puzzle I'm handing to you. Distribute photocopies of the Teaching Resource Page.

Step 2 (3-5 minutes): Regain students' attention and ask each pair to share one or two answers. Go around the room until all answers are given. Sum up the contents of Daniel 6, pointing out Daniel's exceptional example in his work, his relationship with God, his principles, and his faith in light of tough circumstances.

Step 3 (5-7 minutes): Use questions such as the following to help clarify Daniel's qualities:

What are some words that might be used to describe the kind of job Daniel was doing in his position as an administrator?

What was the conclusion that Daniel's enemies came to about his character?

What do you know about Daniel's relationship with God from this passage of Scripture?

Describe what Daniel's attitude might have been toward his whole situation as a foreign captive in a pagan society.

Where do you think Daniel got the strength and power to be the person he was?

Wrap up the discussion by summarizing students' contributions. Make sure learners have a clear picture of Daniel's public faith and exemplary character.

Step 4 (8-10 minutes): Write the following list of Daniel's characteristics in a column on the chalkboard: No corruption in him, trustworthy, not negligent, prayed often, thankful to God, willing to disobey king when the law went against God, didn't hide his faith from others, servant of God, innocent of wrongdoing, trusted God. Quickly define each significant word in the list to be sure students understand their meaning and importance.

Explain to your learners that you are now going to read some typical situations faced by people their age. Students are to tell which characteristics on the chalkboard would aid them in facing each situation in a way pleasing to God. They should also explain why they chose the characteristics. (You can add more situations to the list. You can also tell students to suggest additional godly characteristics not on the board that might fit each situation.)

Situation #1: A friend asks your help to cheat on a test.

Situation #2: You want to sleep in instead of going to Bible study.

Situation #3: You find a dollar someone in this class obviously intended to put in the collection plate.

Situation #4: Your older sister offers to buy you and your friends a six-pack of beer.

Situation #5: A friend ridicules you for being a Christian.

Situation #6: Your mom refuses to let you come to a fun youth group event because she thinks you're spending too much time "at that church place."

Move to the CONCLUSION by saying

something like this: **We have seen how some of Daniel's qualities might work out in everyday life today. Now let's take some time to think about how we stack up to Daniel.**

Conclusion and Decision

CONCLUSION (3-5 minutes)

Tell students that you are now going to read a list of statements. The students are to individually and privately mark on a sheet of scratch paper (or on the back of their crosswords) their response—either yes or no—to each statement. Here are the statements:

I am like Daniel . . .

. . . in having a consistent time with God.

. . . in a public example that shows others my faith.

. . . in my hard work and responsibility.

. . . in doing what is right even if it is unpopular.

. . . in that I depend on God even when things don't go right.

Finally, to give your students a chance to ask God to help them obtain some of these godly characteristics for themselves, encourage them to write a short paragraph in response to this statement:

God, please help me to . . .

Close in prayer.
Distribute the Fun Page take-home paper.

The next session, Session 5, involves a skit for which you may wish to recruit adult volunteers. See BEFORE CLASS BEGINS for details.

Read Daniel 6 and then try to complete the crossword puzzle. (It works best with the *New International Version* of the Bible.)

ACROSS

1. Daniel was not *careless* (see v. 4).
6. God performs signs in the *skies* (v. 27).
8. Another word for *miracle* (v. 27).
10. The bad guys could find no grounds for these (v. 4).
15. The stone was *secured* with a signet ring (v. 17).
16. Daniel had no *rot* in him (v. 4).
18. Daniel was *less than two* of the administrators (v. 2).
20. The bad guys were *people who tell untruths*.
22. Daniel had exceptional *attributes* (v. 3).
24. The bad guys told *untruths*.
26. Daniel faced toward this city when he prayed (v. 10).
28. The bad guys said they could *not ever* find any basis for charges against Daniel (v. 5).
30. The bad guys wanted the king to issue a *proclamation* (v. 7).
31. God *delivers* (v. 27).
33. The king *projected* that he would set Daniel over the whole kingdom (v. 3).
34. God's kingdom will not be *demolished* (v. 26).
36. The animals with the teeth (v. 16).
37. Daniel was to be set over this (v. 3).

DOWN

2. The *codes* of the Medes and Persians (v. 8).
3. God's dominion will never *come to a finish* (v. 26).
4. Daniel prayed *more than two times* a day (v. 10).
5. The king's name (v. 1).
7. The king's residence (v. 18).
9. The king spent this without eating (v. 18).
10. The laws of the Medes and Persians *are unable to* be broken (v. 8).
11. Daniel did not *even once* do anything wrong before the king (v. 22).
12. The good guy (v. 2).
13. Declaration (v. 7).
14. Daniel served God *without interruption* (v. 20).
17. Daniel did this three times a day (v. 10).
19. Daniel did this continually (v. 20).
21. *Believes in*. Daniel was not wounded because he believed in God (v. 23).
23. The king ordered the people to *honor* God (v. 26).
25. Over a hundred of these are mentioned in verse 1.
27. The bad guys had done this falsely to Daniel (v. 24).
29. The laws of the Medes and Persians cannot be *revoked* (v. 8).
32. The king wanted to *place* Daniel over the kingdom (v. 3).
35. The lion's home (v. 7).

Fun Page!

The TOWN CRIER

FERROCIOUS LIONS ATTACK REPORTERS!

Babylon—*Town Crier* staff reporters Typo and Pifont and their mascot mutt claim to have been attacked by killer lions as they attempted to locate government official Daniel.

"There was hunnerts of 'em," said a frightened and shaken Pifont. "Thousands!"

"We were surrounded by 'em," spoke up Typo. "If it wasn't for my bravery and daring, we never would have survived."

Their mascot mutt was unavailable for comment.

WELL, MAYBE TYPO AND PIFONT **EXAGGERATED** A BIT. YOU'RE PROBABLY FAMILIAR WITH THE STORY OF DANIEL IN THE LIONS' DEN (SEE DANIEL CHAPTER 6). MANY PEOPLE MIGHT THINK DANIEL WAS THROWN TO THE LIONS BECAUSE HE REFUSED TO WORSHIP A **FALSE HUMAN GOD.** THAT'S TRUE, BUT THERE'S MORE TO IT THAN THAT. HE WAS THROWN IN BECAUSE HE **PUBLICLY ADMITTED** HE WOULDN'T WORSHIP A FALSE GOD.

THE POINT IS, ANYONE CAN WORSHIP GOD PRIVATELY BUT PUBLICLY **DENY IT.** (BUT READ MATTHEW 10:33 TO SEE WHAT HAPPENS!!) DANIEL HAD GUTS. HE BELIEVED GOD AND WAS PROUD OF IT! BE LIKE DANIEL!

The incident of Daniel in the lions' den proved to everyone involved that God is forever in control. The bad guys learned that lesson once and for all when they were thrown to the hungry lions and eaten up! Now that's truth with teeth!

Follow the instructions on this Fun Page "fold-up" to see what eventually happens to a person who fails to recognize the power and authority of Almighty God, and thus becomes "Satan's chump."

Instructions: Fold the bottom section of this page up along the lines until **"A"** meets **"A"** and **"B"** meets **"B,"** as shown in the illustration.

What becomes of "Satan's chump"?

Remember:

"Be self-controlled and alert. Your enemy the devil prowls around like a roaring lion looking for someone to devour"

1 Peter 5:8.

Today's Good News:

"Now when Daniel learned that the decree had been published, he went home to his upstairs room where the windows opened toward Jerusalem. Three times a day he got down on his knees and prayed, giving thanks to his God, just as he had done before." Daniel 6:10

DAILY THINKERS

Day 1 Read Genesis 42:1-7. Describe what Joseph's feelings might have been upon seeing his brothers.

Day 2 Genesis 42:8-20. Describe the feelings Joseph's brothers might have had during this incident.

Day 3 Genesis 42:21-24. Describe what Joseph must have felt about Reuben at this time.

Day 4 Genesis 42:25-38. What kind of family problem did Joseph's request cause?

Day 5 Genesis 43:1-34. Make a brief outline of this whole chapter.

Day 6 Genesis 45:1-11. Sum up Joseph's outlook on the events of his life. What events in your life could you say God directed?

Session 4

THEME: A public relationship with God.

BIBLE STUDY OUTLINE

Read 1 John 1:1-4 to your students. Make the following remarks as time allows.

Introductory remarks: The first step after becoming a Christian is to establish a personal relationship with Jesus Christ. You get to know Him more and more by praying, reading your Bible and centering your thoughts and actions on Him. Another step in your relationship with God is to "go public." By that I mean, tell others about Jesus.

First John was written by the apostle John, a man who walked closely with Jesus, saw His miracles, heard His teachings and witnessed His death, resurrection and ascension into heaven. He was among the very first disciples to be baptized with the Holy Spirit so that the world could know about God (Acts 1:2-8).

Verse 1: John states the purpose of the letter in this verse—but it also can be taken as a motto for his whole life. His job was to "proclaim . . . the Word of life." He makes it clear that he had firsthand knowledge of the Son of God, for he had "heard . . . seen . . . looked at . . . touched" Jesus as he walked with the Lord on the dusty paths of Israel.

Verse 2: John describes Jesus as "the eternal life." That is, Jesus is eternal and the provider of eternal life. It was John's job to "testify to it, and . . . proclaim" that life to the people around him, including anyone who read his letter.

Verse 3: The first reason John gave for telling people about Jesus was that they could join him in salvation and a personal fellowship—or friendship—with God and with Jesus.

Verse 4: The second reason John gave for speaking about Jesus was that it made him happy to lead others to a growing, vibrant relationship with God.

The apostle John is our example. We, too, can tell others about Jesus. We can bring others to Jesus and experience the joy of seeing our friends discover for themselves the eternal life that God gives. None of us is in the unique position that John was in as an apostle of Jesus. On the other hand, John never had the chance to talk to a modern–day junior high kid! You can do that. You can help lead your friends to Jesus. You don't have to be a great preacher. Just invite a friend to a fun youth group activity or to our Bible study. Something as simple as that can be the first link in a chain that leads to a brand new life in Jesus Christ for your friend. (Now do the Object Lesson.)

OBJECT LESSON: LINKS IN A CHAIN

Show your learners a chain. Point out the various links. Describe some of the "links" in a chain of events that you experienced as you came to know the Lord better and better. Explain to your students that no one person will help a friend experience all the links of a growing relationship with God—that is, one person won't necessarily invite a friend to a Bible study, drive the friend there, explain what the Bible is all about, explain the gospel, pray with the person and so on. Those steps might happen through many people over a period of weeks or even years. We can rest assured that God is in control of the chain and that He will assign individual links to individual people.

The important truth behind all this is that we should be willing and able to do what God wants us to do, however big or small it may seem, to help a friend get to know Jesus Christ.

DISCUSSION QUESTIONS

1. **Is it easy or hard for an average Christian your age to let people know that he or she is a Christian? Why?**

2. **What do you suppose would happen if everyone was too embarrassed to admit that he or she is a Christian? What do you suppose would happen if everyone was willing to tell others about Jesus?**

3. **Here at our youth group meetings we tell others about Jesus. If you bring your friends here, we can help you tell them how to become Christians. What are some things that you and we could say or do to help more people learn about how to become Christians?**

Here are two more postcards to go with the ones on the previous *Games and Things*. These two cards have room for a short personal note from you to your students.

HAPPY VALENTINE'S DAY!

Did you know that in the days of Jesus, people thought that the emotions were centered in the intestines rather than in the heart? I wonder what their valentines would have looked like?!

JUST A NOTE . . .

. . . to let you know how glad I am that you've joined our group!

Moses' Relationship

SESSION 5

WHAT THE SESSION IS ABOUT

A close relationship with God makes a vital difference in people's lives.

SCRIPTURE STUDIED

Exodus 3:1-4:17; 13:21,22; 33:12-17; 34:29-32; 40:34-38

KEY PASSAGE

"The Lord replied, 'My Presence will go with you, and I will give you rest.' " Exodus 33:14

AIMS OF THE SESSION

During this session your learners will:

1. Examine several personal encounters Moses had with God;
2. Compare God's presence with the Israelites to His presence in Christians' lives today;
3. Describe how they can express God's presence in their lives.

INSIGHTS FOR THE LEADER

Throughout world history there have always been men and women of unusual influence over events and people. But the number of those who have actually changed the course of history is much, much smaller. There is no question that Moses is one of the select few.

Let's review Moses' place in biblical history. We have studied Abraham's life. Abraham's grandson, Jacob, had twelve sons. The older boys hated the next-to-youngest son, Joseph, and sold him into slavery. He ended up in Egypt, and eventually became the second-in-command to Pharaoh. When famine hit that whole part of the world, a series of events resulted in Joseph being reunited with his family and bringing them to Egypt so that they could survive the hard years of limited food and water.

Four hundred years later, Abraham's descendants had increased in number so that there were six hundred thousand men, plus women and children (see Exod. 12:37). But now the people were in bondage, enslaved by Egyptian rulers who feared them because they were so populous. This is where Moses comes in.

Moses Was Close to God

The purpose of this session is to guide students in discovering some of the things that made Moses so special, and to apply them to life today. One main point to emphasize is the importance of Moses' close walk with God.

The development of Moses' character is left to guesswork, with no details given in the Exodus record. But it appears that quite a struggle must have gone on within him as he realized that for all his privileged position in the royal household, he was "different," and his own people were living in conditions horrifyingly opposite to his own luxurious surroundings. If he had not had such a struggle he could not have responded as he did to the circumstances oppressing the enslaved Hebrews. The writer of Hebrews sums it up: He "refused to be known as the son of Pharaoh's daughter. He chose to be mistreated along with the people of God . . . . He regarded disgrace for the sake of Christ as of greater value than the treasures of Egypt" (Heb. 11:24-26).

These verses in Hebrews pinpoint the essential twin commitments of the true servant of God: One is to the Lord Himself, and the other is to His people. We shall see over and over again that this is the mark of Moses. His commitment to both is total. The strength of these commitments becomes clear in Moses' desperate distress when the two are in conflict. See, for example, his plea in Exodus 32:32 after the dreadful debacle of the golden calf. Moses was filled with anguish at the thought of what Israel had done. On the one hand, he longed for God to be vindicated and he knew that atonement was required, but on the other

hand he ached for his people to be forgiven. So he went back up the mountain to pray. His inner conflict was resolved in a most amazing prayer. He asked nothing less than that he should be blotted out of God's book of life. Whether he was seeking to become a substitute for the sinning nation, or whether he was simply expressing his identification with them is not absolutely certain. But either way, it is an astounding prayer. It is very similar to the longing of Paul in Romans 9:3.

Moses and Prayer

Prayer is one important measure of how much we really care about anything or anyone, and there is no question that Moses was a man who cared deeply. Although he was a stern leader who could let fly in blazing, white-hot anger when needed, he also had the tender desires of a father for his children, caring not only for them in the present while he was with them, but also for their future when he was gone. Because of this concern we see the blessing he pronounced upon the tribes of Israel just before his death (see Deut. 33), showing concern for their acceptability to the Lord and their protection from their enemies.

Moses' life of prayer must have been continuous, but there were high peaks of special prominence. The Everest among those peaks was surely the time he spent with God on Sinai, receiving the laws that were the basis of God's covenant with Israel and which have shaped not only that nation, but the world, down to this very day.

In Exodus 24:12-16 we are shown the specialness of this revelation. It was not a man communing with his own thoughts and producing the product of his subconscious mind. This was God unveiling His will. The stone tablets were visible evidence of that (see v. 12). Nor was the covenant based on a committee's deliberations. The people and their elders stayed behind. Even Aaron was excluded. Moses, apart from his assistant Joshua, went alone (see vv. 13,14).

But even Moses could not rush into such close communication with his Creator. There was a six-day waiting period; only on the seventh day did the summons come to advance into the cloud.

Parallels for Our Day

Moses' relationship with God can teach us essential principles for our own relationship with God. First, there is the divine initiative. He calls us to meet Him; it is a divine summons. We are not doing the Lord a favor by meeting with Him; it is we who are privileged. And we are disobedient if we don't meet Him.

Second, there is the importance of solitude. Public worship is important and must never be neglected, but it is never intended to be a substitute for private daily communication with the Lord (see Matt. 6:6).

Third, Moses' six days of patient waiting are a rebuke to all of us, for we rush in and out of the Lord's presence as though He is a fast-food stand. We need to relearn the ancient art of meditation on the Word and of listening to God. We must allocate the needed time for something so important. God has given us 1440 minutes to fill every day. They are there for the taking.

It was in this unhurried waiting on the Lord that the secret of Moses' authority lay. Our lasting effectiveness as believers also has its mainspring here.

Effects of Time with God

One effect of Moses' consistent meetings with God was physically visible. His face shone! So much so that he put on a veil to hide the phenomenon from the people. Paul takes up this incident in 2 Corinthians 3:12-18 to make the point that a similar transformation can take place in the Christian. The more time we spend in Christ's presence, the more we reflect the Lord's glory, not so much in a shining face (though there can be a visible effect) but in a Christlike life.

The remarkable character of Moses' life continued right to the very end. Deuteronomy 34:6 tells us that God "buried him" after his death, and no one knows exactly where his grave is. In a sense, that is the way it always was with him throughout his life: hidden in God.

SESSION PLAN

BEFORE CLASS BEGINS: There is no Scratch Sheet this time, but there are several Teaching Resource pages. Happily, little photocopying is required. The first two Teaching Resource pages following this Session Plan are simply torn out of the book and taped together to form a poster. The poster is a quick description of Moses' early life. As you discuss it with your class, hold the poster up for all to see, or display it on the wall and allow students to gather around for a closer look. If your copy machine will make enlargements, you may want to copy the poster sheets before you tape them together. The next Teaching Resource page is the "I Believe You, But . . . " skit. You should make two copies of the skit; one for each of two actors. (You might want to have older students or leaders present the skit. If so, give them fair warning before class.) Keep the original because you will read the part of the Narrator. The skit requires a stick to serve as Moses' rod. The final Teaching Resource page is a series of questions that you are to cut out and hide in various parts of the classroom before students arrive. As always, photocopy the Fun Page. The ALTERNATE CONCLUSION requires materials for making fancy invitations: paper, colored pencils, scissors, glue, tape, glitter, paper lace and similar items.

Attention Grabber

ATTENTION GRABBER (5-10 minutes)

This session is about Moses' relationship (and our own) with God. Here is a simple but tough game to introduce your students to the idea of relationships. Read the questions below out loud. The first student to shout out the correct answer to each question wins the round. Each question is followed by the answer in parentheses.

Use the first question and answer as an example of how to play the game. Draw a family tree chart on the board to help students grasp how each person is related.

1. **What relation to you is your mother's brother's son?** (Your cousin.)
2. **What relation to you is your aunt's father's wife?** (Grandmother.)
3. **What relation to you is your father's stepson's mother?** (Stepmother.)
4. **What relation to you is your uncle's father's only grandchild?** (Self.)
5. **What relation to you is your brother's son's sister's mother?** (Sister-in-law.)
6. **What relation to you is your sister's husband's sister?** (No relation.)
7. **What relation to you is your nephew's sister's son?** (Grandnephew.)

When all questions have been answered, say something like this: **Congratulations to the winners of our game. I wanted to get you thinking about relationships because today**

we are going to take a look at Moses, a man who had a very special relationship with Almighty God.

Bible Exploration

EXPLORATION (30-45 minutes)

Materials required: The skit requires a stick for Moses to hold; everything else can be left to the imagination of the audience. Optional: A public address system.

Step 1 (3-5 minutes): Use the Teaching Resource poster you assembled to provide a brief background sketch of the life of Moses up to his encounter with the burning bush. Then spend a couple of minutes reviewing the events of Moses' life from this point on for your students.

Step 2 (5-10 minutes): Using the Teaching Resource script ("I Believe You, But . . . "), present a skit that will give your students a picture of the events at the burning bush. You might have someone read God's lines from offstage or outside the room using a microphone so that the voice comes through a speaker in the room. (Have the "reverb" on the amplifier turned up high.) A student actor or someone from outside your class portraying Moses can interact with this voice. Or have volunteers from your class rehearse ahead of time and perform the skit.

Step 3 (12-15 minutes): Write the following Scripture assignments on the chalkboard:

1. Read Exodus 13:21,22; 40:34-38. How did God guide His people?
2. Read Exodus 33:12-17; 34:29-32. What did Moses ask God for? What happened to Moses as a result of being in God's presence?

Have students form pairs and work together to complete each assignment. (You may want to read the passages aloud.) After they have had time to work, regain their attention and ask them to report what they have found. Make sure students understand that God made His presence known to the Israelites and to Moses personally in a very real way. Today our experience of God's presence, while usually less dramatic, is no less real and personal.

Step 4 (10-12 minutes): Tell students that you have hidden slips of paper containing questions all around the room. Have students work together in their pairs to search for the questions. When a question is found, the pair returns to their seats with the paper and answers the question. Say, **I want you to answer these questions carefully. One word answers don't count. You have about ten minutes to find and answer one of the questions. If you finish early, locate and respond to another question.**

After students have had time to work, regain their attention and ask them to read their questions and share their responses. The ideas your students are working on may be a bit abstract for some of them. Be prepared to amplify their responses by preparing answers to the questions before class.

Move on to the CONCLUSION by saying something like this: **We have seen that God's presence is with us today and that we can radiate His love and glory by spending time in prayer, Bible study, worship, meditation and so on. The difficult thing is putting our priorities in order so that we take the time to do these things and hear Him speak to us. Let's take some time to think about this.**

Conclusion and Decision

CONCLUSION (3-5 minutes)

Tell students, **Moses had such a glow about him that people could not look at him without squinting. His glow came from being in the presence of God. It was a miraculous sign of his special relationship with the Lord. We can glow too—not like Moses did (unless we hang around toxic waste dumps), but from the inside out.**

Ask your learners to write down their responses to these statements:

My light is brightest when . . .

My light is dim when . . .

I can increase the brightness of my light by . . .

After allowing students time to write, close in prayer.

Distribute the Fun Page take-home paper.

ALTERNATE CONCLUSION (5-10 minutes)

Materials required: Items for constructing fancy invitations (see BEFORE CLASS BEGINS for suggestions).

Tell students, **Use paper, glue, pens and other materials to create a fancy invitation that God might send to invite you to come into His presence. Be sure you include a specific way by which you could come into His presence this week.** Students can work individually or in their original pairs.

Allow volunteers to display their invitations.

Close in prayer. Remain available for any who might wish to discuss further their experience of or need for God's presence in their lives.

Distribute the Fun Page take-home paper.

MOSESoooo
THE EARLY YEARS
CRACK
THE PEOPLE OF ISRAEL, ONCE GUESTS IN EGYPT, HAVE NOW BECOME THE SLAVES OF THEIR HOSTS.

THE PHARAOH BECAME ALARMED AT THE INCREASING NUMBER OF JEWS.
LET'S KEEP OUR NATION SAFE FROM A SLAVE REBELLION IN FUTURE YEARS! I WANT EVERY BABY HEBREW BOY KILLED AT BIRTH.
SWISH

WHEN MOSES WAS BORN, HIS MOM MADE A DESPERATE ATTEMPT TO SAVE HIS LIFE BY LAUNCHING HIM DOWN THE NILE RIVER IN A WATERPROOF BASKET.
THE PHARAOH'S DAUGHTER (TAKING A BATH) SAW MOSES, HAD PITY FOR HIM AND ADOPTED HIM.

Moses killed the guard and tried to hide his body in the sand. He obviously didn't do a very good job because ...

.... The next day he stumbled upon two Hebrews fighting with each other and when Moses tried to stop them one said, "Are you going to kill me like you did the Egyptian guard yesterday?" Moses knew that the cat was out of the bag (or sand).

HEY!!! UH..

BONK!

POKE!

- BUNDSCHUH -

I Believe You, But . . .

Narrator: This skit is taken from the familiar story of Moses at the burning bush, as found in Exodus 3. Let's eavesdrop on the conversation between God and Moses and imagine ourselves in Moses' feet (since he wasn't wearing sandals at the time).

The scene is the desert where not much happens. Moses turns a corner and is confronted with a burning bush that does not burn up. Not only that, the bush talks!

God: Moses! Moses!
Moses: (Surprised.) Who is it?
God: It is God, the God of your forefathers. (Moses covers his eyes in fear.)
God: Don't come any closer. Take off your shoes, for you are standing on holy ground. (Pauses while Moses complies.) Let's get right to the point. The Hebrew people, my chosen ones, are really suffering hardships under the Egyptians . . .
Moses: Well, everyone knows that. Especially me. That's how I got stuck out here in the first place.
God: Yes, I know. You see, it is time for me to put a stop to all their sufferings. I am ready to rescue them.
Moses: That's nice. They could sure use your help.
God: Hold on, guy—it's you who are going to help me!
Moses: (In disbelief.) Are you kidding? I'm not the person for a job like that. Besides, I'd have to go to Egypt and I'm not too popular there. I think it's a great idea, but . . .
God: Moses, that incident with the guard was close to forty years ago. All your enemies are dead.
Moses: But why me?
God: Moses, I'll be right there with you . . .
Moses: Oh, sure. Don't tell me the bush walks, too.
God: No, but it is a sign to help you believe.
Moses: Don't get me wrong, Lord. I really believe you, but I'm not sure it will work. I don't even know who to say sent me.
God: Just tell them, "I AM sent me to you." This is my name forever and they have used it for generations down to this day.
Moses: It's great for you to have a plan, but I don't know where to go or who to tell.
God: Faith starts with obedience. It might be a good idea to head in the direction of Egypt and to tell the Israelites' leaders. They will listen to you, I promise.
Moses: Lord, I'm still not too sure . . . . Well, I don't even know what to say.
God: Do you believe me?
Moses: Sure, but I'm not too good with words. I think you want a man who likes to talk . . .
God: Moses, tell them about my appearing to you here in this burning bush and that I am going to rescue them as I promised.
Moses: They won't believe me! They won't do what I tell them to!
God: I have told you they will listen. You need to have faith.
Moses: But, I do believe you . . . uh . . . . um . . . (Embarrassed.) Could I have some proof? In case someone else doesn't believe . . . you know?
God: Take your staff and throw it on the ground. (Moses throws staff on the ground, looks astonished, and begins to run.)
God: Wait! Pick it up.
Moses: But . . . no way! I'm not gonna touch that! It turned into a snake!
God: (Interrupting.) Pick it up. (Moses picks it up very cautiously and then sighs in relief.)
Moses: How did you do that?
God: Never mind. Put your hand in your robe and pull it out again.
Moses: (Moses puts his hand in his robe and pulls it out again, looks amazed.) It's white with leprosy! (He puts his hand back into his robe and pulls it out again.) Phew! It's OK again.
God: If they don't believe one sign they will believe the other.
Moses: But, Lord, I'm just not a good speaker. I have a speech impediment.
God: Who made mouths? Trust in me with all your heart and don't depend on yourself.
Moses: I do trust you, but please send someone else to do it.
God: Blessed is the man who trusts in the Lord and whose trust is the Lord. Moses, I'm getting tired of your unbelief.
Moses: Well, OK, I'll go . . . but, but, you gotta stick by me. Please don't leave me—even for a second!

(Lights fade out as does Moses' voice, as he bows in reverence and submission.)

TEACHING RESOURCE QUESTIONS

Cut apart these cards and conceal them in relatively easy–to–find locations around your classroom (taped to the wall behind trash cans, taped under the chairs, tacked to the bulletin board, inside a potted plant and so forth). If necessary, give hints as students search. There is more than one copy of each question so that several pairs of students can work on the same problems.

Since God has probably not guided you with a cloud or fire, how might He do it?	**Since God has probably not guided you with a cloud or fire, how might He do it?**	**Since God has probably not guided you with a cloud or fire, how might He do it?**	**Since God has probably not guided you with a cloud or fire, how might He do it?**
In the bush, cloud and fire, God's presence was obvious to Moses and to the children of Israel. In what way is God's presence obvious today?	**In the bush, cloud and fire, God's presence was obvious to Moses and to the children of Israel. In what way is God's presence obvious today?**	**In the bush, cloud and fire, God's presence was obvious to Moses and to the children of Israel. In what way is God's presence obvious to you today?**	**In the bush, cloud and fire, God's presence was obvious to Moses and to the children of Israel. In what way is God's presence obvious to you today?**
The glow that Moses had after he spent time with God was noticed by everyone. In what ways do you think a Christian glows, shines or demonstrates that he or she has been with God?	**The glow that Moses had after he spent time with God was noticed by everyone. In what ways do you think a Christian glows, shines or demonstrates that he or she has been with God?**	**The glow that Moses had after he spent time with God was noticed by everyone. In what ways do you think a Christian glows, shines or demonstrates that he or she has been with God?**	**The glow that Moses had after he spent time with God was noticed by everyone. In what ways do you think a Christian glows, shines or demonstrates that he or she has been with God?**
Moses spent time with God. How do we spend time with God and what do we do when we are with Him?	**Moses spent time with God. How do we spend time with God and what do we do when we are with Him?**	**Moses spent time with God. How do we spend time with God and what do we do when we are with Him?**	**Moses spent time with God. How do we spend time with God and what do we do when we are with Him?**

Session 5

The TOWN CRIER

JUDAS BETRAYS JESUS!

By staff reporters Typo and Pifont   Based on Luke 22:47,48

Jerusalem—When we arrived in this wonderful town, it was a beautiful, sunny morning. We checked into the little hotel and had a bite to eat.

We were here to get the story on Jesus and His twelve disciples. What was it like to be one of those disciples? How did it feel to walk and talk with the Lord Jesus Christ all day, every day? How were their lives influenced by the presence of the Son of God?

We decided that it would be best to interview just one disciple. We wanted a typical one—not too young, not too old, not too rich, not too poor. After checking out all the disciples, John, Peter, Matthew, etc., we decided that the perfect, most typical apostle was a nice guy named Judas Iscariot.

As it turned out, that was a bit of a mistake.

Later that night, when we first came upon Judas, he was kissing Jesus on the cheek. (That was OK back in those days. Times have changed!)

We thought that was a friendly thing to do, but as it turned out, it was a kiss of death.

With that kiss, Judas betrayed Jesus to the Roman soldiers. Jesus was crucified, and Judas Iscariot joined the ranks of history's most famous traitors.

Why would anyone become like Judas? How could anyone follow Jesus for as long as Judas did, and remain unmoved in his or her heart?

We attempted to find the answers . . .

"The Lord replied, 'My Presence will go with you, and I will give you rest.'" Exodus 33:14

You can buy insurance for anything today. You can buy homeowners' policies to insure your house against fires, floods, tornadoes, junior high kids, etc. You can buy car insurance to cover accidents, injury and theft. There's airplane insurance. Earthquake insurance. If you're a rancher, you can insure your prize pigs. If you're a piano player, you can insure your fingers.

But what do you do when you want to insure that your relationship with God is going to grow and mature every day? How can you insure that your Christian life is going to be the very best day by day?

There are TWO ways to insure that you grow to become a successful Christian. One is the right way. And then there's THIS way:

The Acme Insurance and Mail Order Contact Lens Company

HOLINESS POLICY

The Acme Insurance and Mail Order Contact Lens Company insures the below-signed policyholder forthwithly: Acme will pay $100,000.00 in cash or contact lenses to the policyholder should he or she ever fail to be absolutely holy and wonderful.

However, this Acme policy will be null and void if the following qualifications are not met by the policyholder:

1. **Policyholder must not be between six months and 178 years old;**
2. **Policyholder must not be six months or less of age;**
3. **Policyholder must not be 178 years or older;**
4. **Policyholder must not be male;**
5. **Or female;**
6. **Policyholder must not be animal, vegetable or mineral;**
7. **Policyholder must not be larger than a breadbox;**
8. **Policyholder must not be smaller than a breadbox;**
9. **Policyholder must not be a breadbox;**
10. **Or anything else.**

Happily, for those of us Christians who do not qualify for Acme's Holiness Policy, there is a way to genuinely be sure that our relationship with God is growing and improving as time goes by. Here's what to do:

1. Pray. Talk to God, not just when you're desperate, but always. He likes you, and He likes to hear from you!
2. Put your nose in the Bible. Attend Bible studies, but don't forget to spend a lot of time alone with God and His Word. Obey His Word.
3. Worship God. Tell Him why you like Him.
4. Meditate. It's fun to turn off the music, skip the TV and just spend time thinking about God, His blessings, heaven and so on.
5. Serve God. Get involved in actually doing good things. Your minister can help you come up with some good service projects.

Make a habit of doing all these things and you'll get to know God better and be a successful Christian. And that's what we want, that's why we do the Fun Page for you.

DAILY THINKERS

Day 1 Read Joshua 1:1-5. What promises did God give to Joshua?

Day 2 Joshua 1:6-9. Make a list of what God asked Joshua to do.

Day 3 Joshua 1:10-18. What "conditions" did the Israelites ask for in return for following Joshua?

Day 4 Joshua 2:1-13. Why did Rahab offer to help the spies?

Day 5 Joshua 2:14-21. What was the deal between the spies and Rahab?

Day 6 Joshua 2:22-24. What was the spies' conclusion based on the fearfulness of the land's inhabitants?

THEME: A close relationship with God makes a vital difference.

Session 5

BIBLE STUDY OUTLINE

Read Genesis 4:1-14 to your students. Make the following remarks as time allows.

Introductory remarks: Most of us have heard the story of Cain and Abel, the two sons of Adam and Eve. Cain killed his brother Abel, becoming the first murderer. Why did he do this terrible thing and what lessons can we learn from the lives of Cain and Abel? Let's find out.

Verses 1-5: We see a few similarities between the two men in these verses: They were brothers; they worked on a "ranch"—one taking care of the crops, the other in charge of the animals; they both brought an offering to the Lord. This is where the difference begins. Cain "brought some of the fruits of the soil" to the Lord, but Abel brought "fat portions from some of the firstborn of his flock." The difference is not that one brought plants and the other animals, but that Cain's offering was careless and thoughtless while Abel's was the very best he had to offer. He loved God and showed it with his choice of animals. As it says in Hebrews 11:4, Abel's offering was one of faith. It's possible that Abel's act of sacrificing the best animals made it less likely that his flock would flourish. This didn't bother Abel, however, for he trusted God. Because Abel had faith and Cain did not, God readily accepted Abel's offering but disregarded Cain's. At this, Cain became infuriated.

Verses 6,7: God responded to Cain's anger with words of advice and comfort: Watch out for sin, it will get the best of you if you do not protect yourself from it.

Verses 8-14: Cain killed his brother and received the ultimate punishment—banishment from God's presence (see v. 14).

The real difference between Cain and Abel was in their relationship with God. Abel had a good relationship with God, cemented by faith. Cain was not close to God, indicated by his sins—his deficient offering, anger, jealousy, deception, murder, lying to God, self-pity and lack of repentance. It's the relationship with God that made the vital difference. The same is true for us today. Our relationship with the Lord, or lack of one, will make all the difference in the world.

OBJECT LESSON: PADLOCK

Show your class a large, open padlock. Say something like this: **If you want to have a relationship with Almighty God, you must have faith in Him. The kind of faith we are talking about is the strong faith required to make a life-changing commitment to Him. This padlock is like our faith. Our faith in God is what locks us together with Him.** Snap the lock shut.

DISCUSSION QUESTIONS

1. **What is faith? How is it related to forming and maintaining a relationship with God? How is it like a padlock?**

2. **Which do you think came first: Cain's bad actions or his poor relationship with God? How do you think things would have worked out if Cain had listened to God's warning to do what is right? How do you suppose establishing a good relationship with God would affect the sinful behavior of a person?**

3. **What is a good relationship with God like? What are some things we can do to improve our relationship with God?**

Have you ever conducted a Bible study "out in the field?" A small group of kids, an interesting location and a pertinent word of wisdom from the Bible can make an unforgettable Scripture message. Here are some ideas:

AN AIRPORT

Seat your kids where they can see and hear the planes landing and taking off. Spend a few minutes describing the various instruments in a plane's cockpit (e.g. radar, radio, altimeter, compass, fuel gauge, various engine gauges) and the controls needed to safely fly the plane (stick and pedals to control the plane's direction, throttles, flaps, landing gear levers and so forth). Point out that all these instruments and controls are there to insure that the pilot can safely arrive at the intended destination. The destination is the runway—small and narrow, but of inestimable importance. This thin strip of concrete is the only safe place to land.

Tell your listeners that Jesus is like that runway—His way is narrow, but it's absolutely essential that Jesus is each person's ultimate "destination." He provides the only safe landing for a person traveling through this life. Without Jesus, there is only a disastrous end.

You can base this study on Matthew 7:13,14, John 14:6 or similar passages.

A FAST-FOOD RESTAURANT

After ordering some food at a busy fast-food restaurant, set your kids down and tell them the story of the feeding of the 5,000 (see Matt. 14:13-21).

Challenge the kids to figure out how many pounds two fish would have to weigh to make a "McTrout" sandwich for each person who listened to the Lord, and how long five loaves of bread would have to be to make enough burger buns. Let your kids try to calculate how long it would take the restaurant to serve 5,000 meals (judging from how long it takes the lines of people to be served and how many cars get past the drive-thru window in a given amount of time).

Contrast the situation at the restaurant with the miraculous presence of God's power that day with Jesus.

A POWER PLANT

Drive your kids to the site of an electrical substation or the foot of a tall high voltage transmission tower. Discuss the nature of electrical power. Ask your listeners to relate any "shocking experiences" they have had with electricity. Compare the power of electricity to the power of the Holy Spirit—starting with Acts 1:8 for example. The story of Ananias and Sapphira in Acts 5:1-11 also speaks of the power of God.

Moses' Dependence

SESSION 6

WHAT THE SESSION IS ABOUT

All of us need to give and receive support as part of our growing experience.

SCRIPTURE STUDIED

Exodus 4:10-16; 17:8-13; 18:13-26

KEY PASSAGE

"Therefore encourage one another and build each other up, just as in fact you are doing."
1 Thessalonians 5:11

AIMS OF THE SESSION

During this session your learners will:

1. Search out the ways in which Moses depended upon other people;
2. List ways Christians today can be supportive of one another;
3. Select one way to put helping others into practice.

INSIGHTS FOR THE LEADER

Moses was a man who was able to strengthen others with his leadership. But as his experience as leader grew, he learned his own need of the strengthening power of human fellowship. He grew to depend upon people. In fact, at the very beginning of his call, when God ordered him to bring the Israelites out of Egypt, Moses argued with the Lord about his ability and would only obey when he was promised the help of his brother Aaron (see Exod. 4:10-16).

Once he had led the people out of Egypt and into the wilderness, Moses found his work had only just started. When Jethro, Moses' father-in-law, came on a visit he saw Moses on his judge's seat from morning to night wearing himself out with no time for the other vital tasks of leadership (see Exod. 18:17-23). His advice was simple—delegate! And so Moses, bowing to the wisdom of the older man, appointed officials over thousands, hundreds, fifties and tens to look after the minor cases for him. He depended upon these officials for their much-needed support.

Moses Seeks Help—Again

Numbers 11:4-17 records a similar incident. Moses had found himself unable to cope when the rabble—fellow travelers with the true Israelites—began to moan and groan about their limited (though miraculous) diet (see Num. 11:4). The infection of dissatisfaction soon spread throughout the camp and in no time Moses found he had a rebellion on his hands (see v. 10).

Moses talked to the Lord about it (see v. 11). Moses summed up his problem as "the burden of all these people." That was what was bringing him to his breaking point (see vv. 14,15). It is significant that the apostle Paul in 2 Corinthians 11:28, having listed all the terrible sufferings he endured from floggings, imprisonments, shipwrecks and the like, makes the painful crown of thorns of them all "the pressure of my concern for all the churches." The taut string of the tension of leadership has not changed much over the centuries.

Qualities Needed for Spiritual Service

Moses felt he was about to snap. So the Lord gave the solution. It was to share the leadership. Seventy elders who had already proven their qualities (see Num. 11:16), probably drawn from the previous division of labor proposed by Jethro, were to be selected.

But the fact that they were already known as leaders and that Moses had selected them was not in itself sufficient. They must have the same Spirit of God on them as Moses had (see v. 17). With the Spirit on them, they would support Moses in his burden of leadership.

The case has a distinct parallel in the New Testament with the choosing of the first deacons in Acts 6. Once again, the immediate

cause was grumbling among the people of God. There too, the overburdening of the leadership was part of the problem, and the solution was delegation. And there too, those who had already shown the right qualities were chosen. But they were not set loose on their task without the laying on of hands by the apostles, which was the means of that special anointing of the Spirit essential to their success.

Literal Support

Exodus 17:10-13 is another passage your students will study. While his people fought against the Amalekites, Moses held up his hands—symbolizing his dependence on God for help. He found that his people prevailed as long as he held up his hands, but began to lose when his weary arms dropped. So Aaron and Hur held up his arms. Moses knew when he needed the strength of supportive friends.

Moses never let go, either of his Lord or his people. He depended upon God and people for support.

The Need for Christian Support

It is the most precious of human relationships to have a fellow Christian with whom you can be perfectly frank, who can share your joys and sorrows, your virtues and faults, without envy and without judging. To be able to confess failings to one another, to be listened to in love and then to pray for one another (see Jas. 5:16) is not just a formula for spiritual and mental health; it is the very essence of Christian fellowship. And it is often the key to keeping a leader leading.

For many junior highers the call to independence is so blaring that they reject the idea of being dependent upon anyone. At the same time they are actually extremely dependent upon those around them for food, care, shelter, love, understanding, financial aid, companionship and even transportation.

As you consider the message of this session, remember that your students have much to learn about the give and take of living. Pray that learning to give, encourage and build others up may become an integral part of their lives.

SESSION PLAN

BEFORE CLASS BEGINS: Photocopy the Fun Page. Make one copy of the "Reweaving a Basket Case" Teaching Resource page for each group of three or four students. See step 2 of the Exploration and Teaching Resource Cards for further details. There is no Scratch Sheet this time. Provide a container (hat, can or the like). Cut apart the Teaching Resource Cards and place them in the container. The CONCLUSION calls for a brick.

Attention Grabber

ATTENTION GRABBER (5-7 minutes)

Give a pencil and a piece of paper to each person. Tell your students, **You are going to draw a picture of a house. But you have to close your eyes and draw the house without looking**

and without having anyone help you. Let students draw. Then let them look at their results and have a good laugh.

Have students form pairs. Say, **Now try again. This time, one person will draw with eyes closed, and your partner will help you. Partners, give directions such as, a little to the right, sharp left and so on. Go ahead and try it.** Let students draw again, then check results. If time permits, let partners trade roles and try again.

Say, **It is often necessary to have help in order to accomplish what we wish. Today we are going to take a look at the life of a very great person who also found it impossible to do everything himself. He had to depend on the help and encouragement of others.**

Bible Exploration

EXPLORATION (30-35 minutes)

Step 1 (12-15 minutes): Write these three headings across the top of the chalkboard: The Problem; What Moses Did; Who Helped Him Do It. Allow room at the left of the chalkboard to write these references in a column: Exodus 4:10-16; Exodus 17:8-13; Exodus 18:13-26.

Tell students, **I'm going to read each Scripture passage to you. As I do, we'll fill out this chart on the chalkboard.** Jot down the students' responses under the appropriate columns. The chart should look something like this when completed:

	The Problem	What Moses Did	Who Helped Him Do It
Exodus 4:10-16	Moses afraid to speak	Asked God to get someone else	Aaron his brother
Exodus 17:8-13	War with Amalekites	Held up the staff of God	Aaron and Hur
Exodus 18:13-26	Too much work	Delegated authority	Jethro (Moses' father-in-law)

Summarize students' responses. Point out that God, as well as others, was there to help and support Moses in these situations.

Step 2 (12-15 minutes): Say, **Moses was a unique and capable person, but he was not above needing the help and support of others. Let's think for a moment about situations in which people today could use our help and support.**

Assemble students into groups of three or four. Distribute the "Reweaving a Basket Case" Teaching Resource page, one copy per group. Have a representative of each group pick five cards (more or less depending on time remaining) from the container (see the Teaching Resource pages for complete details). Explain, **Read the cards you've received. The cards list areas in which a person might need support. Your job is to list ways people your age could help this person by showing support and encouragement. List your ideas on the "Reweaving a Basket Case" sheet. Go into detail on your answers; please no one-word responses.** To motivate students to think more deeply, ask them to list at least two or three suggestions per card.

Step 3 (5-7 minutes): After students have had time to complete the activity, regain their attention and ask several to share their work. Add your own insights as needed. Encourage students to be alert to people who need encouragement.

It is important to stress the fact that a person with severe problems in any of the areas discussed should be steered toward professional and ministerial counseling. Be sensitive to the possibility that a student with deep needs is sitting in your class.

Conclusion and Decision

CONCLUSION (3-5 minutes)

Show your students a brick. Say something like this: **Helping others is like building a house. The bricks you add will make the shelter stronger and more durable. Getting along with people can be easy (and even fun), but relationships also need to be strengthened by our kind deeds, helpful encouragement and lending a hand. I want you to think of a specific person you can show support to this week: your best friend, your worst friend, your mom or dad, your brother, your teacher—anyone you want to choose. Then, on paper, I want you to draw three bricks. On the bricks, write some specific and practical things you will do this week to show support to the person you chose.**

After allowing time for students to work, close in prayer.

Distribute the Fun Page take-home paper.

ALTERNATE CONCLUSION (5-7 minutes)

Work together as a class to develop a plan that will help build the body of Christ. It can be as simple as an agreement that each class member will make an extra effort to be friendly to older people or lonely people in the congregation. It may be a project that will help the whole congregation, such as a work day to clean up the grounds or to make items needed in the nursery. After agreeing on a plan, write it up as a contract and let everyone who wishes to cooperate sign it.

Close in prayer.

Distribute the Fun Page take-home paper.

Give the contract to the minister or other appropriate leaders to let them know what your students are planning. They may wish to respond in person or with a note to your class.

Reweaving a Basket Case

This beautiful person needs encouragement, friendship and support—just as we all do. The cards you've drawn tell you in what areas this person needs help. Work together in your group to think of detailed, practical ways people your age could support and encourage this person. Write your ideas on this page and be prepared to share your efforts with the rest of the class.

Teaching Resource Cards

There are 20 cards on this sheet, enough for four small groups of students to have five cards each. If you have more than 16 students, you should photocopy this page. Or, you could distribute less cards per group (do this if you have a short time period) or form larger groups (more than four students per group).

After any copies are made, cut out and shuffle all the cards (keep the sets separate if you have more than one copy of the cards). Place each set in a container from which students can draw cards. When one container is empty, allow the remaining groups of kids to begin drawing from the next container.

Has just started a smoking habit	**A false but very bad rumor is spreading about this person**	**Says, "God never answers my prayers"**	**Holds a bitter grudge against someone**	**Has to go to summer school!**
Parents fight all the time	**Stuck in bed with a broken leg**	**A major gossiper**	**Borrows things and doesn't return them**	**Complains and criticizes a lot**
"Killer Klonski" pushes this person around	**Has just moved here and seems ill at ease**	**Known as a person who exaggerates the truth**	**Feels ugly all the time**	**Always wants to borrow people's homework**
Has shoplifted several times	**Has just lost a friend in a car accident**	**Wants to tell a friend about God, but is chicken**	**Rarely joins in with friends**	**Won't help you work on this assignment!**

The TOW

Today's Good News:

"Therefore encourage one another and build each other up, just as in fact you are doing."
1 Thessalonians 5:11

The Town Crier Early Edition

TWELVE DISCIPLES LOST IN BOATING ACCIDENT, FEARED DEAD

Based on Matthew 14:22-34

Gennesaret—Eyewitnesses report that all twelve of the close disciples of Jesus Christ climbed into a small boat to cross to this side of the lake, not realizing that a fierce windstorm was approaching. Jesus Himself did not board the boat, but His whereabouts remain unknown.

"They should have arrived some time this evening," said one bystander, "but they are long overdue." Storm conditions still make it impossible to mount rescue operations. The Jerusalem Weather Bureau reports that the unexpected storm may last several days. All hope for the twelve's survival has been abandoned.

The Town Crier Late Edition (Well, nobody's perfect)

DISCIPLES RESCUED!

Peter sits in rear of boat as disciples look on.

Gennesaret—The citizens of this small lakeside community were amazed this morning when the twelve disciples, feared lost in a freak storm, calmly rowed ashore—all apparently in good health (except Peter, who was seasick).

Contrary to Weather Bureau predictions, the storm lasted only a few hours. Also contrary to earlier reports, Jesus was on board the boat after all. The twelve disciples claim that Jesus came to them walking on the water, but many local townsfolk scoff at this.

This reporter interviewed eleven of the disciples (Peter being seasick). I asked them what it was like to be all alone on board a tiny boat in a raging storm.

"Wet," they all agreed.

"We are all great friends," they said. "Before Jesus arrived, we did everything we could to encourage each other. We helped each other row, John told entertaining fish stories and Andrew passed around some leftover pizza he had. That's when Peter started turning green. We helped each other bail out the water and Peter's pizza, and as the storm grew worse, we prayed for each other and attempted to cheer each other up as much as possible."

OK, I ADMIT SOME OF THE DETAILS IN THE STORY ABOVE ARE NOT **COMPLETELY** ACCURATE! READ MATTHEW 14:22-34. AS YOU PROBABLY KNOW, JESUS ARRIVED ON THE SCENE (BY WALKING ON WATER) AND RESCUED THE POOR DISCIPLES.

SOONER OR LATER, EVERYONE FEELS TOSSED HERE AND THERE BY THE STORMS OF LIFE. PROBLEMS BEYOND CONTROL. TROUBLES AND TRIALS.

SURROUND YOURSELF WITH CHRISTIAN FRIENDS. THEY CAN HELP YOU AND YOU CAN HELP THEM WEATHER THE STORMS.

AND DON'T FORGET: JESUS IS YOUR FRIEND, TOO!

"Etiquette": proper social behavior

The theme of this Fun Page is FRIENDSHIP. How can you be a better friend, a person that others just love to like? Follow the simple rules in the

ACME BOOK OF SOCIAL ETIQUETTE

Always brush your teeth at least once a month. Following this simple advice will allow others to get near you.

Change your socks after every bath, or 50,000 miles, whichever comes first.

There is an old saying: "Never put anything in your ear except your elbow." If you should happen to embarrass yourself in public by getting your elbow stuck in your ear, act nonchalant and sneak out the back door. If you have both elbows stuck in your ears, you may as well move to another country.

Making noise in worship services is rude, unless you're the minister.

Etiquette for boys: Young boys tend to hit or punch the arm of their favorite girl. This is fine. However, do not bite, throw things at the girl or destroy her personal property.

Etiquette for girls: When a boy drives up to pick you up for a date, it is proper to point out that thirteen-year-old boys don't have drivers' licenses.

Etiquette for hardened criminals: When stealing a car, always open the car door for female members of the gang.

One of the nice things about a true friend is this: He or she will forgive you when you mess up. A true friend will also help you be or do the best you can. Do you qualify as a good friend?

DAILY THINKERS

Day 1 Read Joshua 6:1-5. If you were a general in Joshua's army, what would you think of this plan?

Day 2 Joshua 6:6-14. Write an imaginary page in the diary of one of Jericho's inhabitants.

Day 3 Joshua 6:15-19. What instructions did Joshua give about items of gold and silver?

Day 4 Joshua 6:20—7:1. What was Achan's sin?

Day 5 Joshua 7:2-13. Describe Joshua's attitude. Would you agree with the way he felt? Why or why not?

Day 6 Joshua 7:14-26. What does this incident tell you about disobeying God? How can we avoid God's anger at our disobedience to Him?

THE COMPLETE JUNIOR HIGH BIBLE STUDY RESOURCE BOOK #10

THEME: We need to give and receive support.

Session 6

BIBLE STUDY OUTLINE

Read Ecclesiastes 4:9-12 to your students. Make the following remarks as time allows.

Introductory remarks: Having friends is one of the most important parts of anyone's life. Let's take a look at a Bible passage that gives insight into the kind of friend a person should have and be.

Verse 9: Solomon, the author of Ecclesiastes, was a very rich man—the richest man in the world during the time he was alive. To him, one benefit of having a friend was that two people could earn more loot for their efforts! However, the point applies to any form of effort. Two people studying together can often learn more about a difficult subject than one. Two friends fixing a motorbike can do the job better than one. Solomon's point is that when a person encourages a friend, that friend can do better and achieve more. This is called "support," and support is what friendship is all about. We can help and be helped in good times and bad. That's what friends are for.

Verse 10: Solomon felt sorry for the poor guy who has no friends—he's stuck out there by himself when he skins his knees on the rocks of life.

Verse 11: Maybe you've heard of the old Arctic explorers who slept next to their dogs and each other to share body warmth. By themselves they would have died, but together they survived. Friends united can face any problem, but a person alone is in trouble. This is why it's so important to talk to others and seek advice when things are troubling you. That's a biblical principle.

Verse 12: (As you go over this verse, do the Object Lesson).

OBJECT LESSON: CAMERA TRIPOD

Compare the support that friends can lend each other to the support of a tripod. Demonstrate how a closed tripod falls over while an open one easily stands. The tripod needs the support of all three legs in order to stand. Say, **Be in the habit of supporting your friends and seeking their support. God has given friends to us as a gift; be the best friend you can be.**

(If your tripod has a platform on it, you can load some books or other heavy objects to demonstrate the idea that friends can help each other carry the burdens of life.)

DISCUSSION QUESTIONS

1. **Describe an instance when a friend came to your rescue. Describe a time that you feel you were a good, supportive pal.**
2. **How do you feel when a friend helps you or you help a friend? How do you feel when you've been let down by a friend or have let someone else down?**
3. **Describe the kind of friend you can count on to support you. How can you be more like that kind of friend? Do you choose friends that have these qualities?**
4. **Why is it important to seek a friend's advice and encouragement when facing a problem? Name some problems that are better shared. Can you think of any problem that you could face better alone?**
5. **How can the Christians in our youth group better help and support each other in their Christian faith?**

Fun Stunts with Clothespins

BOWL 'N' PINS

Have several volunteers sit at a table. Place a bowl in front of each player and put ten clothespins in each bowl. Lay a rope on the table so that it passes between the bowls and volunteers. The object of the game is to be the first player to pin all ten clothespins to the rope—using only the mouth. Players must sit with hands behinds their backs. If the rope moves out of a player's reach, the leader can slide it back.

You can play several rounds with different volunteers, but be sure to discard the clothespins after they've been in someone's mouth! Try playing the game with blindfolds.

PLEASE PASS THE PLATES

Form teams of ten or more people. Players stand side by side in a row or in a circle. Each player has one clothespin in his or her mouth, positioned so that the clothespin can be opened and closed with the teeth. Players must stand with their hands behind their backs. The object of the game is to be the first team to pass a paper plate from one end of the team to the other (or around the circle a set number of times). Players grab and pass the plate using only their clothespins. Hands must be held behind the back. The leader can retrieve a dropped plate.

RUBBER BAND GUNS

Remember the rubber band guns of yesteryear?

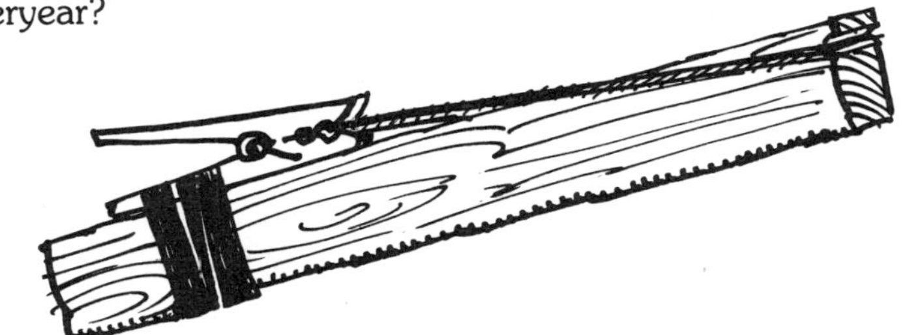

They are easy to make and work great for carnival games. Challenge the players to shoot rubber bands through a hole in a target or knock a paper cup off someone's head (provide eye protection). Guns made to accommodate hefty rubber bands can make fun "weapons" in a lights–out game of tag. Be sure participants wear eye protection.

Moses' Temper

SESSION 7

WHAT THE SESSION IS ABOUT

We must use self-control and respond appropriately when we are angry.

SCRIPTURE STUDIED

Exodus 2:11-15; 32:7,8,15-20,25-28,35; Numbers 20:1-13

KEY PASSAGE

"'In your anger do not sin': Do not let the sun go down while you are still angry." Ephesians 4:26

AIMS OF THE SESSION

During this session your learners will:

1. Identify situations in which Moses lost his temper and the results of his actions;
2. List valid and invalid reasons for anger;
3. Decide on appropriate responses in situations which might make them angry.

INSIGHTS FOR THE LEADER

Anger in itself is not a sin. How can it be, since we often find God Himself expressing anger in the Bible? But it is what makes us angry, and how it is expressed that can create a problem. Things that ought to make us angry, like oppression in Central America or starvation in Africa, can leave us virtually unmoved. But let someone steal my parking space just when I was going to pull into it, and watch out!

The truth is that genuine righteous anger is very, very rare among humankind—though Jesus certainly knew it and vented it from time to time (see Mark 3:1-5; John 2:14-17). Instead, our anger is generally self-oriented, an explosion of our personal resentment. Righteous anger issues from love, not hate.

Moses expressed a mixture. It would be unfair to him to say that his volcanic outbursts were not in part expressing God's own feelings of righteous wrath. Like Jeremiah, he could say "I am full of the wrath of the Lord" (Jer. 6:11). But undoubtedly there was also the very human taint of irritability, impatience and sheer cussedness. It's that side of his anger that we are seeking to isolate in this lesson and hold up to our junior highers as an example of "how not to do it"!

Patience, Moses!

Many examples of Moses' impatience are worth examining, including his panic when everything went wrong in his first attempt to get an exit visa from Pharaoh (see Exod. 5:22,23). And then, of course, there was that incident with the Egyptian when he was young (see Exod. 2:11-15).

Moses also had his occasional arguments with the Lord, as we see from Numbers 11:10-15. From one point of view, this is not a bad thing, for it betokens the complete honesty with God that Moses always maintained. We see the same frankness in Jeremiah, and in many of the Psalms. But we have to be careful that intimacy with the Almighty does not spill over into insubordination or even blasphemy. What Moses had to cope with was provoking enough. The people had become sick of their unvarying diet. Just suppose you had a Big Mac for breakfast, lunch and dinner every day. After a week you probably couldn't look another burger in the sesame seeds. And that's how it was with Israel and their daily menu of manna. Miraculous it may have been, but the novelty had long since worn thin and every time a hungry Israelite ate a bite he dreamed of a melon or a salmon instead.

So they all complained and Moses wearily took their complaints to the Lord. The extent of his exasperation came out in his prayer, which was full of complaining "Whys?" and a general accusation that God had loaded him dangerously low in the water by giving him such a miserable lot of crybabies to carry (see Num. 11:12). In effect he says, "It's all your

fault, Lord!" (see v. 11) and with more petulance than piety tells the Lord to get him out of the mess by killing him, if need be (see v. 15). Ministers and Sunday School teachers know the feeling well!

Water, Water

The incident in Numbers 11 was a foreshadowing of an even more serious occasion—more serious, that is, for Moses, who lost his crowning reward of entering the Promised Land because of it (see Num. 20:1-13).

The argument this time was over water. As usual, the Israelites' complaint was couched in terms of "things were better before—is this the best you can do for us?" Moses and Aaron undoubtedly did right in bringing the complaint to the Lord, and there is no hint of anything amiss in the way they presented the problem. Also there is nothing in the Lord's reply to suggest that He was angry with His servants at this stage. However, something went drastically wrong in the way they implemented the Lord's command. Having got the people together, Moses spoke to them with scorching sternness (see Num. 20:10). He struck the rock and sure enough water gushed out. But the Lord condemned Moses and pronounced judgment: "Because you did not trust in me enough to honor me as holy in the sight of the Israelites, you will not bring this community into the land I give them" (v. 12).

It has always been a puzzle as to what way Moses' trust was deficient. It is obvious that Moses went beyond the letter of the Lord's command: Whereas the Lord had said, "Speak to that rock" (v. 8), Moses both spoke to it and struck it. Psalm 106:33 defines the "trust" problem as being more in Moses' words than his action: "Rash words came from Moses' lips." In that case, it may be the fact that Moses said, "Must we bring you water out of this rock?" (Num. 20:10) and thus took glory from God.

We cannot be certain what the precise problem was and will have to be content with the knowledge that the Lord knew Moses' heart at the moment he spoke and that is the crucial thing (see 1 Sam. 16:7).

Learning to Control Temper

Would Moses have been Moses without that hot blood flowing through his veins? Could he have ever led Israel through those tortuous 40 years if he had not known the flames of passion that flared in his spirit? Certainly not. But he had to learn to control his temper. Twice in the Bible we have the perfect summary of how anger, though not to be denied, must be tamed: "'In your anger do not sin': Do not let the sun go down while you are still angry" (Eph. 4:26; also see Ps. 4:4). Moses knew that the kind of anger that came out of bitterness could bear only the fruit of bitterness (see Eph. 4:31) in its rash, uncontrolled expression.

Because Moses was so teachable, the Bible is therefore able to say of him that he was "very meek, above all the men which were upon the face of the earth" (Num. 12:3, *KJV*). Moses was meek, but not mild!

SESSION PLAN

BEFORE CLASS BEGINS: There is no Scratch Sheet this time. Photocopy the Fun Page. Assemble the two Teaching Resource pages to make a poster. The ATTENTION GRABBER requires that you photocopy the Games and Things page that follows this session. You will need poster board and colored felt pens for the EXPLORATION.

Attention Grabber

ATTENTION GRABBER (5-10 minutes)

The Games and Things page is a special picture puzzle poster. It's theme is anger; solving the puzzle will introduce your students to this session's topic.

This is the solution to the puzzle:

STAR + GET - TARGET + OBL + ROCK - BLOCK + TEAR - TEA + Y, = SORRY,
MITTEN - 10 - MT = I
FILE + N - FIN - E + C + OAR - CAR + STAR + M - ARM = LOST
THUMB - H - TUB + Y = MY
ST + TEMPERATURE - STATUE - R. = TEMPER.

KNOT - KT = NO
NEEDLE + G - LEG = NEED
2 - W = TO
HB + 2 + RAT - BAT - T + RAT - HAT + Y, = WORRY,
MITTEN - 10 - MT = I
P + FOOT - POT + HOUND - HO = FOUND
PIG - PG + T. = IT.

After students have had a chance to solve the puzzle, say something like this: **Today we are going to look at Moses, a man of God who had a strong temper, and some of the difficulties that he experienced because of it.**

ALTERNATE ATTENTION GRABBER (5-7 minutes)

Ask, **How can you tell when a friend or family member is getting angry? What things make that person angry? What are some of his or her facial expressions, some things he or she says or does?** Make the discussion fun. Note the students' responses on the chalkboard.

Say something like this: **Have you noticed anything on this list that makes someone else angry, but doesn't usually upset you? It's interesting that each of us is different. Today we are going to look at a man of God who had a strong temper, and some of the difficulties that he experienced because of it.**

Bible Exploration

EXPLORATION (25-40 minutes)

Materials needed: Poster board, colored felt pens, the Teaching Resource poster.

Step 1 (10-12 minutes): Create a chart on the chalkboard similar to the one in the illustration.

Lead a class discussion based on the chart (or have students work in small groups, making notes to present later to the class). Read each passage and have students debate their answers for the four questions. Students should give reasons for believing that the results were or were not justified. Have students brainstorm any possible alternatives to the poor responses to anger.

Add any thoughts that your learners may have missed, using materials from the INSIGHTS FOR THE LEADER. Make sure students see that Moses often had good reason for his anger—injustice and rebellion or complaining attitudes toward God certainly don't deserve compliments. But Moses also expressed his anger in inappropriate ways, with unfortunate results.

Step 2 (Widely variable time): Attach to the wall the Teaching Resource poster. Tell students, **Work together in groups of two or three people. Walk up to the poster and take a look at each situation depicted. Choose one situation to write about and return to your seats. Then, on your paper, write out (1) a positive response to the situation, (2) a negative response and (3) the possible results of each response you have suggested.** (List these three steps on your chalkboard.) You may want to assign situations to be sure most or all are covered. Tell students to work on additional situations if you want to fill a longer period of time.

After allowing time for students to work, reassemble the class and go through the situations on the poster, letting groups take turns telling what they have written. Wrap up by summarizing some of the negative results that can happen when we respond negatively to an anger-producing situation, and some of the positive results that can happen when we use our creativity to find a more positive response.

Step 3 (10-12 minutes): Provide poster board and colored felt pens. Have students read Ephesians 4:26. (You might wish to write the verses in advance on a sheet of newsprint.) Tell students, **Stay with your partners for this step too. Work together**

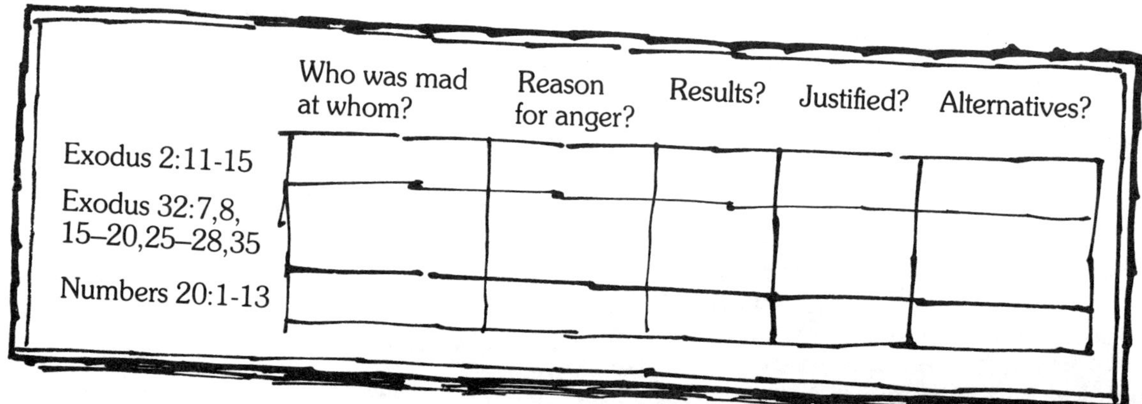

to create a caution sign that could be used to remind people your age about the dangers of inappropriately letting their anger loose.

After students have had some time to create their signs, ask volunteers to show what they have done and explain it to the class.

Move to the CONCLUSION by saying something like this: **Today we have looked at anger from a biblical and a practical perspective. Let's take some time to think about our personal handling of anger.**

Conclusion and Decision

CONCLUSION (5-7 minutes)

There are two suggested CONCLUSION activities this time; you can assign either one or let each student choose which activity he or she wishes to do. The second suggestion requires small pieces of poster board from which students can cut wallet-size cards.

Suggestion #1: Tell students, **Make a chart like the one we had on the chalkboard, with information about the last time you got angry, the results, and some alternatives you might try the next time you get angry. Do this assignment individually. You can be honest with yourself and God because I won't ask you to share your thoughts with the class.**

Suggestion #2: Tell your learners, **Make a small card to carry in your purse or wallet. The card should have the words of Ephesians 4:26 on it, and you might want to put a reminder to yourself on it such as, "When I feel angry I'll read this card."**

After allowing time for students to work on the assignments, close in prayer. Ask God to help students understand the need for self-control in the area of temper. If students have developed relationships as a group that allow for personal sharing, let volunteers share a typical situation or kind of person that tends to cause them to become angry. Then you can support each other in prayer about those situations.

Distribute the Fun Page take-home paper.

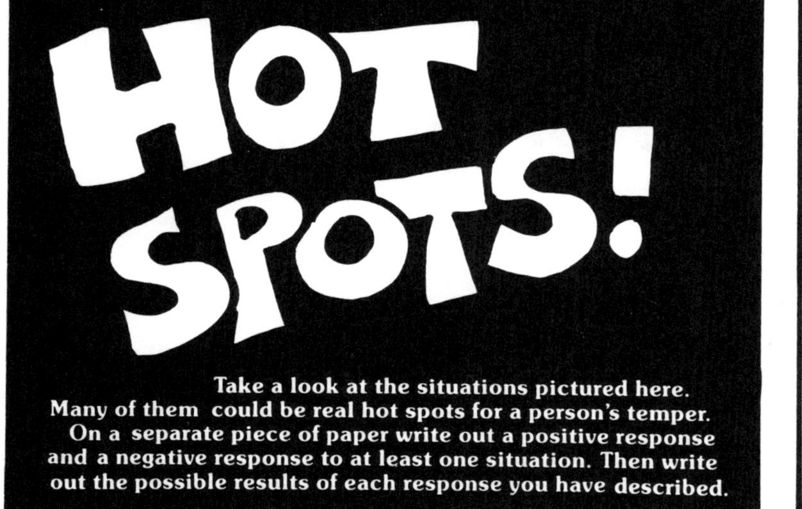

HOT SPOTS!

Take a look at the situations pictured here. Many of them could be real hot spots for a person's temper. On a separate piece of paper write out a positive response and a negative response to at least one situation. Then write out the possible results of each response you have described.

HEY, RALPH! SORRY I WAS A LITTLE BIT LATE!

...AND SINCE I'M SURE ONE OF YOU WAS CHEATING I'M GOING TO HAVE TO GIVE YOU BOTH AN "F" ON YOUR TERM PAPER!
ZERO

LAWRENCE WELK'S HIT PARADE!
OH NO! THE TV PREMIERE OF THE NEW JAMES BOMB SPY MOVIE IS ON NOW!
TV WEEK
—BUNDSCHUH—

Session 7

The TOWN CRIER

Based on Daniel 3 and 4

KING NEBUCHADNEZZAR HAS THE WORLD'S SECOND WORST TEMPER!

Babylon—Hundreds of this nation's top advisors were ordered executed by King Nebuchadnezzar.

"Normally, he's an all right guy," said one official as he was dragged off in chains. "He just has a tendency to fly off the handle."

Shortly after the incident, Nebuchadnezzar became so angry at three young men (Shadrach, Meschach and Abednego) that he ordered a huge oven to be heated seven times hotter than normal, and the three were thrown in. The fire was so hot it fried all the poor soldiers who cast the three into the oven.

Why did the king get so hot under the collar? Probably because he's so full of pride and arrogance.

In fact, he is so full of pride that he spends a great deal of time bragging about what a wonderful king he is and what a wonderful empire he's built.

That sort of pride makes God very angry.

Sources have reported that a voice came down out of the sky and said: "You will be driven away from people and will live with the wild animals; you will eat grass like cattle" (Daniel 4:32).

When asked to comment, the king said, "Moo" and went back to chewing his cud.

Nebuchadnezzar spelled backwards is "razzendahcuben," from which we get the English word "razz," as demonstrated by the king in this photo.

KING NEBUCHADNEZZAR WAS AN ANGRY MAN. HIS ANGER WAS SELF-CENTERED AND DESTRUCTIVE. HIS ANGER DESTROYED RELATIONSHIPS AND FRIENDSHIPS. GOD WAS ANGRY, TOO. BUT HIS ANGER IS CONSTRUCTIVE: HE GETS MAD AT WRONGS AND INJUSTICES. HE SETS THINGS RIGHT!

WHAT ABOUT YOU? NEXT TIME YOU'RE MAD, LIST THE REASONS WHY. SEE IF IT'S BECAUSE OF YOUR OWN EGO, OR BECAUSE YOU CARE FOR OTHERS.

Today's Good News:

"'In your anger do not sin': Do not let the sun go down while you are still angry." Ephesians 4:26

Here's a fun game! Play it alone or with a friend. Object of the game is to get the highest score by being the "nicest" person.

1. Cut out the five cards below. Read the phrase printed on each card. Pick the one card with the phrase you like best and LAY IT OFF TO THE SIDE.
2. Shuffle the remaining four cards and then divide them into two pairs, faceup, like this:

Pair A  Pair B

3. Look at Pair A. Do the colors of the eyes (black or white) match? 4. Look at Pair B. Do the eyes match?
5. Add up the numbers of PAIRS with matching eyes. If Pair A *or* Pair B is a matching pair, you have one matching pair. If both A and B match (THEY DO NOT HAVE TO MATCH EACH OTHER!), then you have two matching pairs. Write down the number of matching pairs. For example, if you have no matching pairs, write down a "0."
6. Now follow steps 2 through 5 again (remember to shuffle), only this time look for matching EXPRESSIONS (happy or angry). When you've determined the number of pairs that match, write it down next to the first number.
7. Follow steps 2 through 5 one last time, but look for matching BOW TIE colors. Write down that number next to the other two. You should now have a three-digit number, for example "020."
8. Look up the number in the "Glad or Mad List" below. You'll find an answer to the card you laid to one side! That answer applies only to that one card. Write down the number of points you win or lose.
9. Now pick a second card to lay aside and then follow steps 2-8. Continue playing until you have found an answer on the "Glad or Mad List" for all five cards. Add up your total score. The winner is the one with the highest number of points.

When my girlfriend/boyfriend broke up with me, I . . .

When I smashed my finger in the door, I . . .

When my chemistry teacher said she was going to flunk me, I . . .

When my dad wouldn't let me have the keys to the car, I . . .

When I discovered that my best friend was telling lies about me, I . . .

GLAD OR MAD LIST:

000. calmly spoke with my friend and straightened out the situation. +10 points.
001. ripped the door off its hinges and threw it through the neighbor's window. -10 points.
002. poured ten pounds of wet plaster of paris into my friend's locker. -10 points.
011. determined that I would study some next time. +10 points.
020. forgave and prayed for my friend. +10 points.
021. gently opened the door and kissed my finger until it stopped throbbing. +10 points.
022. tied my friend's shoelaces to the leg of his/her school desk. Ha,ha! -10 points
100. humbly obeyed his decision. After all, I won't be old enough to drive for two more years. +10 points.
102. picked up my date with the rider lawn mower. It's better than nothing. -10 points.
110. pushed the ring he/she gave me over his/her pointy head and around his/her throat. -10 points.
112. smiled calmly because I know the next girlfriend/boyfriend I have will be a lot better than this creep! +10 points.
120. humbly obeyed his decision. He's right about what happened LAST time I borrowed the car! +10 points.
122. pushed the car over to my date's house, and made him/her push me and the car to the party. -10 points.
200. asked my friend to forgive me for what I had done to offend him/her. +10 points.
201. slammed the door on the fingers of the next person to come along. -10 points.
202. told everyone in school that he/she was a Barry Manilow fan! -10 points.
211. forced her to drink my experimental shrinking formula. -10 points.
220. told my friend that I would always love him/her no matter what he/she did. +10 points.
221. smiled at my clumsiness and promised to be more careful next time. +10 points.
222. soldered his/her braces shut. -10 points.

If you've played this game, you realize that it's a fun way of looking at some good things and some dumb things people might do when they are in a maddening situation. But always remember, nobody likes a hothead. Keep close to the Lord. He can help you with your temper.

DAILY THINKERS

Day 1 Read Ruth 1:1-22. What do you think was the difference between Orpah and Ruth that caused Orpah to turn back while Ruth stayed with Naomi?

Day 2 Ruth 2:1-13. If Ruth had stopped at this moment to write in her diary, what might she have written?

Day 3 Ruth 2:14-23. Boaz did much more for Ruth than the law required (compare Leviticus 19:9,10; 23:22; Deuteronomy 24:19). What do you think was his reason?

Day 4 Ruth 3:1-18. Ruth's actions may seem strange today, but they were appropriate in the culture of her time. Afterwards, Naomi told Ruth to wait. Have you had times when you've had to wait for the Lord to work?

Day 5 Ruth 4:1-12. Write a newspaper article describing the transaction between Boaz and the other man.

Day 6 Ruth 4:13-21. What relation was Ruth to King David? And she was a more distant ancestor of whom? (See Matthew 1:5-16.)

THE COMPLETE JUNIOR HIGH BIBLE STUDY RESOURCE BOOK #10

THEME: Anger and other problems.

Session 7

BIBLE STUDY OUTLINE

After relating the background given in the introductory remarks below, read Jonah 3:10—4:11 to your students. Make the following comments as time permits.

Introductory remarks: Nineveh was a powerful, pagan city. Its warriors were known and feared for the ruthless ways they tortured and murdered their enemies. God was sick and tired of Nineveh's wickedness, so He told Israel's prophet Jonah to "preach against it" (see Jon. 1:1,2). Jonah, angry that God would give the hated Ninevites a chance to repent, headed in the opposite direction. With the help of a big fish, God managed to get Jonah back on track. Jonah did as he was told; he preached repentance in the streets of the city. The king got the message and ordered everyone in Nineveh to fast, pray and repent.

Jonah 3:10: God saw their repentance and demonstrated His compassion. He let the Ninevites off the hook.

Jonah 4:1: One would think that a man of God would be happy to see his enemies turn in repentance to the Lord. Not Jonah. He was mad! Why? Possibly because he was afraid God's special love would no longer be centered on Israel. Whatever the reason, Jonah's angry words toward God were not at all the appropriate response.

Verses 2,3: Jonah knew the Lord well; he knew God is gracious, compassionate, slow to anger, abounding in love and willing to give repentant people another chance. But though Jonah knew these things, he did not practice them himself. No, he would rather die!

Verses 4,5: God questioned Jonah's reason for being angry; Jonah left God's question unanswered. Instead he went out from the city to sit and wait—he was hoping God would do something rotten to Nineveh.

Verses 6-11: God realized that Jonah needed to be taught a lesson. The Lord miraculously caused a vine to grow to shade Jonah, who very likely had sensitive skin after sharing stomach space with the fish's digestive juices. Then God destroyed the vine. Again, Jonah was furious with God. The lesson was simple: Jonah cared more about a worthless vine than he did about the more than 120,000 people of Nineveh.

We see several big problems in Jonah's life. First, we see his resentful anger. Then we notice how unlike God he was—God was compassionate, slow to anger, loving and all the rest. Jonah was none of these. Jonah was also vengeful. He camped outside the city, hoping God would do something horrible to the repentant Ninevites.

The key to Jonah's problems was how unlike God he was. As Christians, we need to diligently seek to be like Jesus. The word "Christian" means "little Christ." It is up to us to learn all we can about our Lord and to put into practice what we learn. As we become more and more like Him, we will have less and less of the problems Jonah had.

OBJECT LESSON: MODEL

Show your students a plastic model kit. Say, **This model is designed to look like the real thing, only smaller. It would have been stupid if the designers of the kit didn't really care what it looked like. It would also be stupid to assemble it haphazardly, without trying to fit the parts together properly. It's supposed to end up looking as much like the real thing as possible.**

In the same way, those of us who have given our lives to Jesus should strive to be like Him. He is the object we are trying to model with our lives. It's wrong not to care about how we behave or think because we are supposed to act and think like Jesus. It takes time and effort to put together a model perfectly and it takes time and effort to become like Jesus. If we don't model our lives after Jesus, the pieces of our lives won't fit together properly. This is the job God has given us and He has promised to help us.

Variation: Show your students two versions of the same model kit: one properly assembled and one with the parts glued together in a big mess.

DISCUSSION QUESTIONS

1. **What was Jonah's real problem? Is it one many people have?**
2. **What is the meaning of the word "Christian"? Why is its meaning significant?**
3. **How can we become more like Jesus? What are some of His traits that we should imitate?**
4. **What happens when we don't model our lives after Jesus?**

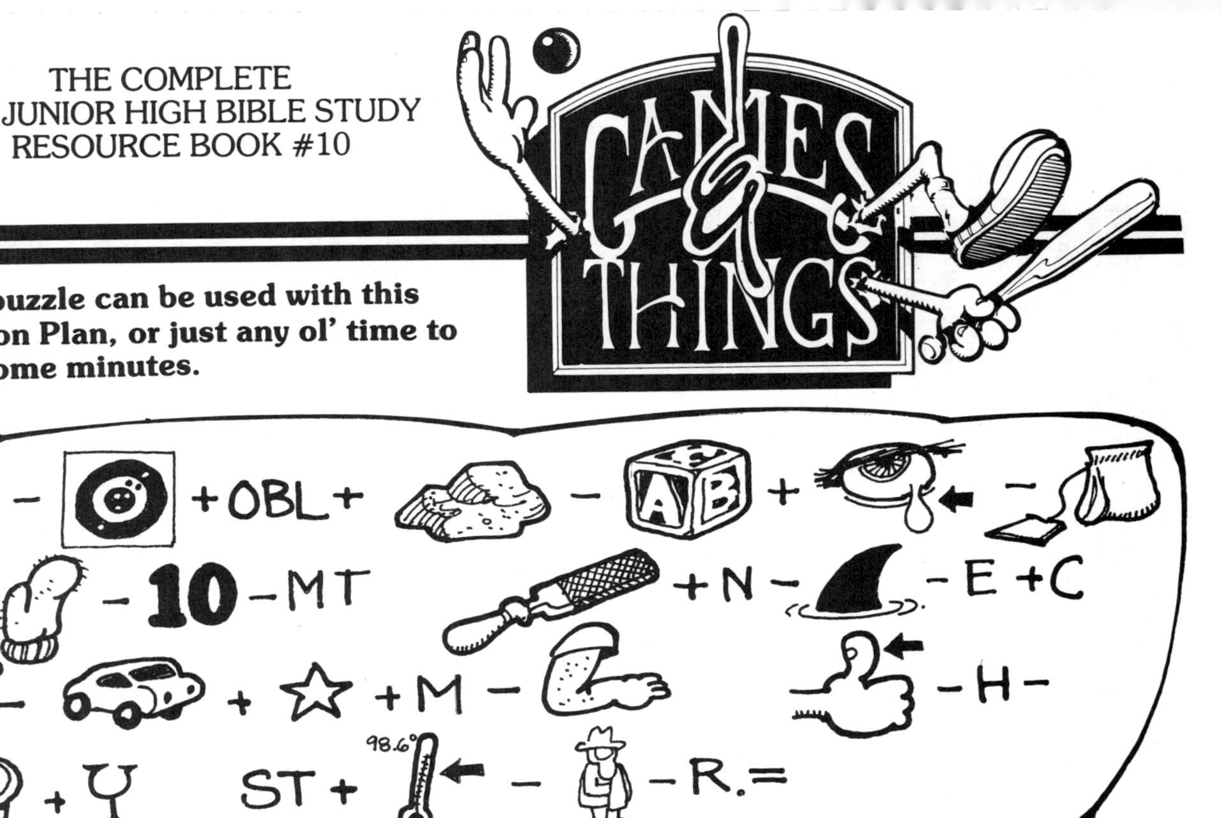

This picture puzzle can be used with this week's Session Plan, or just any ol' time to while away some minutes.

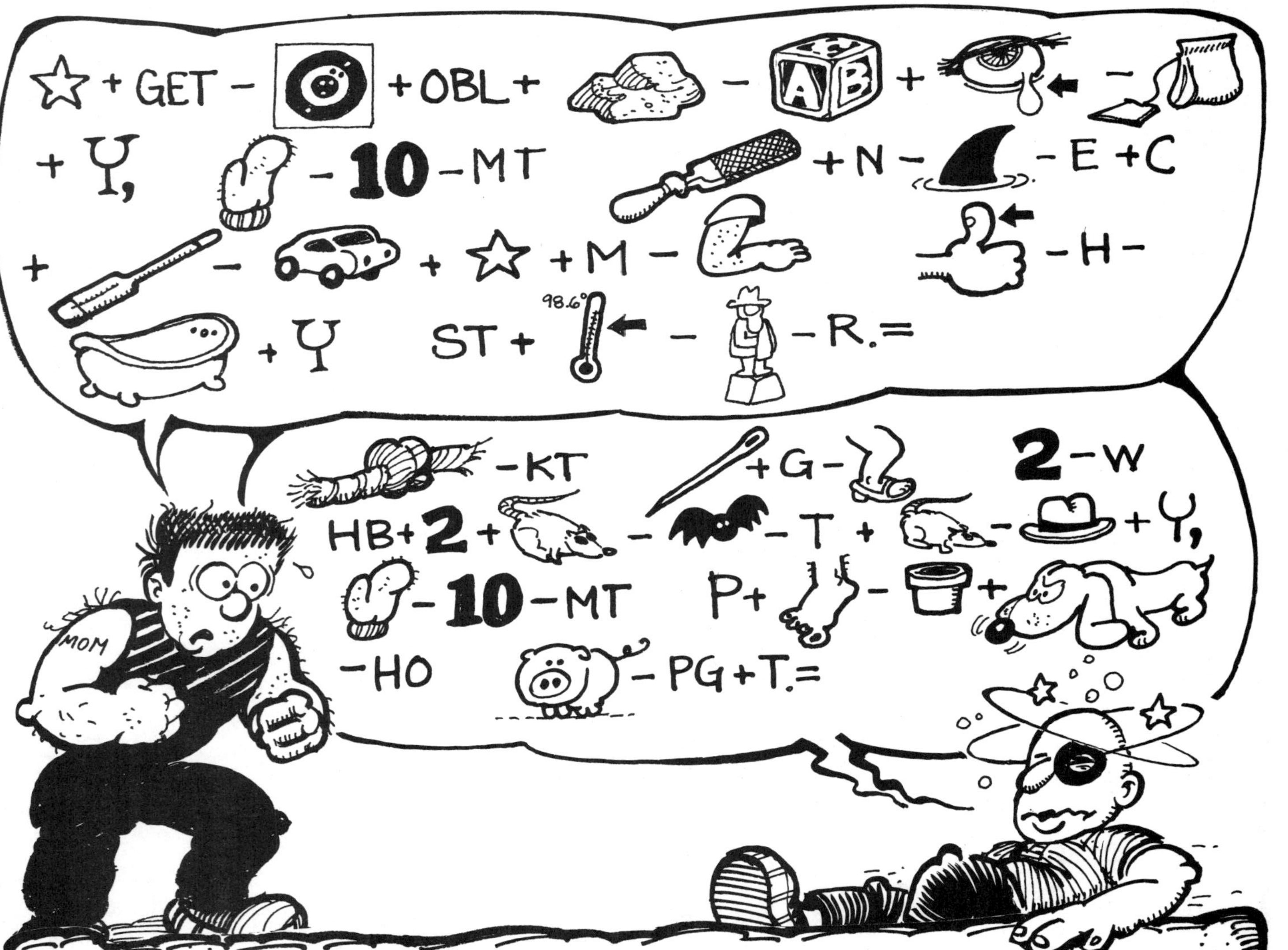

Proverbs 14:17 says, "A quick-tempered man does foolish things." Take God's advice from Ephesians 4:31: "Get rid of all bitterness, rage and anger, brawling and slander, along with every form of malice."

Moses' Value

SESSION 8

WHAT THE SESSION IS ABOUT

God can make nobodies into somebodies.

SCRIPTURE STUDIED

Exodus 2:10-22; 3:1-12;
Acts 7:20-38; Philippians 1:6;
Hebrews 11:23-29

KEY PASSAGE

"Being confident of this, that he who began a good work in you will carry it on to completion until the day of Christ Jesus." Philippians 1:6

AIMS OF THE SESSION

During this session your learners will:

1. Describe specific times in the life of Moses when he was a "nobody" and when he was a "somebody";
2. Compare the qualities that give a person value in the world's eyes and those that give value in God's view;
3. Evaluate their own qualities.

INSIGHTS FOR THE LEADER

In the second century, a pagan writer called Celsus attacked Christianity on the grounds that it attracted all the riffraff of society. He considered it must be false if it appealed to such people. He said, "They want and are able to convince only the foolish, dishonorable, and stupid, and only slaves, women, and little children." But Paul showed that this is the very glory of Christ's way. "God chose the foolish things of the world to shame the wise; God chose the weak things of the world to shame the strong. He chose the lowly things of this world and the despised things" (1 Cor. 1:27,28). The gospel, then, is good news for nobodies!

Nobody or Somebody?

Long before Paul wrote, God showed that He loved to take a "nobody" and make him a "somebody." This is what He did with Moses. First He had to take Moses from being a "somebody" in the world—a prince in Egypt—and turn him into a "nobody"—a shepherd in the middle of nowhere. Then He could make Moses the leader of a nation which was itself a bunch of nobodies, a slave people. God turned Moses and these people into the privileged bearers of His self-revelation to the world. Moses had to come down from being a somebody in the world to being a nobody before God, in order that he could be turned into a real somebody for the Lord!

God's dealings with men and women have not changed since Moses' time. We have to have our self-righteousness and pride broken before we will turn to God with a repentant and obedient heart. Sometimes that may come through disappointment, personal failure, even heartbreak and tragedy. But then God picks us up, dusts us off, gives us His big hug of love and sets us on our way with the assurance of His never-failing strength. In a world that is full of people trying to bluster their way through, masking their terrible insecurities, Christians can walk with confidence and an inner serenity that keeps us relaxed when everyone else is tense.

Why? Because we have squarely faced the fact not just of our own inadequacy and insecurity, but of our downright sin (see Rom. 3:23). We dare not claim to have any credits in our account with God once we have seen the depravity of our own hearts. So we don't try to pretend anymore. That sounds like the open door to dark despair. But it isn't, because we have realized that is not the end of the story. We know that even while the human race is in full rebellion against God, Christ died for us for love's sake (see Rom. 5:8). So Christians have confidence that in Christ we have the ultimate in security; we are released from fear, for our security depends on God, not ourselves.

The apostle Peter speaks for all Christians when he says "you are a chosen people, a

royal priesthood . . . a people belonging to God" (1 Pet. 2:9). No matter that once we "were not a people" (v. 10). It's what the Lord has made us now that counts.

In your class you will possibly have some who are in the first "somebody" stage of pre-Christian experience. Their need is to know conviction of sin and their complete spiritual nakedness. Then there may be others who have reached that position and are waiting for the cheerful, encouraging word of the gospel that says "Believe in the Lord Jesus, and you will be saved" (Acts 16:31). But there may be yet a third group who, though they have believed and been saved, still feel themselves "nobodies" and need encouragement to realize their new status in Christ. Perhaps God will use you through this lesson to encourage your "nobodies" to realize they are "somebodies" in Christ!

Moses the Somebody

Let's now see how this somebody-nobody-somebody pattern worked in Moses' life.

Stephen gave a summary of the great man's life when he spoke before the Sanhedrin in Acts 7.

From verses 20 through 22 he sketches the worldly privileges that Moses enjoyed. Through the providence of God he was brought up in Pharaoh's household and learned Egypt's wisdom and ways, knowledge which would surely stand him in good stead.

In verses 23 to 29 Stephen recounts how Moses tried to use his position and comparative security to help his fellow Israelites. However, as we've seen in the previous lessons in this series, it all went wrong, and the episode ended with his having to flee for his life.

Ordinary human reasoning would say this was a tragedy. Moses had "blown" his golden chance. It was potentially a marvelous opportunity for Moses the Hebrew to be right there in Pharaoh's court. Surely if help was to come for the oppressed Israelites that was the one place to be.

But God planned otherwise! Moses had some more learning to do, this time in the university of the wilderness. And he was a long time at his studies—40 years! But the time of his graduation came at last (see vv. 30-32). It was time to put what he had learned into practice and start work (see vv. 33-38). It was no easy task. Israel had once rejected Moses when he was "somebody" when they might have received him with open arms (see v. 35). Would they listen to him now that he was a "nobody"? He himself had his doubts and told God so (see Exod. 3 and 4). In fact the people did rumble away in rebellion against his authority many times, as we've seen throughout this series. Nevertheless, he achieved the impossible and brought Israel out of Egypt. How and why did he do this? Because he was God's man, appointed by Him, raised up in leadership by God's command. His own inadequacy and fears were overcome by the power and grace of God.

You and your students are not Moses, but in your Christian lives you have Moses' God to love you, care for you and empower you.

SESSION PLAN

BEFORE CLASS BEGINS: Photocopy the Scratch Sheet and the Fun Page. Photocopy the two Teaching Resource game pages (enough copies for each group of three or four students to have one), then tape each copy of both pages together to create the game board. If your copier is able, enlarge the game pages. Provide a paper clip for each group of players to use with the spinner, and scissors to cut out the tokens. The CONCLUSION requires slips of paper, a container and some simple preparation.

Attention Grabber

ATTENTION GRABBER (3-5 minutes)

Tell students, **Turn to the Scratch Sheet section titled "The Qualities of a Winner" and follow the instructions you find there. Answer the questions in that section and be prepared to share your answers.**

After students have had time to work, regain their attention and ask for their responses.

Say something like this: **Today we are going to take another look at a person whose background and personality did not meet some of the qualifications that we think are necessary for a winner to have. His name, as you have probably guessed, is Moses.**

ALTERNATE ATTENTION GRABBER (5-7 minutes)

Say, **Suppose you were on your way to lunch at your campus. As you walked by the tables three members of the opposite sex held up score cards like they use in the Olympics. They had scored your appearance on a scale of one to ten. What would be your reaction?**

Many students will probably say, "It depends on the score." Ask them to comment on how it would make them feel if they received a low score. Ask other questions such as: **On what basis do you think these people measured the worth of another person? What is wrong with this system of determining a person's "score"? What are some other problems with this kind of judgment call?**

Say, **We are going to take one last look at Moses today. If he had been judged by a group like the one we have been talking about, he may have received a low score. He did not have many exceptional external attributes that would make him a "10"—but God chose to make him someone special anyway.**

Bible Exploration

EXPLORATION (35-50 minutes)

Materials needed: The "Nobodies into Somebodies!" Teaching Resource game, paper clips and scissors.

Step 1 (8-10 minutes): Ask students to form pairs. Assign, or let pairs select, at least one of the three assignments from "A Premature Burial . . . " section of the Scratch Sheet. Read the definition of an obituary from the Scratch Sheet and check to make sure students understand the meaning. Then explain, **You are to write an obituary that might have been printed about Moses if he had died at the end of the time period assigned to you. Read the Scriptures listed and then write the obituary.**

After students have had time to write, regain their attention and ask them to read their obituaries. Summarize what they have said and point out any of the following material that they may have missed. Moses was an important person—a "somebody"—while he was being raised in the court of Pharaoh. He was considered the son of Pharaoh's daughter. He probably had great wealth and status. Then Moses experienced being a "nobody" for forty years. He watched sheep and lived fairly isolated in the wilderness. Had he died during that time he would have been a mere footnote in history. God wanted Moses to be a somebody, but He wanted Moses to be a somebody because of Him. It was in the last forty years of Moses' life that the changes that made him a somebody took place.

Note: If you have only a short amount of time to teach class, you can skip the next two steps and go directly to step 4.

Step 2 (3-5 minutes): Ask students to help you make a list of all the things people their age might think would make a person a "somebody." List their suggestions on the chalkboard. Then ask, **How do these values compare with what Moses experienced in the first forty years of his life? What are the similarities? The differences?** Let students respond.

Step 3 (3-5 minutes): Ask students, **What makes a person a somebody to God?** List their responses next to the list from step 2. Point out some of the following ideas as your students share.

1. It makes little or no difference to God what the "package" looks like on the outside; He is concerned about the quality inside.
2. God values things according to their eternal significance. To illustrate, aiming to acquire material possessions has a temporal, temporary significance because "things" wear out, break, go out of fashion or become boring. On the other hand, what we do through our care and concern for others lasts forever, and can lead to the salvation of the people to whom we show our Christian love.
3. Being close to God was the secret of being a somebody for Moses—and it is the same for us today as well.

Step 4 (15-20 minutes): Have students form groups of no more than four members. Give each group a copy of the Teaching Resource game, a paper clip and scissors. The game is designed to show the qualities that make a person a "somebody" and the poor results of trying to be a "somebody" without doing it God's way. Read the instructions and be sure everyone understands them. Tell your learners, **Play as many rounds of the game as you can in the time limit. Then we'll discuss what you learn from the game.**

When time is up regain students' attention and ask, **From playing the game, what did you learn about some of the things that make a person "somebody" in the eyes of the world? What are some of the things that make a**

person a real "somebody"? As you discuss these questions with students, review the three major points listed under step 3.

Step 5 (5-8 minutes): Read Philippians 1:6 to your class and ask, **What kind of hope do you think Christians can get from this verse?** Let students respond. The verse shows that if God is working in our lives, we can be confident that He is going to make us into His kind of "somebodies."

Make a transition to the CONCLUSION by saying something like this: **It is pretty obvious that God is the one who makes us "somebodies," and that trying to prove our worth and value by achieving wealth, fame, education or any other accomplishment that leaves God out is worthless.**

Conclusion and Decision

CONCLUSION (5-10 minutes)

Materials needed: A small slip of paper for each student and a container. Prepare some extra slips of paper as described below.

Give each learner a small slip of paper. Explain, **I want you to write one important quality that you've learned will help a person become a true "somebody." Think about it for a minute, write your response and then I'll collect the papers.**

Collect the papers in a container. Scan the slips as they are collected to be sure everyone has written something valid. If some slips must be rejected, replace them with slips upon which you've written qualities. Then have each student take a slip from the container.

Say, **I want you to individually and prayerfully consider the quality you've received. Is it a quality you demonstrate well, or do you need to work on that area? Ask God to help you demonstrate that quality daily.**

Close in prayer.

Distribute the Fun Page take-home paper.

> *"Being confident of this, that he who began a good work in you will carry it on to completion until the day of Christ Jesus."*
> *Philippians 1:6*

Session 8

The Qualities of a Winner

Circle the qualities that you think would most likely be found in a "winner" or successful person.

Criminal history **Poor home situation** **A "zero" in the eyes of others**
Respected by others **Eloquent in speech** **Good self-image**
Youthful **Lousy self-image** **No criminal history**
Uneducated **Good home life**
Good education
Poor communicator **Elderly**

1. Which quality do you think is most important?
2. What would you add to this list?

A Premature Burial

In the obituary column below, write a description of what might have been said about Moses in one of the following 40-year spans of his life. (An obituary is a description of a deceased person that tells about his or her contributions while alive.)

1. **If Moses had died at 40, what might have been written about him?**

   Exodus 2:10
   Acts 7:20-22
   Hebrews 11:23

2. **If Moses had died at 80, what might the people who had known him for the last 40 years have said about him as a result of the last 40 years?**

   Exodus 2:11-22
   Acts 7:23-29
   Hebrews 11:24-27

3. **When Moses finally did die, what do you think could have been said about him based on the last 40 years of his life?**

   Exodus 3:1-12
   Acts 7:30-38
   Hebrews 11:28,29

NOBODIES INTO SOMEBODIES!

Object of the game: To be the first person to go from being a "nobody" to being a "somebody."

To play: Cut out the tokens. Each player chooses a token. Player #1 goes first. Spin the paper clip spinner as shown in the drawing to see how far to jump along the path. Follow the instructions you find near the square you land on. Some squares will have you rocket ahead, some will have you crash back down. Two or more players may land on the same square.

To win: The "Somebody!" square at top must be reached by an exact spin of the spinner. First person to get there wins.

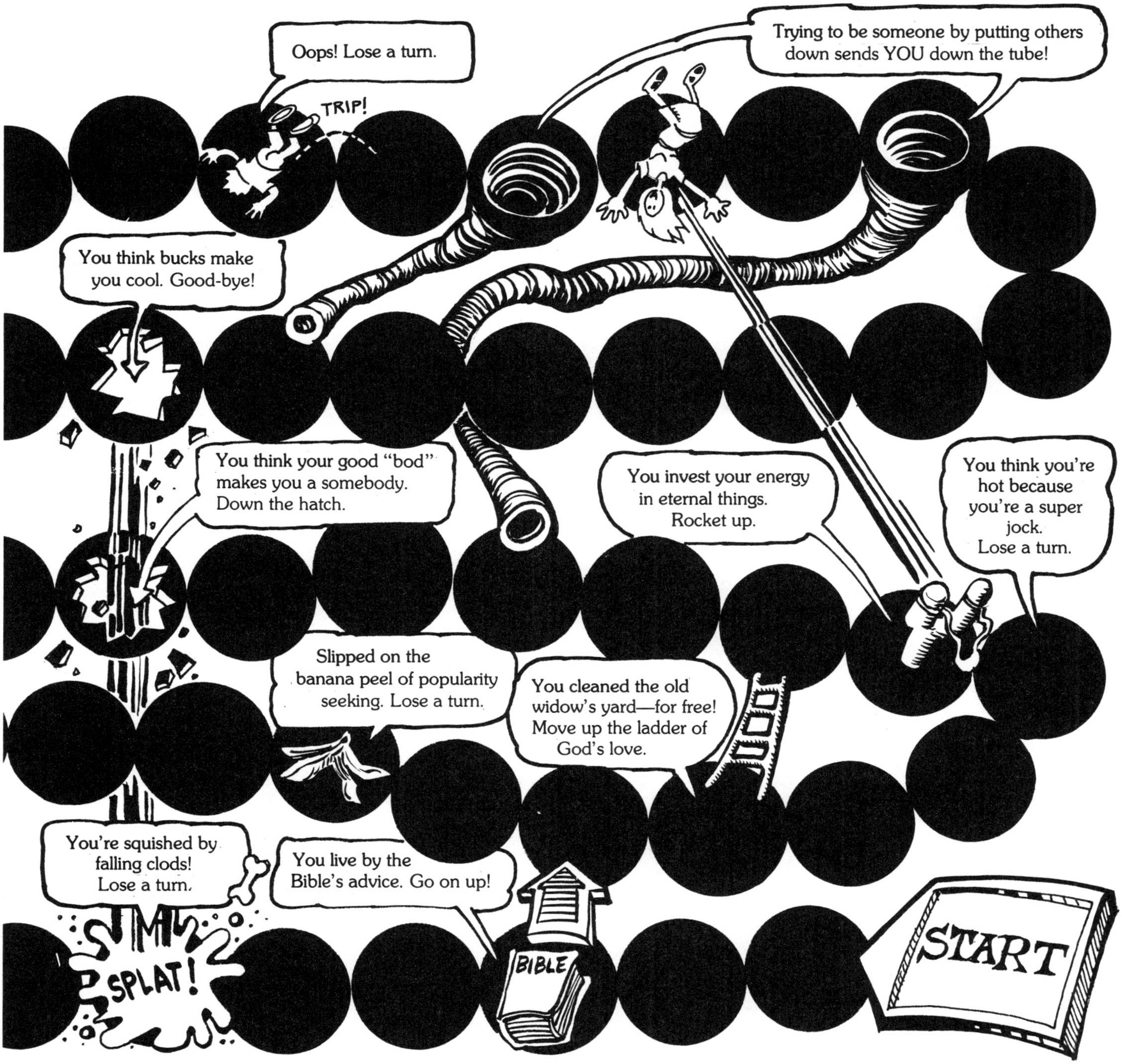

Oops! Lose a turn.

TRIP!

Trying to be someone by putting others down sends YOU down the tube!

You think bucks make you cool. Good-bye!

You think your good "bod" makes you a somebody. Down the hatch.

You invest your energy in eternal things. Rocket up.

You think you're hot because you're a super jock. Lose a turn.

Slipped on the banana peel of popularity seeking. Lose a turn.

You cleaned the old widow's yard—for free! Move up the ladder of God's love.

You're squished by falling clods! Lose a turn.

You live by the Bible's advice. Go on up!

SPLAT!

BIBLE

START

Place paper clip and pencil or pen as shown. Spin the paper clip; whichever number most of the clip lands on is the number of jumps to take.

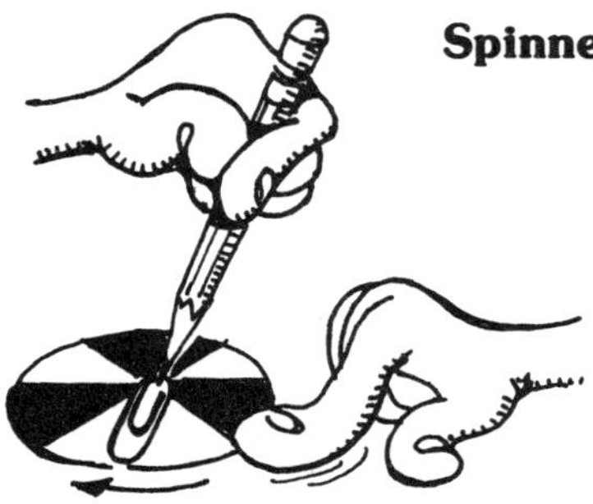

Spinner:

Tokens:

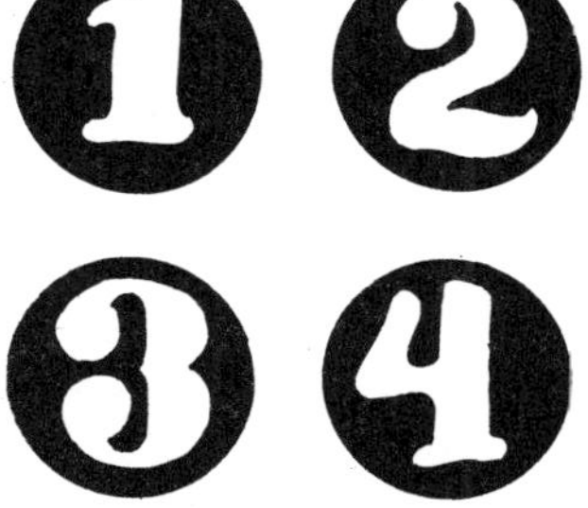

1 2

3 4

Session 8

The TOWN CRIER

CHRIST TURNS LITTLE MUNCHKIN INTO BIG GIANT!

Based on Luke 19:1-10

Before

After

Jericho—Jesus visited Jericho today and was immediately surrounded by a huge crowd of screaming admirers.

The citizens had heard the rumors and the stories of the many miracles performed by Jesus. They had heard of the healings, of the raising of the dead, of the feeding of the thousands. But they never expected to see the miracle that occurred here today!

It all started when Zacchaeus, a very short man, was unable to see Jesus because of the crowd. Everyone was too tall for him to see over, so he climbed up a tree and waited for Jesus to pass by.

Now, Zacchaeus was a very rich man. He was a tax collector, so all the people hated him! But when Jesus saw him in the tree, He asked Zacchaeus to come down, and they both went to Zac's house for a visit.

This made the people very angry, for Jesus was a famous and righteous man, and Zacchaeus was a scummy creep.

Jesus and Zacchaeus talked for awhile, and that's when the miracle happened. Zacchaeus became a believer in Jesus. He repented of his sins and said, "Look, Lord! Here and now I give half of my possessions to the poor, and if I have cheated anybody out of anything, I will pay back four times the amount" (Luke 19:8).

Thus, little Zacchaeus became a giant in the sight of God.

Jesus (on the left) with Zacchaeus (arrow).

ZACCHAEUS BECAME A BELIEVER AND HE PROMISED TO SET RIGHT ALL THE CRUMMY STUFF HE HAD DONE. NOW **THAT'S** A CONVERSION!

I REALLY LIKE THE VERSE WE CALL **"TODAY'S GOOD NEWS."** IT MEANS THAT WHEN A PERSON BECOMES A CHRISTIAN, GOD TAKES A PERSONAL INTEREST IN SEEING THAT HE OR SHE IS CHANGED FROM JUST A FACE IN THE CROWD TO, WELL... SOMEONE WHOSE LIFE COUNTS FOR **ETERNITY**!!

Today's Good News:

"Being confident of this, that he who began a good work in you will carry it on to completion until the day of Christ Jesus." Philippians 1:6

On the other side of this page, the News Hound said that God can take people like you and me and make our lives count for **eternity.** The Bible speaks of eternal life. Eternity in heaven is an exciting part of Christianity. Have you ever wondered just how long eternity is? Oh, sure, it's forever, but just what does that mean? Well, to help you get a handle on it, read this article called

"ETERNITY IN HEAVEN IS . . . "

1. **Eternity is almost twice as long as it takes you to sit through English class.**
2. **Eternity is about half as long as it takes to wait for next week's allowance.**
3. **Eternity is almost as long as it takes for summer vacation to arrive.**
4. **Eternity is more "billions and billions" than the number of stars you can count in the night sky.**
5. **Infinity × forever = eternity.**
6. **Eternity is how long you have to wait to get that driver's license.**
7. **Since God is infinite, it will take an eternity to discover all the wonderful things about Him.**
8. **Eternity is enough time to explore the universe—and then some. Move over, Captain Kirk.**
9. **In heaven, you can spend four billion years talking to a friend—and still not be late for dinner.**
10. **There are no calendars in heaven; there's plenty of time to do everything.**
11. **Eternity in heaven is not boring. You won't be standing on a cloud strumming a harp—unless you want to!**
12. **Everything in heaven is new. New colors, new scenery, new music, new people to meet.**
13. **Eternity in heaven is the best of everything. Nothing bad—or even second best—in heaven!**
14. **Eternity in heaven is better than anything we can imagine—don't miss it!**

Don't forget: your life on earth is **extremely short** compared to eternity. Make sure you're ready NOW to spend eternity in heaven!

DAILY THINKERS

Day 1 Read Esther 1:1-22. Write a newspaper story that might have appeared in the "Susa Times" describing these events.

Day 2 Esther 2:1-23. What do you think Esther's thoughts and feelings were when she was crowned queen?

Day 3 Esther 3:1-15. Why would a king let a man like Haman get away with a plot like this?

Day 4 Esther 4:1-17. One interesting thing about the book of Esther is that God is not directly named in it. Can you see any hints in this chapter that show Esther's trust in God?

Day 5 Esther 5:1-14; 6:1-14. God worked by causing the king to receive Esther and let her live. Have you ever had to do anything hard and frightening? How did God help you?

Day 6 Esther 7:1-10; 8:1-17. How did God protect His people? Has He ever protected you from harm?

THEME: God can make a "somebody" into a "nobody"!

Session 8

BIBLE STUDY OUTLINE

Read Acts 12:18-24 to your students. Make the following remarks as time allows.

Introductory remarks (based on Acts 12:1-17): King Herod wanted to be popular with his Jewish subjects. In order to make them happy, he began to persecute the Church. He beheaded the apostle James and, when he saw that the Jews were thrilled about that, he arrested Peter with the same intention. However, Peter was miraculously released from jail by an angel.

Verse 18,19: When Herod was informed about Peter's escape, he enforced the law; the guards were made to serve Peter's sentence. They were killed.

Verses 20-23: According to Josephus, an historian who lived about that time, Herod and other dignitaries gathered at Caesarea to celebrate a festival. Early in the morning of the second day the king appeared to the people in a "garment made wholly of silver and of a texture truly wonderful." The people (probably to butter him up) shouted "This is the voice of a god, not of a man" (v. 22). Herod, being a vain man, did not deny it. The Bible says that he was immediately struck down by an angel, "eaten by worms and died" (v. 23). Josephus says that after five days of agony, Herod "departed this life." (Now do the Object Lesson).

Verse 24: Despite Herod's attempt to halt the growth of the Church, it continued to blossom by the spreading of God's Word.

So we see that God can make a "somebody" into a "nobody." A person, no matter how powerful and important, who ignores God is in danger of losing it all at the hand of God. It's interesting to note that, shortly before he was made king, Herod had been put in chains and imprisoned by Tiberius, the imperial ruler of Rome. When Tiberius died, Caligula became emperor and immediately released Herod from jail. He exchanged Herod's iron chain for a gold one of equal weight. Herod was then made king of Palestine. Herod, according to Josephus, placed the gold chain in the temple at Jerusalem to demonstrate that God can raise up the one who has fallen down. Too bad Herod didn't learn that God can also do the reverse!

OBJECT LESSON: EARTHWORM

Show your students a rubber earthworm, which can be purchased in the fishing department of a sporting goods store (cut off the hook to prevent injuries). Say something like this: **This is NOT the type of worm that ate Herod. It would be pretty silly for a crowd of people to stand around long enough to watch their beloved ruler consumed by a herd of earthworms! The type of worm that killed Herod was the inside kind: parasites that infected his digestive system. The real cause of Herod's downfall was his prideful arrogance that caused him to accept glory deserved only by Almighty God.**

Alternate Object Lesson: If you want to give a lesson that is *guaranteed* to be unforgettable, try this one (it's not for the squeamish!). Many veterinary clinics keep preserved dog hearts that have been invaded by worms—a graphic way to encourage pet owners to medicate their dogs against fatal heart-worm. If the vet will let you, bring the dog heart in its bottle for your students to see.

DISCUSSION QUESTIONS

1. **Why is it important to remember the words of Proverbs 16:18, "Pride goes before destruction, a haughty spirit before a fall"?**

2. **If God can turn a "somebody" like a king into a worm-eaten "nobody," can He also do the reverse? How might He take someone who is not particularly important in the world's eyes and turn them into someone great in God's eyes?**

3. **What are some of the qualities in a person that are important to God? How can people your age develop these qualities?**

Wacko Party Ideas

Use these ideas at a party for someone who is moving away, who is returning from a long stay at the hospital or for any good reason.

MONEY IN THE CAKE

After baking the cake, but before frosting it, insert coins wrapped in wax paper down through the top of the cake. Party goers get to keep whatever money they find in their pieces of cake. Be sure to warn them about the "hidden surprise" before they start eating!

You can also put in slips of paper with short messages (trivia about the guest of honor, for example) Or you can use this as a way to pick "volunteers" for a stunt.

THOSE WERE THE DAYS

Without the guest of honor's knowledge, arrange with his or her parents to show and narrate old family photos, movies or videos. Lots of fun and very embarrassing!

TESTIMONIALS

Contact several of the invited guests a few days before the party to prepare "This Is Your Life" testimonials. Ask them to describe an embarrassing moment or a "secret" fact about the guest of honor.

MYSTERY FAIRY

Get someone the party goers won't recognize and dress him or her up in a silly mask and costume. During a quiet moment at the party (at testimonial time, for example), the fairy suddenly pops into the room, runs around shouting the praises of the guest of honor and hands out Popsicles and candy to the guests, then makes a hasty retreat.

David's Service

SESSION 9

WHAT THE SESSION IS ABOUT

God chooses and prepares us to live for and serve Him.

SCRIPTURE STUDIED

1 Samuel 16:13,18,21; 17:15,37; 18:5,13,14,16,30; Acts 13:22

KEY PASSAGE

"In everything he did he had great success, because the Lord was with him." 1 Samuel 18:14

AIMS OF THE SESSION

During this session your learners will:

1. Examine the qualities possessed by David that made him God's choice for king;
2. Chart their own qualities and determine how these can be developed and used in the Lord's service;
3. Create a slogan representing God's advice in the use of their abilities.

INSIGHTS FOR THE LEADER

During this session—the first of four about David—your students will discover that God chooses people with particular qualities, both internal and external, to accomplish His work in the world. Not everyone will be chosen to do the same tasks, but each is assigned tasks according to his or her abilities and spiritual maturity. Junior highers are still in the developing years. God can still change and refine their characters. You, as their teacher, are an important part of this process.

Before we look at the information about David to be covered in this session, let's quickly sketch in the historical background. Moses died before the people actually entered the land of God's promise, but his trusted assistant Joshua took over the leadership of the Israelites and led them into their new country. After this stage of their history, they were ruled by a series of judges. But the people wanted a king, and God let them have their way. The first king was Saul, but he proved to be disobedient to God. So the Lord selected a new king—David, the son of Jesse—to take his place.

Carefully study 1 Samuel 13:11-14 and 15:2-11 so that you will be able to briefly explain the circumstances surrounding God's rejection of Saul, Israel's first king. David, the youngest of Jesse's eight sons, was a young man, perhaps still a teenager, when Samuel anointed him king (see 1 Sam. 16:1-13; 17:33,42).

David's Character Qualities

Your students will identify in Scripture the qualities in David's character that made him God's choice for king. Help students understand that it was the combination of several of David's qualities that made him a suitable king.

Let's take a look at five qualities that David possessed. These qualities are found in many junior highers.

1. *Skill.* David was an excellent musician and poet. He probably developed his skill on the harp during the long hours he spent tending his father's sheep. His ability to play soothing music on the harp led him into the employ of Saul. David's music would temporarily relieve the king of the inner torment that periodically plagued him (see 1 Sam. 16:14-23). However, David's musical abilities unfold most vividly in the Psalms. He is credited with writing at least 73 of them.

David was also skilled in the use of a slingshot. This crude instrument was used by shepherds as a weapon against animals that would attack the grazing sheep. David used his slingshot to kill a lion and a bear that attacked his father's sheep (see 1 Sam. 17:34-36). Because he was a shepherd throughout most of his childhood and teenage years, he had mastered the skill of precision shooting by the time he killed the giant Philistine named Goliath (see 1 Sam. 17:4-10,48-50).

2. *Wisdom.* David's maturity and his ability to handle himself wisely made his fame spread.

He was loved and respected for his cunning (ingenuity) and his prudence (good judgment) as seen in 1 Samuel 18:5,16,30.

In the court of Saul, David learned proper etiquette and court procedures, and was able to converse with great and able government leaders.

3. *Handsome.* He is described as "ruddy, with a fine appearance and handsome features" (1 Sam. 16:12). However, David is not shown in Scripture as being vain. He did not rely on his good looks for success, as many people do today.

Remind your students that while people look on the outside, God looks on the inside (see 1 Sam. 16:7). He cares more about character than about appearance. Furthermore, one's outward appearance is often greatly influenced by one's inner qualities. A grouchy person will tend to develop a frowning face, while a cheerful person will more likely have an open, happy appearance.

4. *Leadership.* David was a leader. Saul made him a high-ranking army officer and David led his men wisely, winning the respect and admiration of all the people. David naturally drew people to himself—including men of might and power (see 1 Sam. 18:5).

Although the gift of leadership is not given to all, many junior highers possess qualities that make them potential leaders. Often this is reflected in their ability to influence others. You could encourage them to develop their leadership abilities by making them class leaders.

5. *The Lord was with David.* God validated David's call to kingship by "being with him." (See 1 Sam. 16:13,18; 18:12,14.)

David maintained a deep love and reverence for the Lord all the days of his life. Your students should discover that David's love for the Lord was one of the internal qualities that made him God's choice for king.

David's prudence, cunning, bravery and skill were made all the more powerful by God's presence with him. The Lord's presence with David was so pronounced that it caused Saul to fear (see 1 Sam. 18:12,15).

Lives without God's presence lack the meaning that those who know God enjoy. God wants to be a part of the lives of your students. He desires to be with them, helping them develop to their highest potential for His glory.

SESSION PLAN

BEFORE CLASS BEGINS: Cut apart the cards from the two Teaching Resource pages. There are 32 cards total. Tape them number side up (in a rough square) to poster board. Tape each card along the top edge so that you can easily swing the card up to read its reverse side. You can tape the cards in numerical order, but it's not necessary to do so.

Photocopy the Fun Page. There is no Scratch Sheet this time. See the ATTENTION GRABBER for optional preparation. The ALTERNATE ATTENTION GRABBER requires items to play a game. For the CONCLUSION, prepare a slogan that represents God's advice for you regarding the use of your gifts and abilities. For example, "Pray and practice every day, so a better piano you can play."

Attention Grabber

ATTENTION GRABBER (3-5 minutes)

Ask students to name the qualities they think a person holding each of the following jobs should have: airplane pilot, coroner, brain surgeon, ditch digger, spy, fashion designer, diamond cutter.

Option: Instead of a class discussion, hang a sheet of butcher paper near the door with the question and the list of jobs. Students can jot their thoughts on the paper as they enter the room.

Say something like this: **We have seen that there are different characteristics required for different jobs. God has given each of us a variety of skills and abilities that we can develop in different ways if we choose to. Let's take a look at a person that God chose to be a leader, and think about some of the characteristics that he had and developed.**

ALTERNATE ATTENTION GRABBER (5-7 minutes)

Materials needed: Small ball or knotted towel, inexpensive prizes.

Bring a small ball or knotted towel to class and play a game of "hot potato" with your students in the following manner. Seat students in a circle. (With a large class, play several games simultaneously.) Throw the ball or towel to a student. That person has five seconds to tell something that the person sitting next to him or her is good at doing. If the player is unable to give a response, he or she is out and must remove his or her chair from the circle, thus shrinking the circle. The teacher then throws the ball to another player. If the player answers correctly, he or she may throw the ball to another student. (Note: This game can get rowdy, so make sure you keep your students under control.)

Give inexpensive prizes to the last few students in the game.

Say, **We all have some things that we are good at doing. Some of those things are not**

on the surface for others to see. For example, you may be good at math, and the only person who knows it is your math teacher. Today we are going to look at a person who was chosen by God to be a great leader of His people. We'll look at some of the characteristics that enabled him to serve God as a leader.

Bible Exploration

EXPLORATION (30-40 minutes)

Step 1 (2-3 minutes): Give students a brief explanation of David's place in the history of Israel, using material from the second and third paragraphs of the INSIGHTS FOR THE LEADER.

Step 2 (15-20 minutes): Your students are now to play the Teaching Resource game. See BEFORE CLASS BEGINS for preparation instructions.

Have the students assemble into two teams (one side of the classroom against the other or girls against boys). Hang the poster board with the cards taped to it on the wall. Explain: **This is a simple game, but it might tax your memories. I will call on one person from the first team. That person will pick a card for me to flip up. You probably can't see what is written on the card so I will read it. The card will have a Scripture reference on it or it will describe one of David's qualities, such as his bravery. Then you will pick a second card. The second card must correspond to the first. That is, one card must be a Scripture reference and the other card must be a quality that is mentioned in that passage. If the cards correspond, I will tear both of them off the board and give them to the team who guessed correctly. If they do not correspond, I'll leave the cards on the board and go to the next team. The team with the most cards at the end of the game will win. Incidentally, some Scripture references are on more than one card because those references each mention more than one characteristic.**

Important: Nobody is to make notes about the positions of the cards! And no one on a team can help the person who is guessing the cards. If anyone breaks these rules remove two cards from the offending team and give them to the other team.

Tell students that each team should have Bibles open to Acts 13 and 1 Samuel chapters 16,17,18. This will allow quick searches to see if the Scripture cards match the quality cards. The students will be slow at first, but will soon know which qualities are listed in which passages. Here is a list showing the matching qualities and references:

God said, David is "a man after my own heart"—Acts 13:22.
God said, "He will do everything I want him to do"—Acts 13:22.
Spirit of the Lord was upon David in power—1 Samuel 16:13.
Harp player—1 Samuel 16:18.
Brave—1 Samuel 16:18.
Warrior—1 Samuel 16:18.
Speaks well—1 Samuel 16:18.
Good–looking—1 Samuel 16:18.
The Lord was with him—1 Samuel 16:18.
Servant of King Saul; armor-bearer—1 Samuel 16:21.
Tended father's sheep—1 Samuel 17:15.
Believed that God would deliver him from the Philistine (protect him from Goliath)—1 Samuel 17:37.
High rank in army—1 Samuel 18:5.

Leader of 1,000 men—1 Samuel 18:13.
All the people of Israel and Judah loved David—1 Samuel 18:16.
David was more successful than Saul's other officers—1 Samuel 18:30.

Pick a new player to guess the cards each time. As the teams take turns picking cards, discuss how the statements on the cards relate to David's growth and spiritual maturity. How, for example, could the fact that David continued to humbly tend his father's sheep while in Saul's employ have aided his spiritual development? Be sure that students understand the meaning of the more difficult qualities. For example, go into the meaning of God's statement that David was a man after His own heart. See INSIGHTS FOR THE LEADER for a review of David's qualities.

Step 3 (12-15 minutes): Have students help you list all the skills, talents, interests and abilities that your class members possess. Make a special effort not to get just the obvious talents (singing, sports ability) but the skills and interests that lie under the surface of your quieter students (math, good listener, collecting). List these on one side of the chalkboard. Then ask students to suggest actions or activities that would help develop these skills or talents. Write their suggestions in the center of the chalkboard, next to the appropriate skills.

Now ask students to consider ways that these talents, skills, interests and abilities might be used by God to give credit and glory to Him or to help and encourage someone through a deed done in His name. Some may feel that a painting, to glorify God, must portray a biblical scene. Help students expand their awareness that various kinds of expressions can praise God, His creation, His work in people's lives and so on. A "natural" athlete may praise God by playing football or basketball and becoming what he or she was created to be. Some things that seem to have little practical value today may turn out to be of great worth in the future. How long did David fool around with a sling before he stumbled on a bear or a giant? He probably spent many years developing his skill just for the fun of it, without realizing the potential that it would have in the future.

Move to the next part of the lesson by saying something like this: **We have examined some of the qualities that David had that made him God's choice for king. We have also charted our own gifts and abilities and thought of ways they could be developed and used for the Lord. David was not chosen because of his skills alone. As we have seen in Scripture, God chose a man who would be obedient and who would do His will. Because David was obedient and wanted to do what God wanted him to do, he experienced great success—even in small tasks. Let's consider an opportunity this week where we can develop God's gifts to us. With His help, we can experience success.**

Conclusion and Decision

CONCLUSION (5-7 minutes)

Explain, **I want you to take a moment to consider all the things David was able to accomplish because he used the skills, gifts and abilities that God had given him. Then create a slogan or motto that might represent God's advice for you personally regarding the use of your gifts and abilities. Be prepared to share your slogan with the rest of us.**

To give students an idea of what you want them to do, share a slogan for yourself that you have

prepared before class.

After students have had time to work on their slogans, regain their attention and ask volunteers to read what they have written and describe a situation where they can use the advice given by their slogan.

Close in prayer.

Distribute the Fun Page take-home paper.

Your students may wish to see this solution to the Fun Page game.

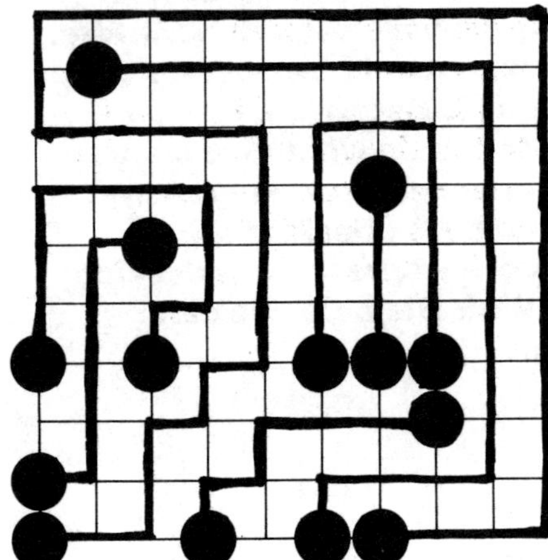

God said, David is "a man after my own heart."	God said, "He will do everything I want him to do."	The Spirit of the Lord was upon David in power.	Harp player
Brave	Warrior	Speaks well	Good-looking
The Lord was with him.	Servant of King Saul; armor-bearer	Tended father's sheep	Believed that God would deliver him from the Philistine (protect him from Goliath)
High rank in army	Leader of 1,000 men	All the people of Israel and Judah loved David.	David was more successful than Saul's other officers.

1	3	5	7
9	11	13	15
17	19	21	23
25	27	29	31

1 Samuel 16:18	1 Samuel 18:30	1 Samuel 18:16	1 Samuel 16:18
1 Samuel 18:13	1 Samuel 16:13	Acts 13:22	1 Samuel 18:5
1 Samuel 16:18	Acts 13:22	1 Samuel 16:18	1 Samuel 17:37
1 Samuel 17:15	1 Samuel 16:18	1 Samuel 16:21	1 Samuel 16:18

2	4	6	8
10	12	14	16
18	20	22	24
26	28	30	32

Session 9

FUN Page!

The TOWN CRIER

SEAFOOD PRICES PLUNGE!

By Typo
Based on Luke 5:1-11

Lake Gennesaret—The price of fish took a dive this week as the local markets were flooded with a huge surplus of fresh-caught seafood.

This reporter interviewed Aaron Benjamin, owner of a local fish market. "It's incredible!" he said. "I've got so many fish, I can't even give them away! The shelves are full, the lockers are full, I've got piles of 'em out back, I've even got 'em stuffed in the glove compartment of my chariot. Hey, you like fish? I'll make you a special deal. Hey, come back!"

Where did all the fish come from? Being a smart little reporter, I went to find the answer.

It all started the day that Jesus was preaching to a huge crowd on the shores of Lake Gennesaret. I should mention that He was preaching to a crowd of people, not fish. The fish came later.

The crowd grew so large that people apparently began to push and shove in order to get close enough to Jesus to see and hear what was going on. It got to the point where Jesus Himself was almost being pushed into the water.

Nearby were two empty fishing boats. Jesus borrowed one from the owners, Simon, James and John, who were on the shore mending their nets. Simon put out a little way from shore and Jesus was able to preach from the boat.

Peter nets unusual seafood delicacies.

When Jesus had finished speaking, He told Simon to put out into deep water and let down his nets for a catch. Simon pointed out that he had worked all night and had caught nothing, but he obeyed Jesus' instructions.

Well, the nets were so full of fish that he had to have help from the other boat. The fish filled both boats so full that they actually began to sink! These were well-built boats, and so they had to be greatly overloaded to be in danger of sinking. Simon, James and John were so amazed at the miracle that they left everything behind and became disciples of Jesus. Simon is now better known as Peter.

Today's Good News:

"In everything he did he had great success, because the Lord was with him." 1 Samuel 18:14

If you've read the *Town Crier* story, you know that Peter was a man who obeyed God, and God helped Peter achieve greatness as an apostle. What sort of personal qualities has God given you that He could use now or in the future?

Here is a game that you may find fairly easy—or extremely difficult. It is built around some of the better qualities you may have.

Instructions: Each circle with a Bible verse inside is to be connected with a pencil line to the appropriate circle with a quality inside. Your job is to determine which verse circle pairs up with which quality circle (there are seven pairs in all), and then to connect them with a pencil line following these rules: (1) The lines you draw must always follow a grid line. You can never leave the grid lines. (You can use the outside grid line, too.) (2) Your line can NEVER touch or cross a line you've already drawn. That's the hard part. (3) Your line can never touch a circle, unless it's the one you wish to connect your line to.

One pair has been done for you as an example. To determine which verses refer to which qualities, use the list below. It'll help if you number each pair 1 through 7 before you begin drawing lines. Have fun!

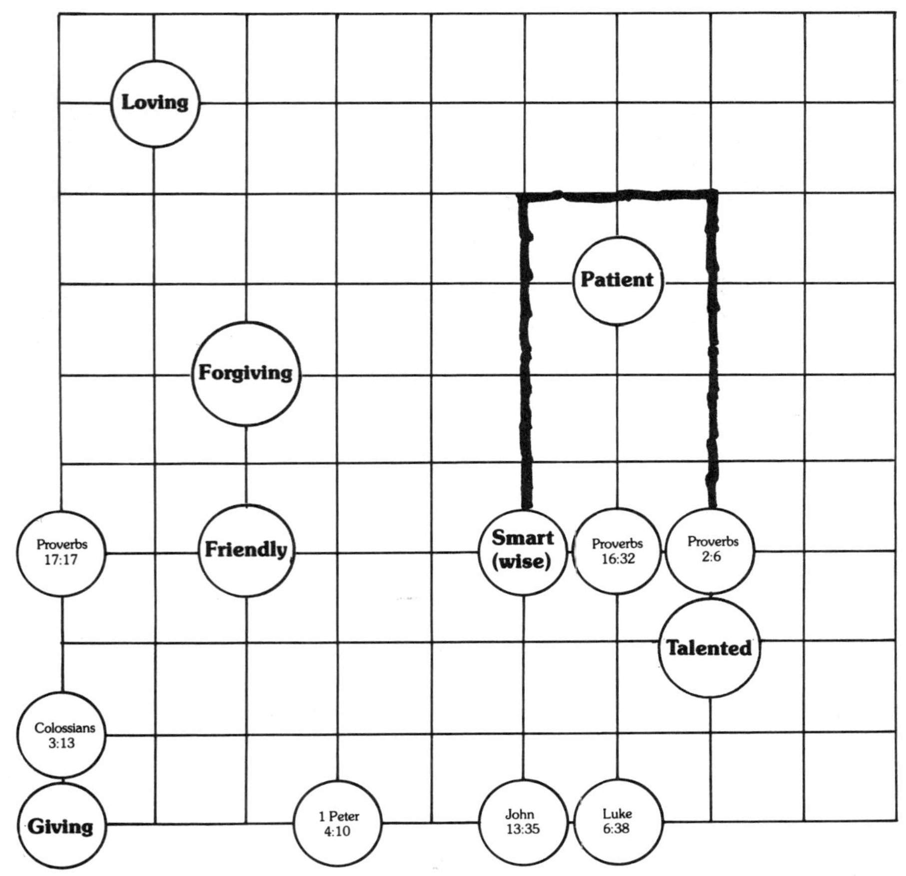

"By this all men will know that you are my disciples, if you **love** one another."
John 13:35

"Bear with each other and **forgive** whatever grievances you may have against one another. Forgive as the Lord forgave you."
Colossians 3:13

"**Give,** and it will be given to you. A good measure, pressed down, shaken together and running over, will be poured into your lap. For with the measure you use, it will be measured to you." Luke 6:38

"Each one should use whatever **gift** he has received to serve others, faithfully administering God's grace in its various forms." 1 Peter 4:10

"Better a **patient** man than a warrior."
Proverbs 16:32

"For the Lord gives **wisdom,** and from his mouth come knowledge and understanding."
Proverbs 2:6

"A **friend** loves at all times."
Proverbs 17:17

DAILY THINKERS

Day 1 Read Psalm 4:1-3. What response does David expect from God?

Day 2 Psalm 5:1-6. What do these verses tell you about God's attitude toward sin?

Day 3 Psalm 8:1-9. How did David feel about God? What is the point of this psalm?

Day 4 Psalm 14:1,2. Do you know anyone whom God might consider a "fool"? Take a moment to pray for him or her now.

Day 5 Psalm 15:1-5. Copy this passage and post it where you will be reminded of what it has to say.

Day 6 Psalm 19:7-11. How does David describe God's laws and rules?

Session 9

THEME: We have God-given qualities.

BIBLE STUDY OUTLINE

The Popsheet lectures are intended to be 5-10 minutes long. This Popsheet has a lot of Scripture to cover, but a simple reading of it without too much additional comment will help to keep the lecture within the time limit. Read Daniel 1:1-7,17-20; 2:1-28,48 to your students and make the following remarks as time allows.

Introductory remarks: (Do the Object Lesson.)

Daniel 1:1-7: Nebuchadnezzar conquered Israel and took captive people he hoped to train as servants. The qualities that he was looking for in the men were: of noble or royal birth, young, no physical problems, good looks, intelligence, well-educated, quick thinking and qualified to serve.

Verses 17-20: In addition to the qualities mentioned, Daniel and his three pals also had the God-given gifts of knowledge and understanding of things important to the king. Daniel was especially good at understanding and interpreting dreams. In those days dreams were considered to be messages from the gods.

Daniel 2:1-13: The king dreamed a dream. He apparently forgot the dream itself, but remembered the troubling impression it made. He asked his magicians not only to interpret the dream, but to tell him what the dream was in the first place! This was humanly impossible, so the magicians begged off. Nebuchadnezzar realized that they and their interpretations were "baloney," so he ordered them all killed.

Verses 14-23: We see additional qualities of Daniel in this part of the story. He had wisdom and tact (see v. 14). He was not afraid to confront his superiors (vv. 15,16). He sought his friend's spiritual support (vv. 17,18). He trusted God and praised Him for His gifts (vv. 19-23).

Verses 24-28,48: Daniel also was straightforward with the king about God's power and abilities, and his own inabilities apart from God (vv. 27,28). Daniel was able to reveal the dream and interpret it to the king (it concerned future kingdoms). The wise men were saved and Daniel was placed in "a high position" (v. 48).

Daniel's qualities were developed through a combination of hard work and God's gifts. We, too, need to seek God and work hard to develop the traits and talents He wants us to display. As we mature in these areas, God will use us to advance His will in our world.

OBJECT LESSON: JUNK FOOD

Hold up a typical fast food hamburger and ask, **What are some of the good and bad qualities of this thing?**

After students have suggested a few explain, **People, as well as hamburgers, are known and judged by the qualities they possess. The prophet Daniel was an amazing man who went through some incredible adventures in his lifetime, not the least of which was his famous trip to the lion's den. Today we are going to examine some of the personality traits he displayed; perhaps this will help us to realize the sort of positive qualities God has given each of us.**

DISCUSSION QUESTIONS

1. **What are some of the qualities Daniel displayed? (If a chalkboard is handy, record students' answers.) Which of these qualities can be seen in people today?**

2. **How did Daniel develop his qualities? What part do you think his faith played in the development of his qualities? Is strong faith in God a quality? What can we do to encourage our faith in God to grow?**

3. **Let's list some additional qualities we admire in people. How can we develop some of them? How is our relationship to God helpful in developing these qualities?**

4. **How can exercising these qualities change the people around us?**

Photocopy and distribute these awards for dubious distinction. The "I DONE GOOD!" award can be used to award points during a contest covering several weeks of activities; the team that earns the most points wins the contest. (Points are earned for attendance, Bible memory, bringing a friend and so forth.)

I DONE GOOD!

Ten Bonus Points for this act of meritorious achievement:

Awarded to: ____________________
Date: ____________________

BIBLE GENIUS!

Memorized this Bible passage: ____________________
Awarded to: ____________________
Date: ____________________

HANDY HELPER OF THE MONTH AWARD!

Awarded to: ____________________

Date: ____________________

Reason: ____________________

OFFICIAL SEAL OF APPROVAL!

Awarded to: ____________________

Date: ____________________

Reason: ____________________

David's Friendship SESSION 10

WHAT THE SESSION IS ABOUT

God cares about our need for friends to help us overcome life's obstacles.

SCRIPTURE STUDIED

1 Samuel 20

KEY PASSAGE

"Love your neighbor as yourself." Mark 12:31

AIMS OF THE SESSION

During this session your learners will:

1. Explore in Scripture David's need for the help of a friend;
2. Determine qualities that good friends possess and evaluate their own qualities as friends;
3. Pray for one another that each will be a good friend.

INSIGHTS FOR THE LEADER

Friendship means a great deal to junior highers. They will often sacrifice other needs, such as education or harmony at home, for the sake of making and keeping friends. However, these so-called "friendships" are often based on external factors, and frequently do not stand the test of time. The loyalty of David's friend, Jonathan, should encourage your learners not only to seek good Christian friends but also to become good Christian friends.

Although chosen by God to be king of Israel, David actually began his reign only after some years had elapsed. The reason for the delay was twofold. It appears that God designed the long period of delay as a time of physical, mental and spiritual growth and preparation for David. From a human vantage point, the delay was caused by Saul's ongoing and bitter pursuit of David.

Saul's Enmity

If you skim 1 Samuel, beginning with chapter 15, you will observe that Saul was obsessed with the idea of killing David. This obsession developed as a result of Saul's fear, jealousy and anger. He feared David because he could see God's power at work in the young man's life. He was jealous of David because God had shown favor to David, choosing him to replace Saul as king. Saul's jealousy grew into uncontrollable anger because David's fame and favor among the people were growing rapidly. Saul resolved in his heart that he would kill David, and he spent many years trying to accomplish this.

David's flight from the enraged Saul took him from place to place (see 1 Sam. 23:13). He spent much time in the wilderness, and even sought shelter in enemy territory. On many occasions, he narrowly escaped death at the hands of Saul. Because God intended for David to become the king of all Israel, God protected him and intervened in each of Saul's plots to destroy him.

As we saw in studying Moses, God provides help when needed. He often worked through other people in order to deliver David from Saul's murder plots. Your junior highers will discover that, just as God sent people to help David, He still sends people to help His children today.

Teenagers, as well as people in general, are often too proud to accept help from others because it means admitting that they can't deal with a situation alone. This session, like the earlier session on Moses, should reconfirm for your learners the fact that needing other people is not a sign of inadequacy or weakness. Even David, a strong and mighty man whom God was with, needed the help of others.

Jonathan's Friendship

As recorded in 1 Samuel 18:1-4, David

became friends with Saul's son, Jonathan, who immediately gave him the garments and weapons from his own person. Jonathan loved God and grew instantly to love His anointed one. He "became one in spirit with David, and he loved him as himself" (1 Sam. 18:1). Naturally, in our culture making a statement that one man loves another will bring giggles and verbal responses from many junior highers. You will need to carefully choose words that will minimize adverse responses and yet clearly convey the fact that there was nothing improper about the friendship of David and Jonathan.

Guide your students to understand that to love another as we love ourselves means desiring the highest good for the other. We want for them no less than we want for ourselves. We treat them as we would like to be treated. At the same time, this kind of love doesn't mean letting the person get away with whatever he or she wants. It is not for a person's highest good to be allowed total self-indulgence.

Jesus Himself said that loving our neighbor as ourselves is the second great commandment of God (see Mark 12:30,31). When we love the Lord, we will love others with this kind of love. This may mean taking risks and making sacrifices, as Jonathan did, for the welfare of another.

First Samuel 20 shows David narrowly escaping Saul's sword because of the help of his devoted friend. Jonathan's decision to disregard his father's command to kill David should not be taken as justification for children or teenagers to rebel against their parents. Jonathan loved his father and treated him with respect; but the thing his father hoped to do, and wanted Jonathan to do, was a sin against God. Jonathan was "grieved at his father's shameful treatment of David" (v. 34). Had Jonathan obeyed his father, he would have been just as guilty of rebellion against God as his father was, and would have been subject to the same punishment: rejection by God.

Jonathan Helps and Encourages

David again received help from his friend when he was a fugitive from Saul (see 1 Sam. 23:16,17). Jonathan knew that Saul's latest plot to kill David was probably causing his friend much distress. He went to David in Horesh and "helped him find strength in God" (v. 16). This involved trying to calm David's fears and to comfort him by assuring him that he would not be killed because he was to be king over all Israel. Your learners should conclude from this passage that true friendship involves offering support and encouragement during times of distress.

As you read the scriptural account of the friendship between David and Jonathan, note the commitment they both had to the relationship, as seen in the number of times they made covenants (promises or commitments) to one another (see 1 Sam. 18:3; 20:16,42; 23:18). Today's teenagers can learn from David and Jonathan's story the importance of that sort of commitment to being a true friend as well as the value of having such a friend.

SESSION PLAN

BEFORE CLASS BEGINS: Photocopy the Scratch Sheet and Fun Page. The CONCLUSION requires index cards and a box or other container. See the EXPLORATION for a recommended but optional requirement.

Attention Grabber

ATTENTION GRABBER (5-7 minutes)

Tell your learners, **Just for fun I'm going to see if you can solve some riddles. If you do so, you should be able to determine the main topic of today's Bible study. I have three riddles—actually, they are famous sayings that I have paraphrased. Your job is to listen to the paraphrased version and see if you can guess the original famous saying. Here is an example: "A feathered creature in the mitt is equal in value to a pair in the shrub." The actual saying is, "A bird in the hand is worth two in the bush."**

Challenge your learners to translate the following paraphrased famous sayings. Allow students to use pencil and paper and work together.

1. A pair of brain holders are superior to a single.
2. Accompanied by a close acquaintance like yourself, who requires adversaries?
3. A confrere in want equals a confederate unequivocally.

The solutions are: (1) Two heads are better than one. (2) With a friend like you, who needs enemies? (3) A friend in need is a friend indeed.

After the solutions have been learned, ask your students to determine what basic subject is mentioned or alluded to in all three sayings. The answer is "friends."

Say something like this: **We all need to have a friend around from time to time, maybe to help with our homework, to play tennis with or to enjoy a hunk of pizza with. In fact, without friends, things can get downright lonely. Today we are going to look at friendship by taking a look at David and his best friend Jonathan.**

Bible Exploration

EXPLORATION (25-35 minutes)

Optional materials: A treat for the members of the winning group in the second step. The treat can be sodas, snacks or certificates offering a small discount on the next youth group special event.

Step 1 (10-15 minutes): Have students form pairs. Direct them to the "Pen Pals" section of the Scratch Sheet. Explain, **Look up the Scriptures indicated and complete the letters that David and Jonathan might have written to each other.**

After allowing time for students to work, regain their attention and ask them to share some of their letters. Quickly read or summarize the events of 1 Samuel 20:35-42. Use the opportunity to review the story of David and Jonathan's friendship, pointing out how Jonathan was willing to take risks for his friend's sake even when it cost him something: his father's favor, for one thing, and perhaps even the possibility of becoming king after his father if David were out of the way. Jonathan knew David was God's choice, and he preferred to go God's way.

Step 2 (10-15 minutes): Ask students to help you come up with a list of qualities a friend should have that they see demonstrated in the story. (A friend should be loyal, trusting, helpful and so on.)

Also ask them to work together in groups of three or four to think of other qualities they feel a real friend should have. Tell them, **I will award 10 points for every word on your list, and five additional points for each word that is over six letters long. The team that gets the most points will win. You can use the words we've already discussed.**

Allow approximately 5 minutes for students to work, then call time. Award the appropriate points to each group and declare a winner. If you wish, give the winning team a treat. Write the students' best words on the chalkboard and discuss how they relate to friendship. Number the qualities as you list them in preparation for the next step. Here is a list of suggested words: supportive, encouraging, gentle, kind, devoted, faithful, nice, hospitable, humorous, likable, Christian, forgiving, patient, respectful, dependable, generous, spiritual, interesting.

Make sure to note that David and Jonathan had a commitment to the Lord as one important basis for their friendship.

Step 3 (3-5 minutes): Say, **I am now going to take a survey of this class. The survey will be a secret one; I won't ask you to sign your names. However, I will read what you write and will get a pretty good idea how well you all think you're doing in the friendship department. I want you all to be honest.**

Explain that as you read the list of qualities of friendship that is written on the chalkboard, students are to write down on scratch paper (or the back of their worksheets) the number of each quality and, next to the number, a plus or minus sign to indicate how well they think they display this quality—plus for doing a good job, minus for doing poorly. Read the list slowly to give students time to consider each quality.

Say something like this: **Thank you for your honesty on this survey. Now let's do something that will help us all be better friends.** Collect the papers when you distribute the index cards as instructed below.

Conclusion and Decision

CONCLUSION (3-5 minutes)

Materials needed: Index card for each student, medium-sized box.

Distribute the index cards. Tell students, **Neatly print your first and last names on the card, then fold it in half.**

When students have finished writing, go around the room with a box and have students place their cards in it. Shake or stir the cards in the box. Then go back around the room and ask each student to take a card from the box and look at the name written on it. (If a student draws his or her own name, he or she should replace the card and draw again.)

Say to students, **Many times we find ourselves in a "closed group" with just our own few friends. This should not be true of Christians. We can grow a lot by making new friends, even when they are people who are not just like us. Our activity involving these index cards will last all week and will be more effective if you do not tell anyone whose name you have. Prayer is a key ingredient in making and keeping friends. Each time you pray this week, I want you to ask the Lord to help this person be a good friend, keep a good friend and find a good friend. Each member of this class can feel good this week knowing that he or she is being prayed for by a very special person.**

Close the session in prayer.

Distribute the Fun Page take-home paper.

Pen Pals

Session 10

SCRATCH SHEET

Imagine that the following letters were sent back and forth between David and his good friend Jonathan (who happened to be King Saul's son as well as David's brother-in-law). The only problem is that some letters were written with invisible ink. Can you fill in the missing correspondence to make the story complete? (The Scripture references in parentheses will help you.)

David,

I think Dad has flipped out. He told all of us at the court that we are supposed to kill you on sight. Be on your guard and go into hiding. I'll tell Dad that you haven't done anything wrong, but that you have helped him greatly.

Jonathan

David,

Good news! You are welcome back. Dad says he's not sore any more.

David,

Sorry about the incident today. I thought everything was OK until Dad chucked the spear at you. I'm glad you weren't hurt. I want you to know it was a shock to me too.

Your friend, Jonathan

Jonathan,

(1 Samuel 20:1)

Dave,

(1 Samuel 20:2)

Jon,

(1 Samuel 20:3)

Davey,

I'll do anything I can to help.

Jon, (1 Samuel 20:5-8)

Dave,

(1 Samuel 20:18-23)

Jonathan,

I'm still out in this field waiting to hear what's going on. How about a memo?

Dave,

(1 Samuel 20:24-34)

Note in my royal journal:

Well, today it happened. The arrows came flying and I heard Jon telling the kid who was picking up the arrows that the arrows were beyond him. I knew that meant trouble. After the servants left, I came out of hiding and Jon and I cried together and said our good-byes. I sure hope we can ride together again, 'cause amigos like him are hard to find.

Session 10

FUN Page! The TOWN CRIER

Based on 1 Samuel 20

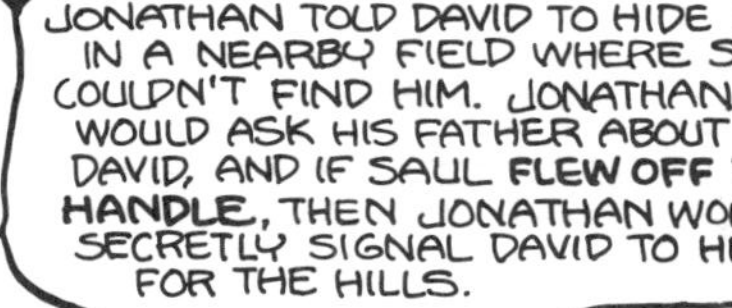

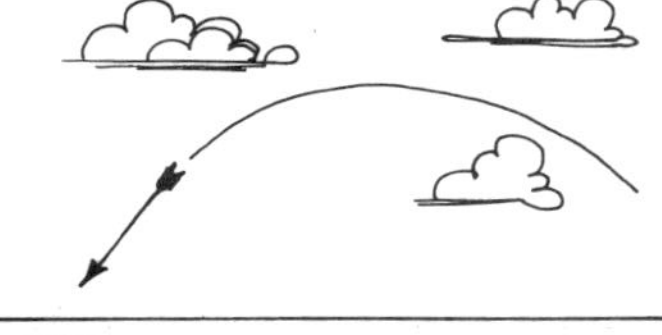

Today's Good News:

"Love your neighbor as yourself."
Mark 12:31

From time to time we run an "Acme ad" for various absurd products. Here's the latest.

Want to be popular? Want to have lots of friends? Find 'em fast with

THE ACME AUTO-FRIEND-FINDER!

Yes! Now even a miserable little clod like YOU can have lots and lots of wonderful friends! Here's how it works:

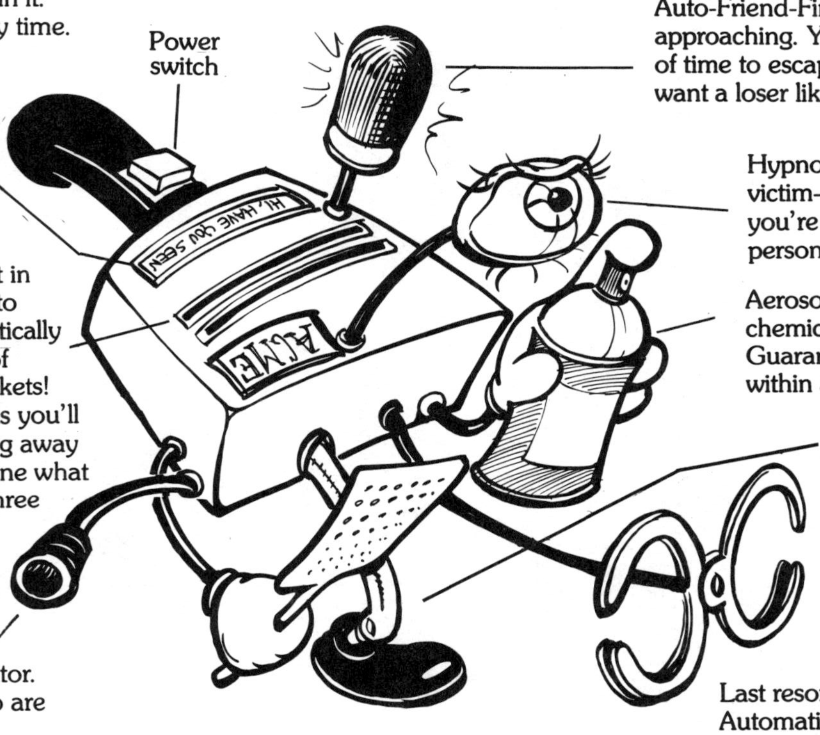

Liquid crystal display feeds you wonderful opening lines such as, "Hi, have you seen my wallet? It had ten thousand dollars in it." Guaranteed to work every time.

Power switch

Discriminator circuit warns you if someone else with an Acme Auto-Friend-Finder is approaching. You'll have plenty of time to escape. After all, who'd want a loser like that for a friend?

Hypnotic eye causes your victim—er, friend—to think you're the world's most fantastic person.

Photocopier slot. Buy a ticket to a red-hot concert in your area. Insert ticket into photocopier slot. Automatically prints unlimited number of exact duplicate concert tickets! Imagine how many friends you'll have when you start giving away free concert tickets! Imagine what sort of fun it'll be when three hundred people all try to share the same concert seat!

Aerosol can sprays secret formula chemical attractant over you. Guaranteed to attract anyone within a block straight to you.

Fly swatter and dog kicker to help keep away pests attracted by chemical spray.

Infrared warm body locator. Helps detect people who are trying to avoid you.

Last resort handcuff device. Automatically traps and handcuffs someone to your wrist. Scientifically-created steel alloy cannot be cut or removed. You have a friend for life!

Yep, that was another ridiculous Acme ad! How does one really go about finding good friends? There's no real formula that will guarantee success. But just remember this: The more you are like Jesus, the nicer you are. And everybody likes a nice person.

DAILY THINKERS

Day 1 Read Psalm 22:1-5. Describe the feelings David had about God, and David's conclusion.

Day 2 Psalm 23. If you don't have these verses memorized yet, try to stick them in your brain now.

Day 3 Psalm 25:8-10. What does God do for sinners?

Day 4 Psalm 26:2. If God did for you what David asked Him to do, what would He find?

Day 5 Psalm 27:14. What does "wait for the Lord" mean? What kind of situation might cause someone to "wait for the Lord"?

Day 6 Psalm 36:1-4. Paraphrase David's description of a wicked person.

THEME: When to leave a friend.

Session 10

BIBLE STUDY OUTLINE

Read Deuteronomy 13:6-11 to your students. Make the following comments as time allows.

Introductory remarks: When Christians talk about friendships, we usually talk about being kind, putting the other person first, encouraging our friends and so on. But the Bible also makes it clear that there comes a time in some friendships when a Christian has to break off the relationship and call it quits.

Verses 6-8: Deuteronomy was written by Moses, the man that God used to communicate His laws to the Jewish people. God wanted His people then and now to live by His laws—doing so keeps God's children close to Him. These verses tell us that if anyone—even our best friend—is endangering our relationship with God, we must choose God over that person.

This choice can be very tough. It's not easy giving up a friend. But it's important to realize that God can never be "out given" by you. If you give up a friend, God will take care of your need for friends. He may even step in and turn that person's heart to the Lord, so that he or she becomes the best friend you could ever have. But the important point is that you must always be willing to put God first in your life. It takes backbone and courage.

Verses 9,10: Should you stone your friend to death? No. This law was for the Israelites, to show how serious God was that they not be turned to worship pagan gods. Though the stoning part is over, the principle remains: God jealously wants us to belong to Him. Hopefully, we can influence our non-Christian friends for good. But if they are causing us to stumble away from the Lord, we must "kill" that friendship. God went to a lot of effort to get the Jewish people out of Egypt; He didn't want to lose them to phony gods. Jesus went to a lot of effort to save us—we must remain true to Him, no matter the cost.

Verse 11: The original purpose of this law was to keep everyone close to God. People don't cause trouble if they know they are going to be buried in a hail of rocks! You, too, should be willing to stand up for what you believe—to throw a couple of stones at people who are trying to hurt your friendship with Almighty God. Tell your friends about your faith in God and the way you live your life. Most of your friends, even the non-Christian ones, will greatly respect you. If not, if they continue to tempt you away from God, walk away from them.

LESSON FROM LIFE: GIVING UP A FRIEND

We suggest that, if you've ever given up a friendship or romantic relationship because of your Christianity, you describe the incident to your listeners. Explain your motivations and the emotions you experienced. Talk about the results of your experience.

Alternately, talk about the influence a person can have over another by showing or telling how a magnet influences a piece of metal. The closer the metal comes to the magnet, the harder it is to tear it away. Our friends can be like magnets that attract us. If we get too close to anyone with wrong ideas, we may not be able to break free easily. Hopefully, the influence our friends have on us will be for good.

DISCUSSION QUESTIONS

1. **Why do you think God was so serious in His condemnation of pagan gods? Why do you suppose He went so far as to demand the death of the bad friend or family member?**

2. **The things of this world can draw us away from the Lord. What are some of the things a friend might draw you toward—things that go against God's wishes?**

3. **The passage we read is the negative side of a Christian's friendships—the Bible of course also talks about the good things that friends can do for each other. What are some things a good friend should do?**

4. **How can Christians win the "battle of influence"—that is, how can they be the ones who do the influencing for good, rather than being influenced for bad?**

Putting Together and Promoting a Library Table

A library table in your classroom can, if done correctly, provide your students with valuable assistance in their Christian growth. Here are a few ideas that will help motivate your students to put the library table to good use.

ON TOP OF THE TABLE

Library tables can and should contain more than just hymnals and old curriculum leftovers! In addition to the standard reference works (concordance, Bible dictionary and the like), spice up your selection with good Christian comics, Christian music tapes (the kinds kids like to hear!), tapes of popular camp speakers, C.S. Lewis novels, easy-to-read paperback Bibles, interesting videos and Christian magazines geared to youth (get a few subscriptions). Add a stack of your handbills and announcement sheets.

MOTIVATING YOUR STUDENTS

The library table is the first thing to be ignored by junior high kids—unless you take the initiative to get them involved.

You can induce your students to become familiar with the table by placing items they use in class on the table. Put worksheets, pencils, scissors, songsheets and other necessary items there, and make the students walk to the table to pick up what they need. Activity sign-up sheets should also be there. Throw on a few "specials" that will attract your students (after class): skateboard magazines, sport action videos, etc.

Build classroom assignments on the contents of your table. Have students listen to and discuss a selection from one of the Christian music tapes. Ask volunteers to look up items in the Bible dictionary. Or have small groups look at various passages from some of the paperbacks. Play a game: Arrange some books so that the first letters in the titles form a word; first person to find the word wins.

ORGANIZATION

To keep track of who checks out what items, design a check-out sheet and place copies of it on a clipboard. Students fill out names, phone numbers, titles, return dates and other needed information. It's best to have someone oversee the process.

Whenever your youth group has an in-house gathering, bring out and promote the library table.

David's Choices SESSION 11

WHAT THE SESSION IS ABOUT

Many important decisions involve two alternatives, one that pleases God and one that displeases Him.

SCRIPTURE STUDIED

1 Samuel 24:1-20; 2 Samuel 11:1-17,26,27; 12:13,14

KEY PASSAGE

"Show me your ways, O Lord, teach me your paths; guide me in your truth and teach me, for you are God my Savior, and my hope is in you all day long." Psalm 25:4,5

AIMS OF THE SESSION

During this session your learners will:

1. Examine the scriptural accounts of two decisions David made;
2. Discuss the results of right and wrong decisions;
3. Follow biblical principles of decision making in dealing with a current decision.

INSIGHTS FOR THE LEADER

In this session your junior high students will examine two of the many decisions David faced during his lifetime. They will discover that David's choices in each of these decisions were in distinct opposition to each other; one pleased God and the other displeased Him. More than simply knowing these accounts, students should be guided to uncover the following information: David's options or alternatives; David's choices; David's motivation for each choice and the final outcome or consequences of his choices.

The Choice that Pleased God

The first of David's choices that your class will examine is recorded in 1 Samuel 24:1-20. Some background information, based on 1 Samuel 8-23, will help you understand the story. In the beginning of God's relationship with the people of Israel, He was their leader. He spoke to them through prophets and provided priests to guide the people in their worship. But they wanted to be like the nations around them; they wanted a king. God warned them that having a king would not be best for them. But He permitted them to have their way. The first king was Saul. He made a promising start as a leader, but then he chose to go his own way in several important instances, disobeying direct orders from the Lord. So God declared him disqualified and selected a new king.

This new king was David. But even after God's prophet had anointed David, Saul was still on the throne. David killed Goliath and entered Saul's service, waiting for God's timing to bring him to his rightful place as ruler. David became so popular with the people that Saul became jealous of him and tried more than once to kill him. So David went into hiding. He collected a group of men who followed and supported him. Every so often Saul would try to find and kill David.

This brings us to chapter 24. David and his men are hiding in a cave, and in walks Saul. Because his eyes were not adjusted to the dark as David's and his men's were, he was at their mercy. David's men urged David to take advantage of the situation. David's options included the following: He could harm Saul, kill him, take him prisoner or do nothing. David refused to harm or capture Saul, but did cut off a corner of his robe (1 Sam. 24:4). Then David regretted even that, and forbade his men to attack Saul (v. 7).

After Saul left the cave, David called out to him and explained how he had refrained from harming the king. In his speech he showed respect and humility toward Saul, assured the king that he meant him no harm (vv. 8-10). David also indicated his intention to wait for the Lord to uphold his innocence, to deal with Saul for his treatment of David and to deliver Saul for his treatment of David and to deliver David from Saul's pursuit (vv. 11-15). David's

decision was based on his respect for and honor of the Lord's anointed and his desire to do what was pleasing in the sight of God (see vv. 6,10).

Because David chose to behave as he did: (1) Saul was convicted by David's righteous act of sparing his life and temporarily repented (see vv. 17-19); (2) The Lord rewarded David by making him king over the nation of Israel (see 2 Sam. 5:3). David had to wait for God's perfect timing, but his patience and good behavior brought him God's blessings.

Unfortunately, David did not always choose the right course of action. He made some wrong choices as well in his lifetime. Perhaps the most well-known is his affair with Bathsheba. Examining this story will require some delicacy on your part. Remember that junior highers have an awakening interest in sex. (Some are wide awake.) They can identify with David's attraction to Bathsheba. This interest in sex is not unhealthy. It is something even junior highers have to wrestle with and learn to keep under control. This study of David's unfortunate choice regarding Bathsheba can help them when they have to choose between God's ways and the world's ways.

The Choice that Displeased God

The story is found in 2 Samuel 11. "In the spring, at the time when kings go off to war, David sent Joab out with the king's men and the whole Israelite army . . . . But David remained in Jerusalem" (v. 1). He had been a mighty warrior, but now, for some unstated reason, he stayed behind while his army was fighting.

One evening David got out of bed and walked around on the roof of the palace. (The roofs of buildings were the cool places in Israel. Perhaps it was a hot night and David couldn't sleep.) From the roof he saw a woman bathing (she was probably on her roof) and he sent someone to find out about her. Her name was Bathsheba, and she was the wife of Uriah the Hittite, a soldier in David's army. Knowing this, David sent for her and slept with her, then sent her home. Later she discovered that she was pregnant, and sent word to David.

The bad choice of adultery was soon followed by another bad choice. He decided to try to cover up his sin. He sent word to the battle front that he wanted to see Uriah. He pretended that he was interested in news of the fighting, but his real goal was to get Uriah to go home and sleep with Bathsheba so that Uriah would think the baby was his own.

Unfortunately for David's plan, Uriah refused to go home. He figured his fellow soldiers were out fighting for their king, and he wasn't going to enjoy comforts and luxuries that they did not have.

Unfortunately for Uriah, David then concocted another plan, one that was even worse than the first. He sent secret instructions that would get Uriah killed in battle. An innocent man lost his life because a king had lusted after that man's wife.

After Bathsheba observed a period of mourning, David had her brought to his house, and she became his wife and bore the son they had conceived in adultery.

Adultery, deceit and murder (however disguised) are totally opposed to the character of God and the character He wants His people to have. David was basically a man who loved God and wanted to obey Him—though he certainly went far astray in this incident. But God knew that David could be brought to repentance over his sins, so he sent a prophet named Nathan to rebuke the king. David accepted the rebuke and repented (see 2 Sam. 12:13)—but the son born out of his liaison with Bathsheba died (see v. 14).

David's Options

The moment David spotted Bathsheba, he had to decide what to do. He could have obeyed God's commandment against adultery. He could have turned his back on the temptation.

Even after the deed was done, he could have taken responsibility for his sin by repenting and confessing both to God and to Uriah. He could have attempted to make restitution for his wrongdoing.

Because David chose to go with his human desires rather than doing what he knew would please God, he committed sin and dragged other people down with him: Bathsheba, the son they conceived, Uriah and Joab who had to follow David's instructions to get Uriah killed in battle. Furthermore, God was displeased, and in order to bring David to repentance, He chastised David. David and a number of other people suffered because of the disastrous choices he had made.

NOTES

SESSION PLAN

BEFORE CLASS BEGINS: Photocopy the two Teaching Resource pages. The students will assemble into small groups; half of the groups will use the first Teaching Resource page, the others will use the second page. Plan accordingly to determine the number of copies to make so that each group will have a page. Also copy the Fun Page. There is no Scratch Sheet this time. The ATTENTION GRABBER requires special preparation and materials.

Attention Grabber

ATTENTION GRABBER (5-7 minutes)

Materials needed: One or more dollar bills, small wrapped boxes with various "prizes" as described below.

Invite a volunteer to help you demonstrate an important idea from today's lesson by being a participant in a "game show." Bring the volunteer to the front of the class. Give him or her a dollar bill and say, **This dollar bill is yours to keep; or you can exchange it for whatever is in this box.** Hold up a wrapped box with some sort of booby prize inside it, such as a chunk of limburger cheese. Most students will go for the box. You can play the game several times with other contestants. If you wish, you can put something of value in one of the boxes, such as gift certificates to a popular store or five candy bars.

When you have finished playing the game, ask your contestants, **Why did you make the decision for the box over the dollar bill?** Let them respond. Then ask the other class members, **Would you have made a different decision? Why?**

We have been playing this game of making decisions for fun. But life is full of decisions, and we often make the wrong choices. Let's take a look at some of the good and bad decisions David made and the effect they had on his life and his relationship with God.

Bible Exploration

EXPLORATION (35-40 minutes)

Step 1 (12-15 minutes): Have students form groups of three to five. Be sure each group has at least one Bible. Say, **Let's take a look at two events in the life of David. In each situation, David was faced with making some important decisions.**

Distribute copies of both Teaching Resource pages, giving the copies based on the 1 Samuel passage to one half of the groups and the copies based on the 2 Samuel passage to the other half. Allow students plenty of time to read the passages and complete the sheets.

Step 2 (8-10 minutes): Reassemble the class. Go over the questions on the first Teaching Resource page, asking students to shout out the correct answers to the multiple choice questions and to share their comments on the questions at the end of the page. Discuss the significance of each thing David did using information from INSIGHTS FOR THE LEADER as needed. Follow the same procedure for the second Teaching Resource page.

Step 3 (3-4 minutes): Ask this question and have students brainstorm answers: **What are some principles we can learn from David's experiences that will help us make sound decisions?** (Point out that even godly people can make big mistakes.) Record students' responses on the chalkboard.

Step 4 (10-12 minutes): Tell students, **Now let's take a look at some typical situations you might face this coming week—situations that require decision-making skills. As I describe each situation, I want you to tell me what options are possible in the situation, the possible results of deciding for each option, what you think God would want a person to do and why He would want that decision.**

Read the following situations, as many as time allows. As students contribute to the discussion, point out any options you can see that they missed, or any consequences they may have overlooked.

1. **Your friend has been stealing things and wants to hide them in your locker.**
2. **You find a paper with the answers to next week's history test on the hall floor.**
3. **You slid into home plate and were tagged out but the umpire called the play safe.**
4. **You've been offered a job that requires you to work on Sunday mornings—and jobs for kids your age are scarce.**
5. **You hear a friend telling tall tales or spreading rumors about another.**
6. **Your folks ask if you went to the arcade last night (you did) when you said that you were going to your friend's house. (You knew they wouldn't let you go to the arcade.)**

Make a transition to the CONCLUSION by saying something like this: **We have seen two significant decisions that David made and some of the decision-making processes that went into them. And we have seen some of the consequences. We have talked about some of the kinds of decisions we have to face today. Now let's take some time to think about our own decision-making processes.**

Conclusion and Decision

CONCLUSION (7-10 minutes)

Tell your learners this: **Take a sheet of paper and follow the five things I tell you to do. (1) Describe a decision that you will have to make in the near or distant future. (2) As far as you can tell, state the choices that you will have in making that decision. (3) List the possible consequences that may result if you make each choice. (4) Write the initials of any other people who will be affected by your decision. (5) Evaluate which alternatives would be pleasing to God.**

Remind students that they may want to ask the advice of a mature Christian as one additional step in their decision-making process. Then direct each student to prayerfully ask God's help in deciding on a proper response to his or her situation.

Close with audible prayer.

Distribute the Fun Page take-home paper.

DAVID'S DECISION 1 SAMUEL 24:1-20

Read 1 Samuel 24:1-20. Then circle the correct answers to these questions.

1. When Saul went looking in the desert for David, what did he take?

   a. Three thousand men.
   b. A dune buggy.
   c. The sacred scrolls.

2. David was in what when Saul entered?

   a. The bathtub.
   b. A special robe.
   c. A cave.

3. What did David cut off?

   a. A piece of Saul's robe.
   b. Saul's servant's ear.
   c. His toenails.

4. Why did David regret what he had done?

   a. Because Saul was God's anointed king.
   b. Because Saul found out about it.
   c. Because he hadn't done it sooner.

5. What did David show Saul?

   a. His high school yearbook.
   b. The way out of the cave.
   c. The piece of robe.

6. What did David call himself?

   a. A flea.
   b. A dead duck.
   c. Davie.

7. Why did Saul call David righteous?

   a. Because God's glory shone upon him.
   b. Because David spared Saul's life.
   c. both a and b.

Now answer these questions in one or two sentences each.

1. What choices did David face when he was in the cave with Saul?

2. What was his ultimate decision?

3. What were some other options he could have chosen?

4. David's motivation behind the decision he made was his desire to please God. David therefore made the right decision and did the right thing. What was the outcome? Was it good or bad?

DAVID'S DECISION
2 SAMUEL 11:1-17,26,27; 12:13,14.

Read 2 Samuel 11:1-17,26,27; 12:13,14. Then circle the correct answers to these questions.

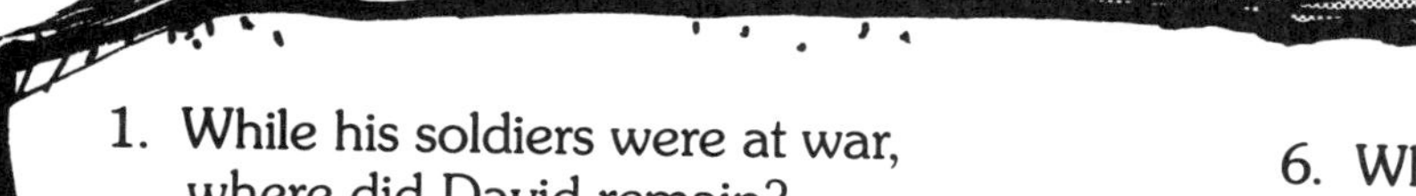

1. While his soldiers were at war, where did David remain?

   a. At the head of the battle.
   b. Back home in Jerusalem.
   c. Under the sofa.

2. What did David see from the roof?

   a. A woman taking a bath.
   b. The soldiers fighting.
   c. Shingles.

3. What was the woman's name?

   a. Uriah the Hittite.
   b. Minnie.
   c. Bathsheba.

4. David made her what?

   a. Pregnant.
   b. A special necklace.
   c. Give back the scroll.

5. What did David want Uriah to do?

   a. Wash his feet.
   b. Sleep with his wife Bathsheba.
   c. Both a and b.

6. What did the letter say?

   a. Send Bathsheba away.
   b. Send money.
   c. Be sure Uriah dies in battle.

7. What happened to Uriah?

   a. He was killed.
   b. He ran away.
   c. He changed his name to Jonathan.

8. What happened to Bathsheba?

   a. She stopped bathing on the roof.
   b. She married the king.
   c. She died.

9. What happened to David?

   a. He admitted his sin to Nathan.
   b. He lied to Nathan.
   c. He resigned.

Now answer these questions in one or two sentences each.

1. What choices did David face when he was on the roof watching Bathsheba?

2. What was his ultimate decision?

3. What were some other options he could have chosen?

4. David's motivation behind the decision he made was his desire to please himself. David therefore made the wrong decision and did terribly wrong things. What was the outcome (there were several bad results)?

Session 11

The TOW

Today's Good News:

"Show me your ways, O Lord, teach me your paths; guide me in your truth and teach me, for you are God my Savior, and my hope is in you all day long." Psalm 25:4,5

THE BAD SAMARITAN

By star reporter Typ
Based on Luke 10:30-37

Jericho—The few small clouds along the horizon were the only signs of moisture as far as the eye could see. The sun was so hot it felt as if someone was focusing a giant magnifying lens upon us, its rays scorching us to our very cores. The arid desert waste surrounded us on every side—which is usually the case when you're surrounded—and our hearts and hopes seemed to melt into the burning sand.

Our final bit of energy was fading with each painful footstep, the path of footprints winding like a desert snake behind us.

My faithful companion, Pifont, fell on his face in the cracked desert soil. His skin was peeling and blistered. With a swollen tongue he murmured something to me as I knelt, nearly exhausted, beside him.

I couldn't make out what he croaked in my ear. He slipped into unconsciousness. I slapped him awake, shook him into consciousness.

"I can't go on," he groaned. "I can't make it."

I would have cried, but I didn't want to waste the water. Our faithful dog, the News Hound, limped over and tried to lick my face. But his tongue was too dry, so instead he just shook my hand. I smiled at him. It hurt.

"This is the last time I go on a cut-rate vacation," I vowed. "When this travel brochure said 'world's largest beach,' it wasn't kidding. The ocean must be a hundred miles from here."

Suddenly we heard screaming and yelling over the next hill. People! We were saved! I clambered up the slope and looked over the peak. Bandits! Desert robbers! They were beating up some poor traveler. They took everything he had, including his water, and left him to roast in the summer sun.

I was scared. They rode off in the opposite direction, but I was afraid to help the poor victim in case they returned and discovered my hiding place.

As I watched, trying to decide what to do, a Jewish priest came along and saw the man. He stopped and glanced at the man, then crossed over to the other side of the desert road and hurried off. Afraid of blood, I guess.

Then another religious leader came along. He hurried off also. This struck me as extremely cruel for them to leave a fellow countryman lying in the road. I tried to make myself more comfortable as I watched from the hill.

I saw another man come. Unlike the others, he was not Jewish. He was a Samaritan and therefore a hated enemy of the Jewish people. But when he saw the poor victim, he stopped. He bandaged the man's wounds. He gave him water to drink. He put him on his own donkey. Together they headed off down the road to safety and civilization.

I lay there smiling to myself until they were long out of sight. A good deed had been done. A life had been saved.

A life had been saved? Uh, oh . . .

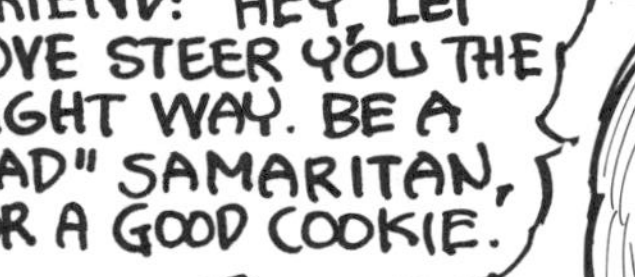

Everyone must make decisions. Some decisions are simple, such as what to wear or where to sit. Others can be more difficult, and are sometimes much more important, such as who to have as a best friend, or how to respond to someone who is mean to you. In order to make an intelligent decision, it pays to have your eyes wide open and a clear view of the facts, as you'll see (or not) when you play

BLINDMAN'S BUFF

Instructions: The object of this game is to "walk" the blindfolded man from the center of the freeway to one of the "Safe Circles." If you hit any of the cars, or fall off the edge of the freeway, the game is over and you lose. The man can only walk north, south, east or west, along the grid lines.

More instructions: (1) Decide which "Safe Circle" you wish to head for. (2) Decide which piece of the "Move Pie" will send you in the direction you wish to go. (3) Hold the point of your pencil or pen on the "Starting Point" star. (4) CLOSE YOUR EYES and then try to move your pencil point from the star to the correct piece of the "Move Pie." Open your eyes. (5) No matter what piece of the pie you land on, follow the instructions in that piece. If you miss the pie or land on a line, do it over again. Or miss a turn if you're playing the game with another. (6) Keep playing until the blindfolded man is safe, gets hit by a car or falls off the edge of the freeway. You can play this game alone or battle it out with another. Try making up some new rules.

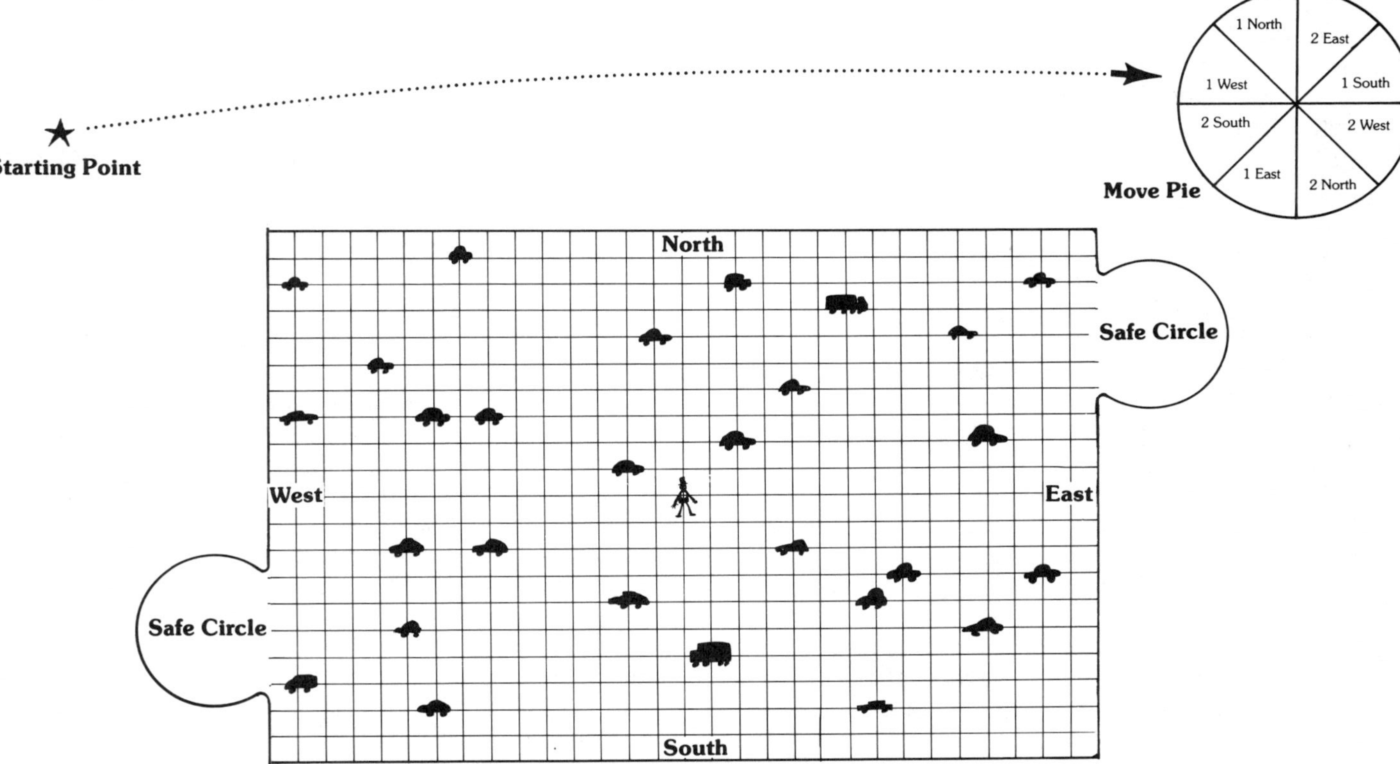

Now that you've played our game, it's simple to see that this game would be ridiculously easy if you could play it with your eyes wide open all the time!

The difficult and important decisions you must make in life would also be much easier if you could see all the "facts and figures." If you could look into the future, you would know now exactly what the best alternative to each decision would be. But, alas, no one can look into the future.

Wait a minute. God can! And that's why it's so important that you let Him advise you on each decision you make. Let Him be your eyes. Let Him be your guide.

DAILY THINKERS

Day 1 Read Psalm 37:1-9. What hope does this passage give for those who feel that everything is going wrong in their lives?

Day 2 Psalm 37:31. What does this verse mean?

Day 3 Psalm 39:4-7. What do these verses tell you about priorities in life?

Day 4 Psalm 40:4. Make a list of "falsehoods" or "false gods" that people turn to.

Day 5 Psalm 40:6-8. What does God desire (see v. 8)?

Day 6 Psalm 40:9,10. What do these verses tell you about David's faith?

Session 11

THEME: Choosing God's way.

BIBLE STUDY OUTLINE

This simple message is based on the Hebrews 11:7 and Genesis 6:22 passages about Noah. You can greatly expand on it by reading much or all of Hebrews 11 (though the first Popsheet was based on this). As in Noah's case, all the people mentioned in Hebrews 11 are not only examples of faith, but of people who made the right decision—to go God's way. Obeying God is, after all, the evidence and outworking of faith. Make the following remarks as time permits. For an opening "crowd breaker," see the first paragraph under the Object Lesson heading.

Introductory remarks: We are all familiar with the story of Noah. He's the guy that built the ark, loaded on the animals and survived the greatest flood in history—happily for us. He made the right decision, and we are around to enjoy the results of that decision. If he had chosen to ride out the flood in his front room like everyone else—well, no more front rooms. No more anything.

Hebrews 11:7 and Genesis 6:22: Notice the progression of events in Hebrews 11:7: Noah was warned by the Lord about the unseen but very real coming flood. Noah responded in faith; though he couldn't see the flood, he chose to believe God. In "holy fear"—which means reverential respect for God more than a fear of the flood itself—Noah chose to do as he was told. He built the boat. Noah's story is one of continual choices. He was always choosing to go God's way. Genesis 6:22 puts it this way: "Noah did everything just as God commanded him." Noah did everything God said, and he did it the way God said to do it.

Because Noah constantly turned toward God when he came to a "decision crossroad," he ended up becoming "heir of the righteousness that comes by faith" (Hebrews 11:7). That is, Noah is a child of God and is entitled to all that involves—simply because he always chose God's way.

This same responsibility falls on us today. We must constantly be choosing to go God's way. Every hour of every day the world confronts us with minor temptations. If we develop the habit of choosing God each time, we too will be like Noah. (Do the Object Lesson.)

OBJECT LESSON: TRAIN TRACKS

Try this "crowd breaker" before beginning your Bible study if you're feeling adventurous (and the weather permits). Just as you are ready to open your Bible and begin, have an accomplice walk up to you holding a small box. The accomplice says, "Knock knock!" You of course reply, "Who's there?" The accomplice says "No" and you say, "No who?"

The accomplice takes a full glass of water out of the box and splashes it in your face saying, "Not 'No who'—Noah!" Be sure to get your Bible out of the line of fire in time. And have a towel on hand.

The Object Lesson: Show your listeners a section of model railroad track (or better still, a track switch that branches off in two directions). Say something like this: **We are like passengers on a train—the train of life. It rolls down the track of our life span. Sometimes we think we know where we are headed, sometimes we don't. But many times we come to a switch. The track of our life branches and we must choose which way to go. Some of these decisions are extremely minor—what shirt to put on, what cereal to eat. Other decisions are very important—how to respond to a classmate's insults, whether or not to become a Christian, how to treat a new stepparent.**

The most important decisions of all are the ones that involve a choice to go God's way or go our own wrong way. In the verses we read, Noah continually chose to go God's way. It certainly wasn't a simple thing to do what God told him to do, but he did it and God blessed him for it. If you want to live for God and experience His blessings, always take the track marked "God's way."

DISCUSSION QUESTIONS

1. **Why do you suppose Noah was so good at making the proper decisions? Do you think it was something he developed over his lifetime? How can you develop the habit of choosing to obey God?**
2. **God doesn't ask us to build arks anymore. What are some of the things that God might ask us to do—things that present us with situations in which we must make decisions to obey or not to obey God?**
3. **God spoke to Noah in an audible voice. How can we today learn what it is God wants us to do?**

Variations on Hide-and-Seek

DOG CATCHERS

This one is like hide-and-seek, but instead of one person against everyone else, it's boys (the dogs) against girls (the dog catchers). The dogs hide and the catchers of course try to find them. Any dog that can return to the starting point without being tagged by a catcher is safe and worth one point to the dogs. Any dog that is tagged is worth one point to the catchers. Catchers must stay at least 20 feet from the starting point once play has begun.

CATS AND MICE

Play a normal game of hide-and-seek, but do not rotate the seeker with each round of play. Instead, any person who is caught must join the original seeker for the next round. As more and more seekers are added, only the very crafty will remain undiscovered. You can call all people back to the starting point after someone is caught and added to the seeker to begin each round. Or, for a shorter version of the game, continue playing as new seekers are added.

MINI HIDE-AND-SEEK

Try this one if you're stuck indoors with not much to do. The rules are the same as hide-and-seek, but the players do not hide—they hide sheets of paper with their names on them. Everyone can watch as the seeker attempts to find a name. Players can find new hiding places after each round; the player whose name goes undiscovered the longest is the winner.

David's Confidence SESSION 12

WHAT THE SESSION IS ABOUT

A rich and fruitful life is the result of a person's total confidence in and reliance upon God's control in all areas.

SCRIPTURE STUDIED

Psalm 27:1-3; 34:1-10; 62:1,2

KEY PASSAGE

"He alone is my rock and my salvation; he is my fortress, I will never be shaken." Psalm 62:2

AIMS OF THE SESSION

During this session your learners will:

1. Play a game based on David's expression of confidence in God and the results of that confidence;
2. Describe areas where trusting God is important;
3. Create a personal psalm that expresses confidence in God.

INSIGHTS FOR THE LEADER

One hundred and fifty psalms have been included in the biblical canon; together they comprise the Hebrew "hymnbook" or "Book of Praises." These hymns were used in both public and private worship. Seventy-three of these psalms are attributed to David, who was an accomplished poet and musician. The psalms of David were usually sung to the accompaniment of the psaltery (an ancient stringed instrument similar to the zither) and/or other instruments.

In this session, your learners will have an opportunity to draw from David's words his innermost trust in and dependence upon God. As your learners read and study the passages, they will begin to understand how the words of David can also relate to their need to place their confidence in the Lord.

Students' Need for God

Some junior highers who attend your class may not be assuming responsibility for their spiritual lives. They may attend Bible studies, worship and other activities only because their parents require that they do so, not because they desire to strengthen their relationship with God through Bible study and personal application of God's Word to their lives.

Other students in your class may possess varying degrees of biblical knowledge which they are applying, at varying degrees, in their lives. These students may not fully understand what it means to depend on God for everything, but they desire to trust Him more.

For learners of both categories, as well as those who may be functioning as spiritually mature Christians, this session will provide the opportunity to see areas in their lives where help is needed that cannot be provided by family or friends. After identifying these areas where God's help is needed, your learners should be led to understand the importance of building up confidence in God, who cares about all aspects of their life and being.

David's Dependence on God

David, as powerful a king as he was, depended on God to supply what he needed in all areas of his existence. As you study the Scripture passages, take note of the symbolic language that the psalmist used to describe the Lord. His choice of words indicates his absolute and unshaken trust in God.

The Lord is my light (Psalm 27:1). To people without the powerful electric lights we enjoy today, the difference between the inky blackness of night and the shining light of day was highly significant. Light became a metaphor of God's goodness and holiness, and the wholeness that He offers to people who trust in Him.

The Lord is my salvation (27:1; 62:2). Salvation means rescue. God rescues us from our sin (through the death and resurrection of

Jesus Christ) because He loves us.

The Lord is my stronghold (27:1). He gives us the strength to live the life He wants us to live.

The Lord is my rock (62:2). A rock speaks of strength and security, not only in ancient times but today. We use the Rock of Gibraltar as a symbol of the ultimate in safety.

The Lord is my fortress (62:2). A fortress is a place of safety and protection. God takes care of and protects His people.

David's Confidence in God

David also had confidence in God's love, power and faithfulness toward him. This trust is expressed forcefully in Psalm 34:4,6,7. When David sought the Lord, God:

Answered him (v. 4). Our Lord is a personal God who cares about us and responds to us.

Delivered him from his fears (v. 4). God can rescue us from the things we fear and from fear itself.

Heard him (v. 6). He has both the ability and the desire to hear His people and to take care of their needs.

Saved him from his troubles (v. 6). All people have troubles of one kind or another. We all need God's help with our problems.

Encamped around him and delivered him (v. 7). God surrounds us, protects us, takes care of us. He is stronger than any other force in the universe, so we can be confident when we are in His care.

David's Response to God

David's character reflected his reliance upon and confidence in God. God's presence produces characteristics in the trusting believer that are not always found in people who do not know Him. David says in the Psalms that, like himself, people who put their trust in God:

Need not be afraid (27:1), for God will take care of them.

Are radiant (34:5)—shining with God's light from within.

Are unashamed (v. 5), for God does not let us down or embarrass us.

Are blessed (v. 8)—happy, whole, full of joy.

Are unshaken (62:2), for they rest upon the unmovable foundation of God Himself.

Furthermore, David says that those who trust God *lack nothing, no good thing* (see 34:9,10) and that their *souls find rest* (see 62:1)—there is no need for restless searching once they have found the ultimate truth in Him.

Junior highers should find these characteristics to be quite appealing. Help them to see that these traits are the outward manifestations of a person's inward trust in God.

Teenagers, like any believer, must grow to the point of depending on God more than on any others. This session should help your students become more aware of their need to give God control of all aspects of their lives. As their desire to trust God becomes a firm commitment, they will begin to take on the characteristics that David possessed and others who trust in God possess today.

SESSION PLAN

BEFORE CLASS BEGINS: Photocopy the Fun Page. There is no Scratch Sheet or Teaching Resource page this time. The EXPLORATION requires special materials and preparation.

Attention Grabber

ATTENTION GRABBER (2-3 minutes)

Write these nonsense words on the chalkboard: cenfodunco, ruleonca, dupindinci, issorinca. Ask students to get together in groups of two or three. Say, **These words describe what David felt toward God. They are not scrambled. Instead, all the vowels in each word have been replaced with wrong vowels. The first group to correctly substitute the proper vowels to form the real words is the winner.**

Give groups a few moments to work. When one group correctly solves the riddle, congratulate them. The words are confidence, reliance, dependence and assurance.

Say something like this: **David, in the Psalms, expressed many of these feelings of trust in God. Let's play a fun game that will help us see some of the things David said about the characteristics of a God-trusting person.**

Bible Exploration

EXPLORATION (30-45 minutes)

Materials needed: Three clipboards, felt marker (dark ink); sheets of construction paper prepared as described below. (The sheets of paper must be thick enough so that no words can be read through them when turned over.) Optional: Treats for the members of the winning team. The alternate third step requires magazines, glue, scissors and poster board.

Your students will play a game based on the three Psalms studied in this session. The game will help students discover the feelings that David expressed toward God and the blessings he received from God. Here is how to prepare for the game:

1. You need three clipboards. The clipboards represent "doors."

2. During the game, students will assemble into two teams. A representative of each team will be given a question and the opportunity to

find the correct answer by choosing one of the clipboard doors. When a door is chosen, the sheet of paper on that clipboard will be flipped up to reveal one of three things: the correct answer, an incorrect answer or a "WILD CARD."

3. There is a list of 13 questions below. Following each question are two answers; the answer in bold print is the correct answer, the other is incorrect. (Note: The answers we have given are from the *New International Version* of the Bible. You may wish to more closely follow another version. Also note that the incorrect answers are not necessarily wrong statements, they simply are not a part of the passage being studied.) For each question, prepare three sheets of paper. On one sheet print the correct answer (in large letters). On the second sheet print the incorrect answer. On the third sheet print "WILD CARD!"

4. The three sheets for each question are to be placed facedown—and upside down—in the clipboards, one sheet for each question per board. (The papers are upside down so that when you lift a sheet up for the students to see what is written, the answer will be right side up.) The three possible answers to the first question should be on top of the stacks in the clipboards. As you place the sheets of paper, randomize which clipboard the proper answer appears on—students will attempt to guess which clipboard has the correct answer to the question being asked.

5. Prepare a place to hang the clipboards on the wall. You can drive three nails into a large board and lean the board against the wall.

Step 1 (15-20 minutes): You are now ready to begin the game. Assemble your class into two teams. Direct students' attention to the three clipboards and say, **Here we have three clipboards representing three doors—doors #1, #2 and #3. I am going to pick a player from the first team. I will then read a passage from the book of Psalms and a question based on that passage. I want you all to follow along in your Bibles as I read the passage. Then the student I picked will attempt to find the answer to my question by choosing one of the doors. I'll flip up the page on that door. If the answer is correct, that team will get a point. If the answer is incorrect, the other team will have about 5 seconds to tell me what the real answer is. If they answer correctly, I will give the point to that team. But if the paper I turn up has "WILD CARD!" on it, the first team gets a chance to say the correct answer. If they answer correctly, I will give them TWO points.**

Pick a volunteer to be the team's representative for the first question. (Choose a new volunteer for each question and alternate teams each time.) Tell your students to open their Bibles to Psalm 27. Read the first question and the proper portion of the Psalm, then allow the student to choose a door. (When a door is revealed, it may not be immediately apparent whether its answer is right or wrong, since the wrong answers are generally very similar to the right ones. Feel free to ask the class in general to judge if the revealed answer is right or wrong—but show from the Bible what is the correct answer. Also, feel free to reveal what is behind the doors not picked.) After you determine which team has earned the point (or points), discuss the significance of the correct answer. Then go on to the next question. Be sure to record the score and to remove the three sheets of paper from the clipboards after each round. Here are the questions:

1. (Bible passage: Psalm 27:1) Question: **What three things did David receive as a result of trusting in God?** Correct answer: **Light, salvation and security.** Incorrect answer: Light, grace and peace.

2. (Psalm 27:2) **What did David receive as a result of trusting in God? Protection against enemies.** Protection against sin.

3. (Psalm 27:3) **What did David receive as a result of trusting God? Courage and confidence.** A courageous army.

4. (Psalm 34:1-3) **What five things did David want to do for God? Extol, praise, boast, glorify and exalt.** Extol, worship, meet, bless and love.

5. (Psalm 34:4) **What did David do before God answered and delivered him? Sought the Lord.** Repented.

6. (Psalm 34:5) **Those who look to God become what? Radiant (with joy) and without shame.** Radiant and ashamed.

7. (Psalm 34:6) **What did David do before the Lord heard him? Called.** Listened.

8. (Psalm 34:6) **What did David have before God saved him? Troubles.** Junior high students.

9. (Psalm 34:7,8) **What did David do before God blessed him? Took refuge in God.** Prayed.

10. (Psalm 34:9) **David feared God. What did he lack? Nothing.** Almost nothing.

11. (Psalm 34:10) **Those who seek God will lack what? No good thing.** Weakness and hunger.

12. (Psalm 62:1) **What two things did David find in God? Rest and salvation.** Rest and redemption.

13. (Psalm 62:2) **God was what three things to David? Rock, salvation, fortress.** Rock, salvation, foundation.

Step 2 (5-7 minutes): Lead a brief discussion to amplify what students have learned. Ask questions like these: **Why do you think David used the word "rock" to describe God? Why did he use "fortress"? Why wasn't David afraid of his enemies? What characteristics did David have?** Use material from the INSIGHTS FOR THE LEADER to help with this discussion. Wrap up by summarizing God's trustworthiness, power and ability to give His people blessings and security.

Step 3 (10-12 minutes): Tell students, **Unlike David, we probably won't be chased by hostile armies or threatened by menacing giants, but we have other things to face. Let's brainstorm a list of things that might happen to junior highers that would cause them to take refuge in God's strength and protection.**

List students' ideas on the chalkboard as they give them. If they need help getting started, suggest one or two of these: A divorce in the family, the death of a loved one, losing a game because of a klutzy move on the last play, being overwhelmed by some subject in school.

After listing ideas, make a transition to the CONCLUSION by saying something like this: **You have given some good reasons to seek God's strength. Isn't it interesting that there are times when no one but God can really give us the comfort and security we need? Let's take some time to think about our personal needs for His help.**

Alternate Step 3 (15-20 minutes)

Materials needed: A large piece of poster board, magazines and/or newspapers with pictures, glue, scissors.

Place materials on a centrally-located table. Say to students, **Each one of us trusts and depends on someone else for the things we need to survive physically, emotionally and spiritually. But ultimately it is our loving God who is really doing the providing, and it is on Him we need to rely.**

Give directions for the activity: **Skim through a**

magazine or newspaper to find one or more pictures that depict or represent something people must trust God for, such as food, good health or salvation. Cut out the picture and glue it to the poster board. Be careful not to cover anyone else's pictures. Be prepared to share what you chose and why you chose it.

When each student has glued at least one picture to the poster, point out the various areas that are represented on the collage. Ask students to explain what their pictures represent and why they chose them.

Make a transition to the CONCLUSION by saying something like this: **We have discussed today some of the ways in which people need to rely upon God. Let's take some time to think about our personal need to rely on Him.**

Conclusion and Decision

CONCLUSION (5-7 minutes)

Ask students to create their own psalm or song that expresses confidence in God for some area of their life. Ask them to sign their papers.

Collect the psalms. During the week, select some of the better ones and reprint them on a large piece of poster board to display in the classroom during the week. Check with the student who wrote each psalm, particularly if there is any personal content, to gain permission to share it in this way.

Close in prayer.

Distribute the Fun Page take-home paper.

FUN Page!

Session 12

The TOWN CRIER

Based on 1 Samuel 17

Question:

What happens when you take one young guy named David, who is too small to fit into a suit of armor . . .

. . . give him a sling and five small pebbles to throw . . .

. . . and pit him against a huge, ugly giant named Goliath, who has a full set of industrial-strength armor, an immense razor-sharp spear and breath that could knock over a goat?

Answer:

Giant rips David into teensie-weensie hamburger patties.

BUT! What happens when you take the same skinny kid named David, give him five pebbles and a sling, AND A HEART THAT TRUSTS GOD?

Answer:

Giant loses head.

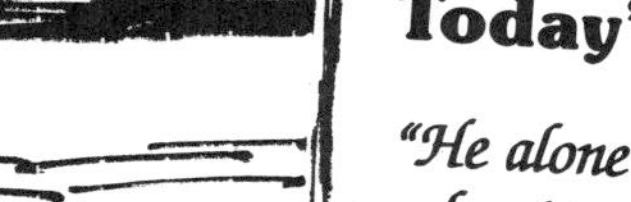

Today's Good News:

"He alone is my rock and my salvation; he is my fortress, I will never be shaken." Psalm 62:2

"Therefore everyone who hears these words of mine and puts them into practice is like a wise man who built his house on the rock." Matthew 7:24

Are you a wise person? Is your life built on Christ, the solid Rock? Are you prepared for anything that may go wrong in life? Just for fun, here's a game about some natural disasters that befall humanity from time to time.

Instructions: Each person below is shouting the name of some natural disaster. Unfortunately, they are all so scared, they've messed up the words! Your job is to split each word into **three parts,** and then stick each part back with two correct parts, to find the actual disasters. For example, *Earthquake, volcano* and *flood* can be split up and rewritten as earcand, flthqo and voloouake! Answers are below, but don't peek until you're finished!

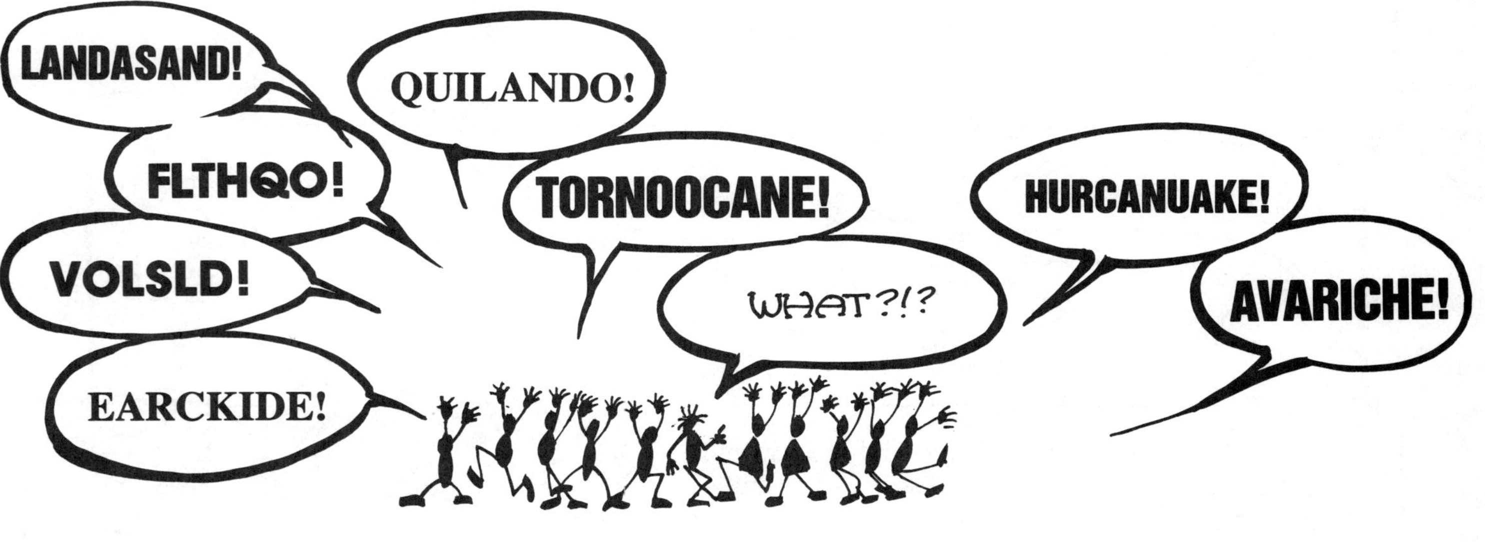

Don't wait until you face a disaster before you get your life straightened out with God. If you haven't done it yet, get right with Him right now!

Answers: Quicksand, earthquake, landslide, hurricane, tornado, avalanche, flood, volcano.

DAILY THINKERS

Day 1 Read Psalm 51:1,2. Does David's request seem sincere? How would you ask God the same thing?

Day 2 Psalm 51:10-12. List what David asks of God.

Day 3 Psalm 103:1. David indicates the depth of his love for God by saying what?

Day 4 Psalm 103:8-13. What are some characteristics of God? What does He do about our sin?

Day 5 Psalm 103:13-18. In light of these verses, what are the things in a person's life that have eternal value?

Day 6 Psalm 108:1-5. Write a song or poem of praise using this psalm as a model.

Session 12

THEME: The Christian who depends on God has five areas of responsibility.

BIBLE STUDY OUTLINE

Read Deuteronomy 10:12,13 to your students. Make the following remarks as time allows.

Introductory remarks: (Do the Object Lesson).

Verses 12,13: Israel was God's chosen people—chosen to live for Him and to spread His truth to the whole world. This is now the job of the Church—all people who have Jesus as Lord and Savior. This passage, therefore, applies to us today as much as it did to the Jewish people back in those days. The passage lists five areas of responsibility:

1. Fear the Lord. The first responsibility is to "fear the Lord your God." This does not mean to cower in the corner from terror. It means to have a reverential attitude of trust and dependence upon God. It is what motivates us to live for Him. A person without this reverential respect would never choose to become a Christian, for he or she would see no need to trust God. Not only does this respect for God begin our relationship with Him, it should stay with us our whole lives through.

2. Walk in all His ways. To walk in God's ways means to be like Him. We are to display the same personality characteristics He displays. Jesus is our example here; we should be loving, forgiving, obedient, behaving wisely and so on, just like Jesus.

3. Love Him. Not only should we respect our God and seek to be like Him, we should feel strongly attracted to Him. People in love want to spend time together, to talk to each other, to get to know each other. People in love are interested in each other. This is the way it should be between you and God. You can talk to Him in prayer. You can get to know Him in Bible study and by responding to what God's Word tells you.

4. Serve God. This love should automatically lead to service. We serve God by serving others. If you say that you love your girlfriend/boyfriend, but refuse to do things with her/him or for her/him, your love is "out to lunch." Service is the natural behavior of someone in love with God. The world needs Christian servants.

5. Observe the Lord's commands and decrees. Simply do what God tells you to do. The Bible is filled with God's wisdom and instructions. If you follow His Word, you will be an obedient and useful servant.

Notice the progression of these five areas of responsibility: First we have to gain an attitude of respect and reverence for the Lord. In other words, we have to recognize that He *is* the Lord and to treat Him that way. That leads to a desire to be *like* Him, to walk in His ways. That means spending time with Him to learn what He is like. The love we begin to feel for Him will naturally pour itself out in service, for love isn't love until it's giving and caring. The servant of God will do what God tells Him to do.

These are the areas of responsibility that each Christian has. Now you know what God wants from you!

OBJECT LESSON: JOB DESCRIPTION

Show your students your job description (or make one up for any sort of job) and read some of the responsibilities listed. Explain to your students that Deuteronomy 10:12,13 is the "believer's job description." Say, **This passage in Deuteronomy is a great summation of what God expects from His children. If you've ever wondered what God wants from you, here's your answer.**

DISCUSSION QUESTIONS

1. **What are some of Christ's characteristics that junior high Christians should display? What are some practical ways to do so?**
2. **What are a few ways we can draw closer to God? How much time would you recommend a person spend doing these things each day?**
3. **Can you think of several areas of service open to Christians your age?**
4. **What are some of the things that God commands us to do or not do?**

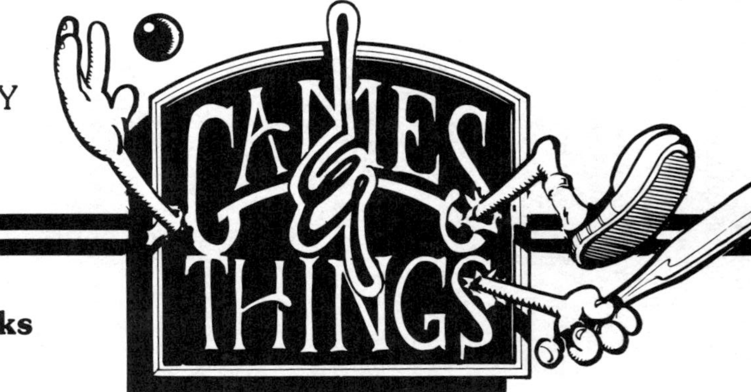

Action Games to Play with Grocery Sacks

BAG HEADS

Give players paper grocery sacks to wear over their heads. Each player should also be given a sheet or roll of inexpensive stickers (the white labels or colored dots available at stationery stores are fine).

Assemble all players on the play area, which can be a circle or square marked with tape on the floor. At the signal to begin, players attempt to attach their stickers to other players' sacks—while trying to avoid being stickered themselves. Because players won't be able to see too well (though they can peek out enough to glimpse the floor), leaders should attempt to steer them back into the playing area when necessary.

Before the game begins, warn players not to intentionally damage or remove another player's sack, or manhandle other players. Each player can hold his or her sack in place but will have to peel and stick the stickers at the same time. The game ends when a set time limit runs out or at least one player runs out of stickers. The winner is the person whose sack has the fewest stickers.

THE PIT AND THE PENDULUM

You are probably familiar with the old game of limbo: Players attempt to squeeze under a horizontal pole without knocking it off its supports. The pole gets closer to the ground each round, eventually making it impossible for anyone to squeak through.

Here's a fun and sloppy version. Tie the two handles of a typical plastic grocery sack to one end of a rope. The rope should be looped over a high tree limb or ceiling rafter in such a way that the height of the sack can be controlled by someone holding the other end of the rope. Partially fill the sack with water and set it in swinging motion, keeping it about three feet above the ground at first.

Instead of letting a person crawl under the "pendulum," which is easy to dodge as it swings back and forth, have that person be seated in a child's wagon. The wagon is slowly pulled under the swinging water bag by a rope tied to its handle. The player can duck or dodge, but not touch the ground in any way. Play several rounds, lowering the sack a bit each time.

Plastic grocery sacks tend to leak and split easily; you may want to put two or more sacks together for strength. When the water-filled sack hits a person, the sack will break or the water will splash out through the handle holes. Either way, a refreshing game!

God's Promises

SPECIAL SESSION

WHAT THE SESSION IS ABOUT

God made and keeps promises to His people.

SCRIPTURE STUDIED

Psalm 34:17; 121:3,4; Isaiah 7:14; 9:6,7; John 11:25; 14:2,3,23; 15:5; 2 Thessalonians 3:3; 1 John 1:9; 3:2; 5:14,15

KEY PASSAGE

"For to us a child is born, to us a son is given, and the government will be on his shoulders. And he will be called Wonderful Counselor, Mighty God, Everlasting Father, Prince of Peace." Isaiah 9:6

AIMS OF THE SESSION

During this session your learners will:

1. Discuss several of God's promises to His people;
2. See how some of these promises can be realized in daily life;
3. Memorize one of the promises.

INSIGHTS FOR THE LEADER

This is a special session designed to give you some flexibility in planning this quarter's studies for your junior highers. Rather than being part of the study of great Old Testament leaders, it deals with some of God's promises to His people. It does not need to be taught as the final session in this course—it may be used whenever you desire a break from your regular sessions:

- When many students are away at camp;
- During a week of special emphasis for your local congregation;
- When your teaching staff must be gone and your substitutes prefer not to try to follow the course sequence.

Because all the required teaching materials are conveniently contained in this manual, you can readily save this session for any "rainy day."

Promises of a Savior

During the centuries before the coming of Christ, God continually gave His people promises that a Redeemer was coming. Many details in these prophetic promises told of specific circumstances surrounding His birth, and other details described His ministry.

For example:

- He would be born of a virgin mother (see Isa. 7:14);
- He would be called Immanuel, which means "God with us" (see Isa. 7:14);
- He would have ultimate authority and power (see Isa. 9:6,7).

Promises to His People

In addition to promises of the Redeemer, God makes many other promises in His Word to His people. Your students will examine a selected few. They will discover that He promises:

- Eternal life (see John 11:25);
- A place in the Father's house (see John 14:2,3);
- Forgiveness and purification from sins (see 1 John 1:9);
- To hear His children's prayers (see Mark 11:24; 1 John 5:14,15);
- To deliver us from trouble (see Ps. 34:17);
- To care for us, never needing to remove His attention so that He can sleep (see Ps. 121:4,5);
- He will strengthen us and protect us from the evil one (see 2 Thess. 3:3);
- That if we abide in Christ, we will bear fruit for Him (see John 15:5);
- If we love and obey Jesus, the Father will love us and the Father and Son will make their home with us (see John 14:23);
- That when He appears to us in the end, we shall see Him as He is, and we shall be like Him (see 1 John 3:2).

Encourage your students to read more of God's promises and to trust Him to fulfill them.

SESSION PLAN

BEFORE CLASS BEGINS: Photocopy the Fun Page in duplex (back to back). If your copier will not duplex, copy each side of the page on separate sheets and tape the sides together back to back. There is no Scratch Sheet this time. Cut out the cards found on the Teaching Resource page (no photocopying is necessary). See the ALTERNATE ATTENTION GRABBER and EXPLORATION for special preparation and materials.

Attention Grabber

ATTENTION GRABBER (5-7 minutes)

Tell students, **Write the name of a person that you feel would be the most likely to keep a promise made to you. Then write a brief statement explaining why you selected this person.**

After students have had time to write, ask for a few volunteers to share their responses. Say, **You have given some good thoughts about who you would trust to keep a promise and why. Of course, the one who can be completely trusted to keep His word is God. Let's look at some of the promises He has given and what happened with them.**

ALTERNATE ATTENTION GRABBER (2-3 minutes)

Materials needed: An inexpensive and easily breakable item such as a small vase; sturdy table; several bricks and a friend to carry the bricks.

You can create a good object lesson by performing this tongue-in-cheek skit. When your students have arrived, say something like this: **I brought this special item to show you, because it has something to do with the subject of today's lesson. It is an art object, a vase made in the 1930s by a sculptor who later became very famous. My grandparents purchased this vase for a few dollars before the sculptor became known. Because the man is now a legend, this signed original is worth a lot of money—a LOT of money. I borrowed it from my folks, who now own it, but I had to promise them I'd be very careful with it. This vase was made by the famous sculptor Mister Korean. It's a Korean vase and says so here on the bottom.**

Put the vase carefully on the table. At this point, your friend should enter and say, **They told me to bring these bricks in here. Where should I put them?** Your friend then plops the bricks down hard on top of your vase. A melodramatic scream ought to be a good way to conclude the skit.

Explain (while your friend cleans up the mess), **The vase is now worthless because it has been broken. Actually, it was worthless before it was broken—but you guessed that, didn't you? This broken vase helps me make a point: Just as a broken vase is worthless, so is a**

broken promise. One of the great things about God is that He can be completely trusted to always keep His promises. Today we are going to look at some of the promises He has given and what they mean to us.

Bible Exploration

EXPLORATION (35-45 minutes)

Materials needed: A six-sided die (number cube); the cards from the Teaching Resource page; the prizes and props listed on the cards.

Step 1 (25-35 minutes): Your students will enjoy this learning activity. It's a simple but active game that will encourage even the most reticent student to join in the class discussion. Your students may have played another version of this game (based on an entirely different subject) because we used it in a previous course. It's worth repeating! Here's how to play:

Seat your students in a circle. Choose one student to begin and give him or her the number cube. Say, **When I give the signal, roll the cube and tell me the number. I have a list of five questions. I will read you a passage from the Bible and ask you a question from the list. The question I ask will be the number you've rolled on the die. There are only five questions but the cube has six sides. The sixth side—the number six—is wild. If you roll the wild number six, I will allow you to pick a card from this stack of cards I hold in my hand. Are you following me so far?**

I am holding two kinds of cards: "Ridiculous Act of Nonsense" cards and "Wonderful Award" cards. If you draw a "Ridiculous Act of Nonsense" card, you must do what the card tells you to do. If you draw a "Wonderful Award" card, I will give you whatever the card says. The awards include money and munchies!

If the first player rolls a number other than the wild six, read the first passage from the following "List of Promises" (or have a volunteer read it). Then pick the question from the following list that matches the number rolled. The five questions follow the "List of Promises."

If the wild six is rolled, allow the student to draw a card from your hand. (Hold your other hand over the cards in such a way that it is impossible for the student to see what is printed.) If you don't want to award a particular prize more than once, throw that card away after a player has picked it. Otherwise, place the card back in the stack and reshuffle.

After a student has completed his or her turn, the next student in the circle rolls the cube. That student is given the *next* passage on the "List of Promises." You can play as many rounds as you like, going through the list several times, asking the questions many times. Be sure to spend a few moments discussing each passage and the answers students give. Add any insights the students may miss. You may wish to ask your own follow-up questions each time a player answers one of the five questions listed.

Note: You will find that students soon warm up to performing the "Ridiculous Acts of Nonsense." In fact, they will be begging to draw the cards. If each question has been asked several times, you can turn an additional number into a wild number, along with

the 6. This will double the chances of rolling a wild number.

List of Promises:

1. John 14:23
2. 1 John 3:2
3. John 11:25
4. Psalm 34:17
5. Isaiah 9:6,7
6. 1 John 1:9
7. 1 John 5:14,15
8. Isaiah 7:14
9. Psalm 121:3,4
10. 2 Thessalonians 3:3
11. John 15:5
12. John 14:2,3

Questions:

1. Is this promise something that has already happened, has yet to happen or can happen every day?
2. Is there something we must do before this promise is fulfilled? If so, what is it and how do we do it?
3. Is this promise good news to the average young Christian? How so?
4. What could be some negative results in your life if God did not keep this promise?
5. If a friend asked you to explain this promise, what would you say or how would you rephrase it?

Wrap up this part of the session (and give the kids a chance to calm down) by summarizing the promises students have discussed.

Step 2 (10-12 minutes): Have your students gather into groups of three or four. Write these two headings on the chalkboard: What to Do; Five Ways to Get It Done.

Explain, **I am going to assign each group one of the promises we've been studying. Be sure that someone in your group writes down the passage I assign. When you've been given your assignment, I want you to do two things. First, I want you to figure out what thing the passage is telling you to do. Then I want you to list at least five things a person your age could do to live up to the passage's instructions. For example, if your passage says to pray, list five good things a kid could pray for. Be prepared to explain your findings to the rest of the class.**

Assign each group one of the following passages: John 14:23; John 15:5; 1 John 5:14,15. Give students enough time to brainstorm, then ask volunteers to describe what they have come up with to the rest of the class. Jot the students' thoughts under the proper headings on the chalkboard. Add any further insights and encourage your students to participate in the joy of God's promises by actually doing some of the things on the list this coming week.

Conclusion and Decision

CONCLUSION (3-5 minutes)

Write John 11:25 on the chalkboard. Tell students, **Work individually to memorize this verse as a way of remembering what Christ has done for you. Write it a few times on some scratch paper to help you learn it. Then try to say the verse for a classmate.**

After allowing time for students to begin learning the verse, close in prayer.

Distribute the Fun Page take-home paper.

SPECIAL NOTE

A great gift for your students in connection with this session would be copies of *Promises to Live By* (Regal Books, 1972), available from your regular Christian supplier.

Teaching Resource Page

Cut out these cards. Supply the props and prizes called for on the cards. If you intend to award each prize more than once, obtain enough items to do so. If you prefer not to award a particular prize simply discard that card.

WONDERFUL AWARD! **A Dollar!**	**WONDERFUL AWARD!** **A Bag of M&M's!**	**WONDERFUL AWARD!** **A Candy Bar!**	**WONDERFUL AWARD!** **A Soft Drink!**
WONDERFUL AWARD! **Peanuts!**	**RIDICULOUS ACT OF NONSENSE!** **Bark five times like a wounded dog!**	**RIDICULOUS ACT OF NONSENSE!** **Laugh like a fool for 10 seconds!**	**RIDICULOUS ACT OF NONSENSE!** **Balance a book on your nose!**
RIDICULOUS ACT OF NONSENSE! **Crow like a rooster!**	**RIDICULOUS ACT OF NONSENSE!** **Act like a monkey!**	**RIDICULOUS ACT OF NONSENSE!** **Eat soda crackers, then whistle!**	**RIDICULOUS ACT OF NONSENSE!** **Place the paper sack over your head for one minute!**
RIDICULOUS ACT OF NONSENSE! **Cry like a baby for 10 seconds!**	**RIDICULOUS ACT OF NONSENSE!** **Hop around the room backwards!**	**RIDICULOUS ACT OF NONSENSE!** **Make five silly faces!**	**RIDICULOUS ACT OF NONSENSE!** **The whole class must stand up and shout, "OOGA-BOOGA!"**

Today's Good News:

"For to us a child is born, to us a son is given, and the government will be on his shoulders. And he will be called Wonderful Counselor, Mighty God, Everlasting Father, Prince of Peace." Isaiah 9:6

Help! One day while our cartoonist was fast asleep at his drawing table, his ink pen went crazy and started drawing all over this copy of the Fun Page! The pen created this difficult maze, which you can solve if you have enough patience.

Instructions: Beginning at the point marked "Start," follow the maze line with your pencil until you've passed through ALL of the "Promise Boxes" and reached the "Final Goal." When the path you're following goes off the edge of the paper, flip the page over and pick up the proper line on the other side. Remember, you must go through ALL the "Promise Boxes." After all, every Christian in the world gets to share in all these promises from the Word of God!

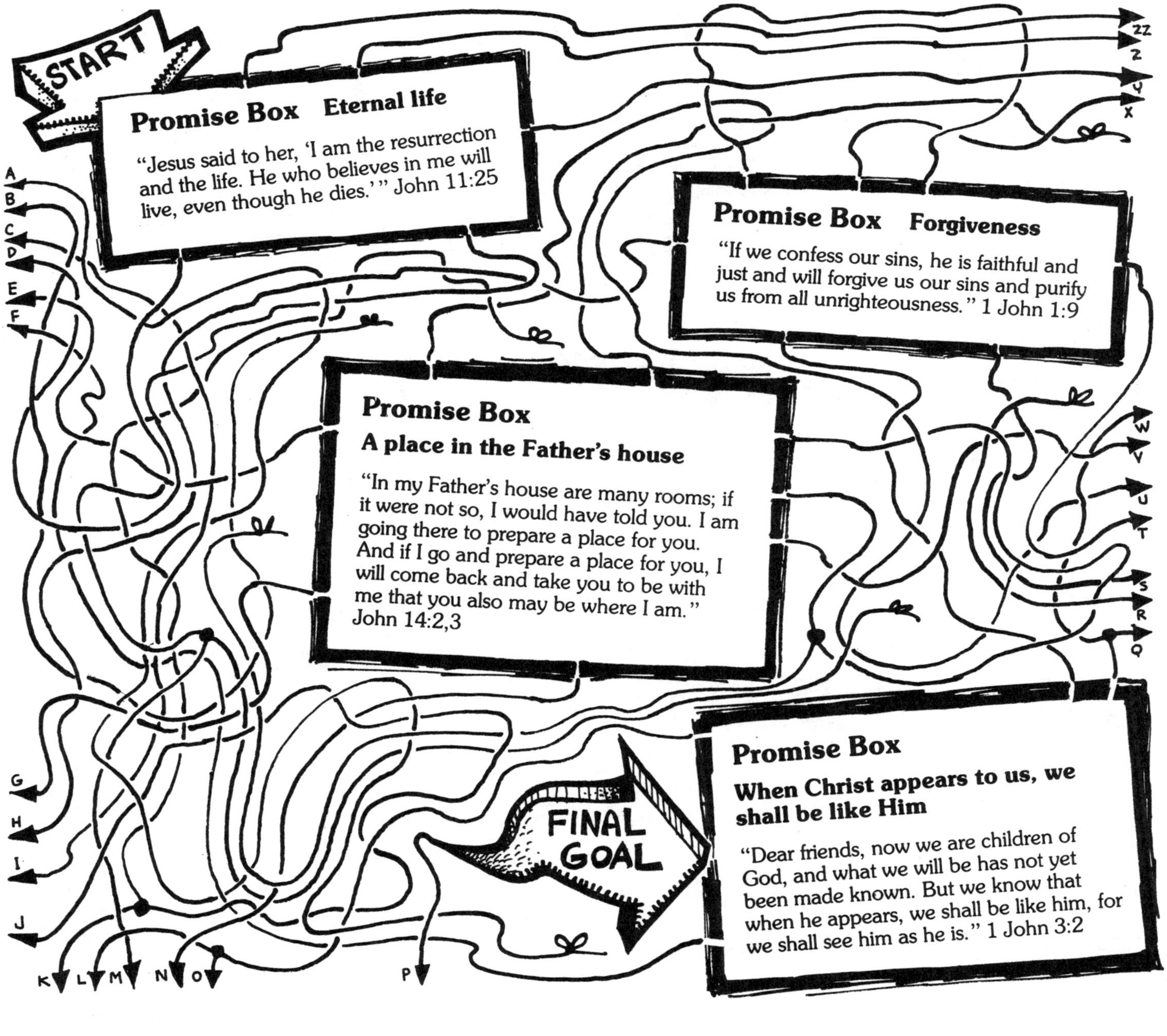

START

Promise Box **Eternal life**

"Jesus said to her, 'I am the resurrection and the life. He who believes in me will live, even though he dies.'" John 11:25

Promise Box **Forgiveness**

"If we confess our sins, he is faithful and just and will forgive us our sins and purify us from all unrighteousness." 1 John 1:9

Promise Box

A place in the Father's house

"In my Father's house are many rooms; if it were not so, I would have told you. I am going there to prepare a place for you. And if I go and prepare a place for you, I will come back and take you to be with me that you also may be where I am." John 14:2,3

Promise Box

When Christ appears to us, we shall be like Him

"Dear friends, now we are children of God, and what we will be has not yet been made known. But we know that when he appears, we shall be like him, for we shall see him as he is." 1 John 3:2

FINAL GOAL

ZZ Z Y X W V U T S R Q P O N M L K J I H G F E D C B A

Promise Box
God hears our prayers
"This is the confidence we have in approaching God: that if we ask anything according to his will, he hears us. And if we know that he hears us—whatever we ask—we know that we have what we asked of him." 1 John 5:14,15
Promise Box
If we love and obey Jesus, the Father will love us and the Father and Son will make their home with us
"Jesus replied, 'If anyone loves me, he will obey my teaching. My Father will love him, and we will come to him and make our home with him.'" John 14:23
Promise Box
God always takes care of us
"The righteous cry out, and the Lord hears them; he delivers them from all their troubles." Psalm 34:17
Promise Box
If we abide in Christ, we bear spiritual fruit
"I am the vine; you are the branches. If a man remains in me and I in him, he will bear much fruit; apart from me you can do nothing." John 15:5
Promise Box
The Lord protects us from the evil one
"But the Lord is faithful, and he will strengthen and protect you from the evil one." 2 Thessalonians 3:3
ZZ
Z
Y
X
W
V
U
T
S
R
Q
A
B
C
D
E
F
G
H
I
J
P
O
N
M
L
K

Session 13

THEME: Keeping promises.

BIBLE STUDY OUTLINE

This message focuses on Matthew 5:33-37. Read it to your students and make the following comments as time permits.

Introductory remarks: God has made many promises in the Bible, and we know that they are true and dependable. But what about our own promises? Are we good to our word? Jesus had something to say about that, too.

Verses 33-36: The principle that the Jewish people lived by was basically the same one many people live by today: If you really want to make a promise that people will trust, swear some sort of oath. The courts of the land require witnesses to either swear an oath on the Bible or to otherwise affirm that they are about to tell the truth. The idea is to attach your word to something of greater power, authority and respect—the Bible, heaven, God and so forth. But Jesus objects to that principle.

Verse 37: Jesus says that our word should stand on its own merit. If we say we'll do something, then we must do it. If we say we won't do something, then we must stay true to our word and not do it. We should be so dependable that people won't ask us to swear by a higher authority. It's very likely that the people Jesus was talking to had the habit of backing out of a casual promise by saying something like, "Oh, I did say I would do that—but after all, I did not swear by heaven that I would do it." Jesus teaches that that habit is wrong and unacceptable. His principle is that we must be dependable. That dependability must extend to all areas of what we say, whether it's something as simple as "I'll take out the trash" to something as important as "I promise to love, honor and obey until death do us part."

This sort of dependability is not natural to our weak human nature. It is the change brought by God's Holy Spirit that makes a person able to be this trustworthy. Get in the habit of being dependable. By God's strength, keep your word and do what you say.

CASE STUDY: WHO'S ON FIRST?

Tell the story of the high school guy who got a phone call from a girl he knew at school. He knew that the girl liked him a lot, though he liked her only as a friend. She asked him to go out for pizza with her and her youth group and he agreed to go that Friday night.

But shortly after he hung up the phone, another girl called. It was that "special someone." He was nuts about her, even though she had hardly said two words to him all year. But here she was on the phone, asking him if he wanted to come over for a family barbecue Friday night. Of course he would. The plans were made and he hung up the phone.

But after jumping and dancing and smiling a big smile, he suddenly remembered the date he had made with the first girl—for Friday night. (Now do the Discussion Questions.)

DISCUSSION QUESTIONS

1. **Does Jesus' principle of being dependable by keeping your word have a bearing on this situation? If so, how?**

2. **What do you think would be the wrong thing for the guy to do? What would be some of the negative results and feelings if he did the wrong thing? What do you think the right thing for the guy to do would be? Is there some way or ways he could make both girls happy?**

3. **What are some typical areas where people your age tend to break their promises? How can a Christian develop the habit of being dependable by keeping his or her word. If you are dependable in small ways now, what do you suppose will happen in the future?**

CHAUFFEURED GETAWAY

The next time you have a special party, game night or retreat, try this one. An adult drives up in front of the meeting place honking the horn. You announce that it's the "Dream Outing Chauffeur" or some such ridiculous title. The chauffeur, who is dressed in formal attire, then takes two or three kids out for a special evening on the town—to a pizza place, a movie or a popular shopping mall. The chauffeur, with help from the youth fund, pays for everything (within reason). To really make it special, have a few people waiting at the destinations with cameras, placards and streamers. Show them special attention but don't embarrass them. It's best if the kids can be returned to the meeting hall before the others leave, so that the "Dream Outing" can be described in glowing terms. (Or else videotape the event for later showing.)

Junior high students are generally not interested in coed activities of this sort so plan one having the group be all boys or all girls. Try picking shy kids who tend not to join in with the usual action—they'll feel special.

VIDEO GREETINGS

We've mentioned this one in a previous edition, but it bears repeating. If someone has recently moved away, get the youth group together to tape a video filled with greetings, news and best wishes. This is also a nice surprise for someone in the hospital.

SURPRISE PARTY

Arrange with a kid's parents to "take over the house" for an evening. On the agreed-upon night, you and a van loaded with youth group members show up at the guest of honor's home. "Throw out" the parents and any brothers and sisters (who go out for their own entertainment), put on the music, roll out the munchies and have a lot of fun. This works best if there is absolutely no reason why this person is being honored! When the party is over, make sure you leave the house as you found it.

See the *Games and Things* for Session 8 for fun party ideas.

CLIP ART
AND OTHER GOODIES

The following pages contain all sorts of fun, high quality clip art. Put it to good use: brighten up your youth group's mail outs, bulletins, posters and overhead transparencies. Cut 'em out, paste 'em up, run 'em off and there you have it!

You'll be happy to know that the LIGHT FORCE publishes several great clip art books for youth workers. These books are the finest on the market. They are made by youth workers for youth workers. Available at your local Christian supply store.

WANT TO PRODUCE GREAT PROMOTIONAL MATERIAL?

TURN THE PAGE FOR EASY INSTRUCTIONS . . .

EASY INSTRUCTIONS

1. **Get a sheet of clean white paper. This will be the master for your promotional piece.**

2. **Choose the art you want from this section. Cut it out and glue it to the master.**

3. **Add headlines with rub-on letters (available at any art store) or with a felt pen. Add body copy with a typewriter or by hand. (Type on a separate sheet and cut and paste.)**

4. **Run off as many copies as you need, hand them out or drop them in the mail. Presto!**

TIPS:

Go heavy on the artwork, light on the copy. A piece with too many words goes unread.

Get in the habit of making a monthly calendar of events. It doesn't have to be an expensive masterpiece; just so it tells your group members what they can find at your church.

Print the calendar on the back of the student worksheet. This will insure that these pages are saved and read.

ALL ABOUT ME

Hi! To help us get to know you, please answer all the questions in the squares below.

Name: ____________________

Address: ____________________

____

____

Phone: ____________ Birthday: ____________

School: ____________ Grade in school: ______

Favorite hobby:

Favorite sport:

Favorite music:

Favorite TV show:

Favorite toothpaste:

FAVORITE TOOTHPASTE?!

YA NEVER KNOW—IT COULD BE IMPORTANT.

I've been coming to this Bible study for this long:

☐ First time.
☐ A few months.
☐ All my life.
☐ I forget.
☐ All of the above.

My relationship with God:

☐ Frankly, I don't believe in Him.
☐ Pretty good; I love Him.
☐ I feel I could do better and would like to know more about Him.
☐ Other (explain):

Thanks for answering these questions! You're invited to join us in all the fun stuff we do, so come on out and enjoy!

VACATION

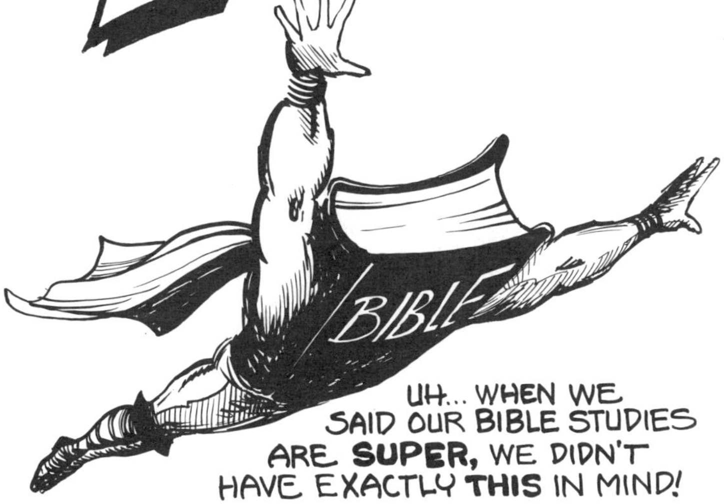
BIBLE
UH... WHEN WE SAID OUR BIBLE STUDIES ARE **SUPER,** WE DIDN'T HAVE EXACTLY **THIS** IN MIND!

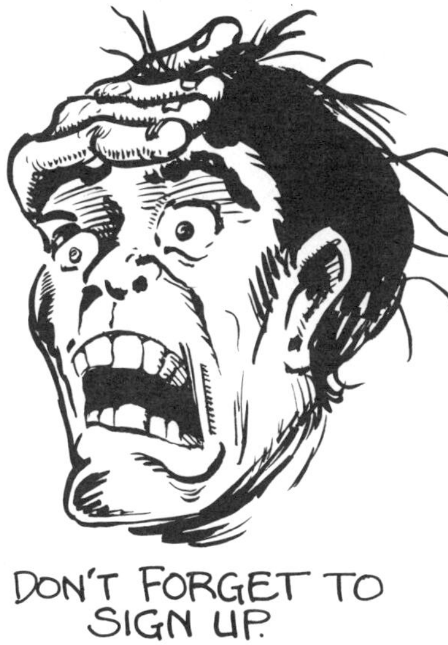
DON'T FORGET TO SIGN UP.

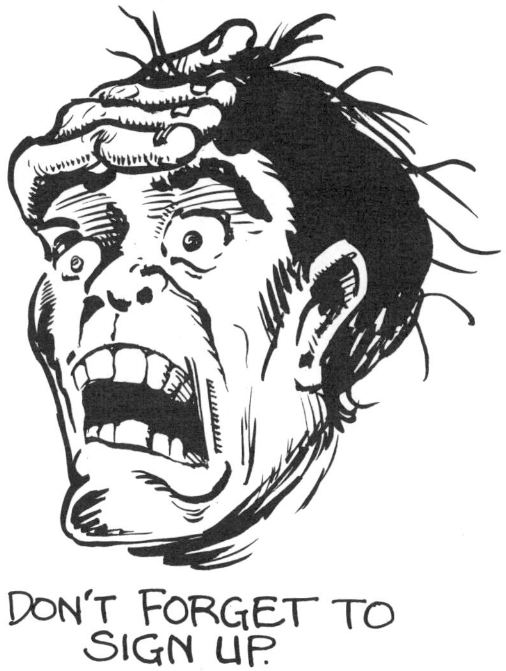
DON'T FORGET TO SIGN UP.

Faith

Faith

RETIREMENT CENTER
MINISTRY—

RETIREMENT CENTER
MINISTRY—

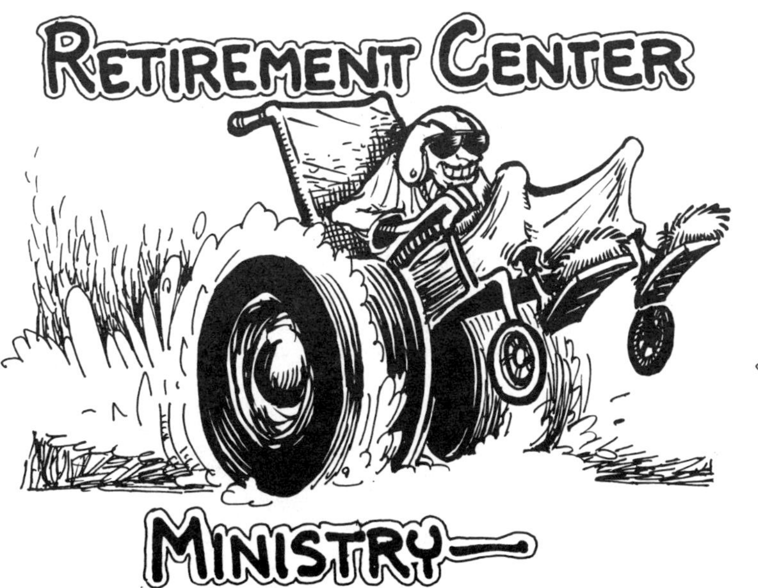

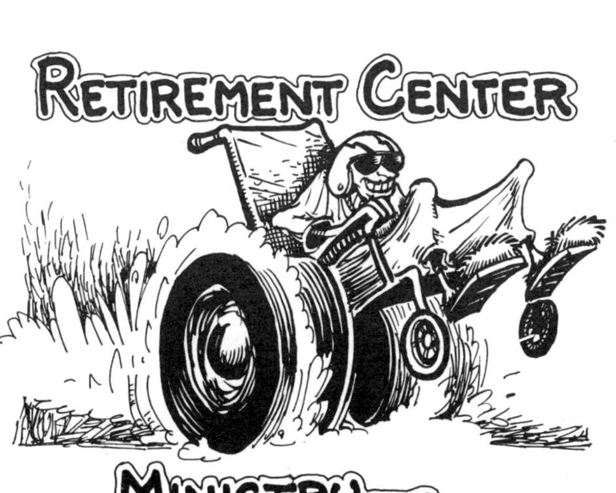